A RING

JOHN BETJEMAN'S OTHER WORKS

POETRY

Collected Poems

Summoned by Bells

High and Low

PROSE

First and Last Loves

A Pictorial History of English Architecture

London's Historic Railway Stations

A RING OF BELLS

Poems of John Betjeman

INTRODUCED AND SELECTED

BY IRENE SLADE

Illustrations by

EDWARD ARDIZZONE

JOHN MURRAY

First published 1962
Reprinted 1964
Reprinted 1967
Reprinted 1972
Reprinted 1974

Made and printed in Great Britain by
William Clowes & Sons, Limited, London, Beccles and Colchester
and published by
John Murray (Publishers) Ltd
50 Albemarle Street London W1X 4BD

Cased 0 7195 0100 8
Paperback 0 7195 0101 6

INTRODUCTION
p. 1

POEMS OF CHILDHOOD
p. 7

DISCOVERING POETRY
p. 17

POEMS OF EARLY SCHOOL
p. 25

POEMS OF HOLIDAYS
p. 31

POEMS OF PEOPLE
p. 47

DISCOVERING ARCHITECTURE
p. 61

POEMS OF PLACES
p. 73

LATER SCHOOL
p. 91

GROWING UP
p. 99

NOTES
p. 107

INTRODUCTION

For myself,
I knew as soon as I could read and write
That I must be a poet . . .

This is what John Betjeman wrote in his autobiographical poem *Summoned by Bells*, looking back on his childhood in Highgate. Yet how few people could ever say, reflecting in middle age, that they had done what they were going to do when they were seven! Seven-year-olds generally want to be engine drivers, space pilots, television stars, jockeys or any one of the countless other glamorous-sounding things that are fashionable at the time. But in the next few years—or months, or weeks—the ambition changes and in the end they grow up to be something quite different.

The rare exceptions are, of course, the infant prodigies whose talents are so great in infancy that there is no doubt about what they will become when they grow up—the young Mozart, the young Macaulay, the young Pope. With John Betjeman it wasn't like that. As a child he had ambition without the corresponding talent:

The gap between my feelings and my skill
Was so immense, I wonder I went on.

But he did go on; he had to express himself in words, however bad his verses were, and although he was no prodigy, he had something else. He had an extraordinary capacity for observation—of objects, scenes and people—and he was acutely sensitive to his surroundings. To him a house was not just a place with four walls and a roof; it was a living thing that had an atmosphere and character of its own; it could feel and think. As he became older he lost none of that sensitivity; it did not become hard and blunted as he grew up. When he did become a poet he remembered his impressions of childhood so clearly that they inspired much of his writing.

John Betjeman became a poet by perseverance and hard work; it was no easy thing for him. His school career was not brilliant—he was far too interested in church architecture and looking at old buildings to concentrate on his lessons properly. At Oxford he was equally carried away both by the atmosphere of the town, with its beautiful medieval colleges, and by the social life of the undergraduates. He left without taking a degree. Then followed a series of jobs as a schoolmaster, then as a journalist.

All this time he was practising writing. He sent his poems to magazines and had most of them rejected. Yet the more he failed the more he wrote, and however disheartened he became, he never gave up. But in those years, from seven to his early twenties, his powers as a writer were maturing, and eventually it became easier for him to express himself in words. As the words came more fluently, his own originality of thought and style developed.

In 1932, when he was twenty-four, he had his first volume of poems published. There were twenty in all, and the book was called *Mount Zion*. ('Hymn', 'Croydon' and 'Westgate-on-Sea', included in this book, are from *Mount Zion*.) After that, small volumes of his poems were published every few years, but his work made very little stir in the literary world. In fact, he remained comparatively unknown as a poet for about twenty years after the publication of *Mount Zion*, except for a small and faithful following of admirers who had recognized his gifts and originality from the very beginning.

It was not until the mid-fifties that things started to change and a wider reading public began to be aware of him. Each of his books of poetry had sold more copies than the one before, but in 1958 all his poems were gathered together into one book—*John Betjeman's Collected Poems*—and no one could possibly have foreseen what a sensational event the publication of this was to be.

Suddenly, almost overnight it seemed, John Betjeman had become the most popular poet of his time. *Collected Poems* sold out so quickly when it appeared that the publishers had to reprint it three times within a month. In the history of John Murray's nothing like it had been known since they published Byron's *Childe Harold* in 1812, when copies were sold to a clamouring crowd through the windows of the publisher's house in Albemarle Street! After their publication the demand for Betjeman's poems continued and has continued ever since, and his enormous popularity shows that many of the people who read him are people who would never normally look at a book of poetry at all. Why is this?

There are many reasons why John Betjeman's verse finds a ready response in so many people, but the two most important ones are these: his writing is direct and uncomplicated, and the things he writes about are the familiar objects and experiences common to most people. The rhythm of his verse, with its prose-like qualities of continuous narrative, is simple to follow:

> I remember the dread with which I at a quarter past four
> Let go with a bang behind me our house front door
> And, clutching a present for my dear little hostess tight,
> Sailed out for the children's party into the night . . .

and

> The sort of girl I like to see
> Smiles down from her great height at me.
> She stands in strong, athletic pose
> And wrinkles her *retroussé* nose.

and

> "Yes, the Town Clerk will see you." In I went.
> He was, like all Town Clerks, from north of Trent;
> A man with bye-laws busy in his head
> Whose Mayor and Council followed where he led.

Another quality in John Betjeman's writing that endears him to his readers is that his is a voice which, in the midst of this 'atomic age' of speed, mass-production and the glorification of material wealth, calls on people to pause and look back awhile on the good things of the past before they are all gone. To him, buildings and places are the things that most reflect the passing of time and the present-day rush towards ugliness. He looks back to the merits of Victorian architecture, at which it was once the fashion to sneer, with its red brick, lavish ornamentation and imitations of the medieval English Gothic style. He sees in it the work of people who really *cared* for what they were doing, and who had an artistic purpose to express. To him it represents the last comparatively tranquil period of British social history before the coming of twentieth-century industrialization with its cheap, shoddy buildings spreading like a plague across the landscape.

But John Betjeman's feeling for the Victorian age is not the dominant theme of all his poetry. He observes life in his own age and writes about it in a way that no one else has done. The mass-produced houses, factories, new towns—even the local gas-works—all have places in his verse, so have the people who live and work in them. He observes them all with compassion and understanding; he never writes in anger about what he sees.

In 1960 *Summoned by Bells*, John Betjeman's story of his early years up to the time of leaving Oxford, was published. When you read this poem in blank verse, you will see how many ideas, subjects and moods of his later verse are drawn from his childhood and school days. In fact the little boy of seven, tramping over Hampstead Heath with pencil and writing-pad, in search of inspiration, is very much present in everything Betjeman has ever written since. His capacity for original observation as a child, his loves, hates, fears, weaknesses and strengths are much the same now as they were then, and it is this which makes it possible for him to communicate his ideas with such ease and directness to other people, for in every human being of whatever age, the sensibilities of childhood lie only a little way beneath the surface of the protective covering of years.

In the present selection of John Betjeman's poems for young readers, I have chosen certain passages from *Summoned by Bells* which set the theme for the group of poems that follow, so you will find that each poem in a section relates in some way to what has been said in *Summoned by Bells.* These extracts, given in the same order as they come in the chapters of the book, without any cuts in the middle, are important because they describe places, people and ideas that had their being in the earlier part of this century. You may already be familiar with the world of gas lamps, carriages, early motor-cars and railway trains; you have probably experienced it in your reading—Wilkie Collins, Robert Louis Stevenson (*Dr. Jekyll and Mr. Hyde*), John Galsworthy, G. K. Chesterton, Sir Arthur Conan Doyle (the Sherlock Holmes stories) and many others. You may live in a town or village which still has Victorian lamp-posts or pillar-boxes, or has the kind of houses and shops that John Betjeman knew as a child. But if you live in a new town or a modern built-up area, John Betjeman's Victorian and Edwardian worlds may be new to you.

Read the poems aloud, either to yourself or to somebody else if you can. If you do not understand a poem at first reading, read it again, and yet again until its rhythm takes a hold of you and its words begin to call up images in your mind. Enjoy the sound and full flavour of words that may be new to you:

the incumbent enjoying a supine incumbency—

or *Ausgang* we were out of love—
Und eingang we are in.

—you can always look them up in the notes afterwards. If you have ever heard John Betjeman read his poems aloud you will notice how often he stops to explain them as he goes along. The notes here are at the back of the book so that they do not distract from your enjoyment of the poems as you first read them. A great scholar and writer, Sir Arthur Quiller-Couch, who, among other things, compiled the invaluable *Oxford Book of English Verse*, once advised young people on reading poetry: 'Just go on reading: the Prince has always to break through the briars to kiss the Sleeping Beauty awake . . . you are the Prince, and she is worth it.'

Irene Slade

I

POEMS OF CHILDHOOD

From SUMMONED BY BELLS

HERE on the southern slope of Highgate Hill
Red squirrels leap the hornbeams. Still I see
Twigs and serrated leaves against the sky.
The sunny silence was of Middlesex.
Once a Delaunay-Belleville crawling up
West Hill in bottom gear made such a noise
As drew me from my dream-world out to watch
That early motor-car attempt the steep.
But mostly it was footsteps, rustling leaves,
And blackbirds fluting over miles of Heath.
  Then Millfield Lane looked like a Constable
And all the grassy hillocks spoke of Keats.
Mysterious gravel drives to hidden wealth
Wound between laurels—mighty Caenwood Towers
And Grand Duke Michael's house and Holly Lodge.

  But what of us in our small villa row
Who gazed into the Burdett-Coutts estate?
I knew we were a lower, lesser world
Than that remote one of the carriage-folk
Who left their cedars and brown garden walls
In care of servants. I could also tell
That we were slightly richer than my friends,
The family next door: we owned a brougham
And they would envy us our holidays.
In fact it was the mother there who first
Made me aware of insecurity
When war was near: "Your name is German, John"—
But I had always thought that it was Dutch . . .
That tee-jay-ee, that fatal tee-jay-ee
Which I have watched the hesitating pens
Of Government clerks and cloakroom porters funk.
I asked my mother. "No," she said, "it's Dutch;
Thank God you're English on your mother's side."
O happy, happy Browns and Robinsons!

Safe were those evenings of the pre-war world
When firelight shone on green linoleum;
I heard the church bells hollowing out the sky,
Deep beyond deep, like never-ending stars,
And turned to Archibald, my safe old bear,
Whose woollen eyes looked sad or glad at me,
Whose ample forehead I could wet with tears,
Whose half-moon ears received my confidence,
Who made me laugh, who never let me down.
I used to wait for hours to see him move,
Convinced that he could breathe. One dreadful day
They hid him from me as a punishment:
Sometimes the desolation of that loss
Comes back to me and I must go upstairs
To see him in the sawdust, so to speak,
Safe and returned to his idolator.

Safe, in a world of trains and buttered toast
Where things inanimate could feel and think,
Deeply I loved thee, 31 West Hill!
At that hill's foot did London then begin,
With yellow horse-trams clopping past the planes
To grey-brick nonconformist Chetwynd Road
And on to Kentish Town and barking dogs
And costers' carts and crowded grocers' shops
And Daniels' store, the local Selfridge's,
The Bon Marché, the Electric Palace, slums
That thrilled me with their smells of poverty—
Till, safe once more, we gained the leafy slope
And buttered toast and 31 West Hill.
Here from my eyrie, as the sun went down,
I heard the old North London puff and shunt,
Glad that I did not live in Gospel Oak.

"A diamond," "A heart," "No trumps," "Two spades"—
Happy and tense they played at Auction Bridge:

Two tables in the drawing-room for friends
From terra-cotta flats on Muswell Hill
And nearer Brookfield Mansions: cigarettes
And 'Votes for Women' ashtrays, mauve and green.
I watched the players, happy to be quiet
Till someone nice was dummy who would talk—
A talk soon drowned . . . "If you'd finessed my heart
And played your diamond . . ." "If I'd had the lead
I might have done." "Well, length is strength, you know."
"Not when your partner's sitting on the ace."
Did they, I wonder, leave us in a huff
After those hot post-mortems? All I knew
Were silks and bits of faintly scented fur
On ladies vaguely designated 'aunts'
Who came on second Thursdays to At Homes.

The sunlit weeks between were full of maids:
Sarah, with orange wig and horsy teeth,
Was so bad-tempered that she scarcely spoke;
Maud was my hateful nurse who smelt of soap
And forced me to eat chewy bits of fish,
Thrusting me back to babyhood with threats
Of nappies, dummies and the feeding bottle.
She rubbed my face in messes I had made
And was the first to tell me about Hell,
Admitting she was going there herself.
Sometimes, thank God, they left me all alone
In our small patch of garden in the front,
With clinker rockery and London Pride
And barren lawn and lumps of yellow clay
As mouldable as smelly Plasticine.
I used to turn the heavy stones to watch
The shiny red and waiting centipede
Which darted out of sight; the woodlouse slow
And flat; the other greyish-bluey kind
Which rolled into a ball till I was gone
Out of the gate to venture down the hill.

"You're late for dinner, John." I feel again
That awful feeling, fear confused with thrill,
As I would be unbuttoned, bent across
Her starchy apron, screaming "Don't—Maud—don't!"
Till dissolution, bed and kindly fur
Of agéd, uncomplaining Archibald.

* * *

GROUP LIFE: LETCHWORTH

Tell me Pippididdledum,
  Tell me how the children are.
Working each for weal of all
  After what you said.

Barry's on the common far
  Pedalling the Kiddie Kar.
Ann has had a laxative
  And Aluréd is dead.

Sympathy is stencilling
  Her decorative leatherwork,
Wilfred's learned a folk-tune for
  The Morris Dancers' band.

I have my ex-Service man and
  Mamie's done a lino-cut.
And Charlie's in the *kinderbank*
  A-kicking up the sand.

Wittle-tittle, wittle-tittle
  Toodle-oodle ducky birds,
What a lot my dicky chicky
  Tiny tots have done.

Wouldn't it be jolly now,
  To take our Aertex panters off
And have a jolly tumble in
  The jolly, jolly sun?

FALSE SECURITY

I remember the dread with which I at a quarter past four
Let go with a bang behind me our house front door
And, clutching a present for my dear little hostess tight,
Sailed out for the children's party into the night
Or rather the gathering night. For still some boys
In the near municipal acres were making a noise
Shuffling in fallen leaves and shouting and whistling
And running past hedges of hawthorn, spikey and bristling.

And black in the oncoming darkness stood out the trees
And pink shone the ponds in the sunset ready to freeze
And all was still and ominous waiting for dark
And the keeper was ringing his closing bell in the park
And the arc lights started to fizzle and burst into mauve
As I climbed West Hill to the great big house in The Grove,
Where the children's party was and the dear little hostess.
But halfway up stood the empty house where the ghost is
I crossed to the other side and under the arc
Made a rush for the next kind lamp-post out of the dark
And so to the next and the next till I reached the top
Where The Grove branched off to the left. Then ready to drop
I ran to the ironwork gateway of number seven
Secure at last on the lamplit fringe of Heaven.

Oh who can say how subtle and safe one feels
Shod in one's children's sandals from Daniel Neal's,
Clad in one's party clothes made of stuff from Heal's?
And who can still one's thrill at the candle shine
On cakes and ices and jelly and blackcurrant wine,
And the warm little feel of my hostess's hand in mine?
Can I forget my delight at the conjuring show?
And wasn't I proud that I was the last to go?
Too over-excited and pleased with myself to know
That the words I heard my hostess's mother employ
To a guest departing, would ever diminish my joy,
I WONDER WHERE JULIA FOUND THAT STRANGE, RATHER COMMON
LITTLE BOY?

CROYDON

In a house like that
  Your Uncle Dick was born;
Satchel on back he walked to Whitgift
  Every weekday morn.

Boys together in Coulsdon woodlands,
  Bramble-berried and steep,
He and his pals would look for spadgers
  Hidden deep.

The laurels are speckled in Marchmont Avenue
  Just as they were before,
But the steps are dusty that still lead up to
  Your Uncle Dick's front door.

Pear and apple in Croydon gardens
  Bud and blossom and fall,
But your Uncle Dick has left his Croydon
  Once for all.

INDOOR GAMES NEAR NEWBURY

In among the silver birches winding ways of tarmac wander
  And the signs to Bussock Bottom, Tussock Wood and Windy
                                                                                    Brake,
Gabled lodges, tile-hung churches, catch the lights of our Lagonda
  As we drive to Wendy's party, lemon curd and Christmas cake.
    Rich the makes of motor whirring,
    Past the pine-plantation purring
        Come up, Hupmobile, Delage!
    Short the way your chauffeurs travel,
    Crunching over private gravel
        Each from out his warm garáge.

Oh but Wendy, when the carpet yielded to my indoor pumps,
There you stood, your gold hair streaming,
Handsome in the hall-light gleaming,
There you looked and there you led me off into the game of clumps.
Then the new Victrola playing
And your funny uncle saying
"Choose your partners for a tox-trot! Dance until it's *tea* o'clock!
Come on, young 'uns, foot it featly!"
Was it chance that paired us neatly,
I, who loved you so completely,
You, who pressed me closely to you, hard against your party frock?

"Meet me when you've finished eating!" So we met and no one found us.
Oh that dark and furry cupboard while the rest played hide and seek!
Holding hands our two hearts beating in the bedroom silence round us,
Holding hands and hardly hearing sudden footstep, thud and shriek.
Love that lay too deep for kissing——
"Where *is* Wendy? Wendy's missing!"
Love so pure it *had* to end,
Love so strong that I was frighten'd
When you gripped my fingers tight and
Hugging, whispered "I'm your friend."

Good-bye Wendy! Send the fairies, pinewood elf and larch tree gnome,
Spingle-spangled stars are peeping
At the lush Lagonda creeping
Down the winding ways of tarmac to the leaded lights of home.
There, among the silver birches,
All the bells of all the churches
Sounded in the bath-waste running out into the frosty air.
Wendy speeded my undressing,
Wendy is the sheet's caressing
Wendy bending gives a blessing,
Holds me as I drift to dreamland, safe inside my slumber-wear.

2

DISCOVERING POETRY

From SUMMONED BY BELLS

For myself,
I knew as soon as I could read and write
That I must be a poet. Even today,
When all the way from Cambridge comes a wind
To blow the lamps out every time they're lit,
I know that I must light mine up again.

My first attraction was to tripping lines;
Internal rhyming, as in Shelley's 'Cloud',
Seemed then perfection. 'O'er' and 'ere' and 'e'en'
Were words I liked to use. My father smiled:
"And how's our budding bard? Let what you write
Be funny, John, and be original."
Secretly proud, I showed off merrily.
But certain as the stars above the twigs
And deeply fearful as the pealing bells
And everlasting as the racing surf
Blown back upon itself in Polzeath Bay,
My urge was to encase in rhythm and rhyme
The things I saw and felt (I could not *think*).

And so, at sunset, off to Hampstead Heath
I went with pencil and with writing-pad
And stood tip-toe upon a little hill,
Awaiting inspiration from the sky.
"Look! there's a poet!", people might exclaim
On footpaths near. The muse inspired my pen:
The sunset tipped with gold St. Michael's church,
Shouts of boys bathing came from Highgate Ponds,
The elms that hid the houses of the great
Rustled with mystery, and dirt-grey sheep
Grazed in the foreground; but the lines of verse
Came out like parodies of *A & M*.

The gap between my feelings and my skill
Was so immense, I wonder I went on.
A stretch of heather seen at Haslemere

And 'Up the airy mountain' (Allingham)
Merged in the magic of my Highgate pen:

> When the moors are pink with heather
>   When the sky's as blue as the sea,
> Marching all together
>   Come fairy folk so wee.

My goodness me! It seemed perfection then——
The brilliance of the rhymes A B, A B!
The vastness and the daintiness combined!
The second verse was rather less inspired:

> Some in green and some in red
>   And some with a violet plume,
> And a little cap on each tiny head
>   Watching the bright white moon.

I copied out the lines into a book,
A leather-bound one given me for verse
And stamped with my initials. There it stood
On the first page, that poem—a reproach.
In later years I falsified the date
To make it seem that I was only seven,
Not eight, when these weak stanzas were composed.

The gap from feeling to accomplishment!
In Highgate days that gap was yawning wide,
But awe and mystery were everywhere,
Most in the purple dark of thin St. Anne's:
Down Fitzroy Park what unimagined depths
Of glade led on to haunts of Robin Hood
(Never a real favourite of mine).
A special Tube train carried Archibald
Northward to Merton, south to Millfield Lane.
A silver blight that made my blood run cold
Hung on a grey house by the cemetery—
So that for years I only liked red brick.
The turrets on the chapel for the dead
And Holly Village with its prickly roofs
Against the sky were terrifying shapes.

"Dong!" went the distant cemetery bell
And chilled for good the east side of the hill
And all things east of me. But in the west
Were health and sunshine, bumps on Hampstead Heath,
Friends, comfort, railways, brandy-balls and grass;
And west of westward, somewhere, Cornwall lay.

Once when my father took me to the Tate
We stood enraptured by 'The Hopeless Dawn',
The picture first to move me. Twenty times,
They told me, had Frank Bramley watched the flame
Expiring in its candlestick before
He put it down on canvas. Guttering there,
It symbolized the young wife's dying hope
And the old mother's—gazing out to sea:
The meal upon the table lay prepared
But no good man to eat it: through the panes,
An angry sea below the early light
Tossed merciless, as I had seen the waves
In splendid thunder over Greenaway
Send driftwood shooting up the beach as though
Great planks were light as paper. "Put it down!
Translate the picture into verse, my boy,
And here's your opening—

> Through the humble cottage window
> Streams the early dawn."

The lines my father gave me sounded well;
But how continue them? How make a rhyme?

> O'er the tossing bay of Findow
> In the mournful morn.

With rising hopes I sought a gazetteer—
Findochty, Findon, Finglas, Finistère—
Alas! no Findow . . . and the poem died.

* * *

GREENAWAY

I know so well this turfy mile,
These clumps of sea-pink withered brown,
The breezy cliff, the awkward stile,
The sandy path that takes me down

To crackling layers of broken slate
Where black and flat sea-woodlice crawl
And isolated rock pools wait
Wash from the highest tides of all.

I know the roughly blasted track
That skirts a small and smelly bay
And over squelching bladder-wrack
Leads to the beach at Greenaway.

Down on the shingle safe at last
I hear the slowly dragging roar
As mighty rollers mount to cast
Small coal and seaweed on the shore,

And spurting far as it can reach
The shooting surf comes hissing round
To leave a line along the beach
Of cowries waiting to be found.

Tide after tide by night and day
The breakers battle with the land
And rounded smooth along the bay
The faithful rocks protecting stand.

But in a dream the other night
I saw this coastline from the sea
And felt the breakers plunging white
Their weight of waters over me.

There were the stile, the turf, the shore,
  The safety line of shingle beach
With every stroke I struck the more
  The backwash sucked me out of reach.

Back into what a water-world
  Of waving weed and waiting claws?
Of writhing tentacles uncurled
  To drag me to what dreadful jaws?

PARLIAMENT HILL FIELDS

Rumbling under blackened girders, Midland, bound for Cricklewood,
Puffed its sulphur to the sunset where that Land of Laundries stood.
Rumble under, thunder over, train and tram alternate go,
Shake the floor and smudge the ledger, Charrington, Sells, Dale and Co.,
Nuts and nuggets in the window, trucks along the lines below.

When the Bon Marché was shuttered, when the feet were hot and tired,
Outside Charrington's we waited, by the 'STOP HERE IF REQUIRED'.
Launched aboard the shopping basket, sat precipitately down,
Rocked past Zwanziger the baker's, and the terrace blackish brown,
And the curious Anglo-Norman parish church of Kentish Town.

Till the tram went over thirty, sighting terminus again,
Past municipal lawn tennis and the bobble-hanging plane;
Soft the light suburban evening caught our ashlar-speckled spire,
Eighteen-sixty Early English, as the mighty elms retire
Either side of Brookfield Mansions flashing fine French-window fire.

Oh the after-tram-ride quiet, when we heard a mile beyond,
Silver music from the bandstand, barking dogs by Highgate Pond;
Up the hill where stucco houses in Virginia creeper drown—
And my childish wave of pity, seeing children carrying down
Sheaves of drooping dandelions to the courts of Kentish Town.

3

POEMS OF EARLY SCHOOL

From SUMMONED BY BELLS

O Peggy Purey-Cust, how pure you were:
My first and purest love, Miss Purey-Cust!
Satchel on back I hurried up West Hill
To catch you on your morning walk to school,
Your nanny with you and your golden hair
Streaming like sunlight. Strict deportment made
You hold yourself erect and every step
Bounced up and down as though you walked on springs.
Your ice-blue eyes, your lashes long and light,
Your sweetly freckled face and turned-up nose
So haunted me that all my loves since then
Have had a look of Peggy Purey-Cust.

Along the Grove, what happy, happy steps
Under the limes I took to Byron House,
And blob-work, weaving, carpentry and art,
Walking with you; and with what joy returned.
Wendy you were to me in *Peter Pan*,
The Little Match Girl in Hans Andersen—
But I would rescue you before you died.
And once you asked me to your house to tea:
It seemed a palace after 31—
The lofty entrance hall, the flights of stairs,
The huge expanse of sunny drawing-room,
Looking for miles across the chimney-pots
To spired St. Pancras and the dome of Paul's;
And there your mother from a sofa smiled.
After that tea I called and called again,
But Peggy was not in. She was away;
She wasn't well. *House of the Sleeping Winds*,
My favourite book with whirling art-nouveau
And Walter Crane-ish colour plates, I brought
To cheer her sick-bed. It was taken in.
Weeks passed and passed . . . and then it was returned.
Oh gone for ever, Peggy Purey-Cust!

And at that happy school in Byron House
Only one harbinger of future woe
Came to me in those far, sun-gilded days—
Gold with the hair of Peggy Purey-Cust—
Two other boys (my rivals, I suppose)
Came suddenly round a corner, caught my arms
And one, a treacherous, stocky little Scot,
Winded me with a punch and "Want some more?"
He grunted when I couldn't speak for pain.
Why did he do it? Why that other boy,
Who hitherto had been a friend of mine,
Was his accomplice I could not divine,
Nor ever have done. But those fatal two
Continued with me to another school—
Avernus by the side of Highgate Hill.

Let those who have such memories recollect
Their sinking dread of going back to school.
I well remember mine. I see again
The great headmaster's study lined with books
Where somewhere, in a corner, there were canes.
He wrapped his gown, the great headmaster did,
About himself, chucked off his mortar-board
And, leaning back, said: "Let's see what you know,
How many half-crowns are there in a pound?"
I didn't know. I couldn't even guess.
My poor fond father, hearing nothing, smiled;
The gold clock ticked; the waiting furniture
Shone like a colour plate by H. M. Brock . . .
No answer—and the great headmaster frown'd;
But let me in to Highgate Junior School.

* * *

AN INCIDENT IN THE EARLY LIFE OF EBENEZER JONES, POET, 1828

"WE were together at a well-known boarding-school of that day (1828), situated at the foot of Highgate Hill, and presided over by a dissenting minister, the Rev. John Bickerdike. . . .

We were together, though not on the same form; and on a hot summer afternoon, with about fifty other boys, were listlessly conning our tasks in a large schoolroom built out from the house, which made a cover for us to play under when it was wet. Up the ladder-like stairs from the playground a lurcher dog had strayed into the schoolroom, panting with the heat, his tongue lolling out with thirst. The choleric usher who presided, and was detested by us for his tyranny, seeing this, advanced down the room. Enraged at our attention being distracted from our tasks, he dragged the dog to the top of the stairs, and there lifted him bodily up with the evident intention—and we had known him do similar things—of hurling the poor creature to the bottom.

'YOU SHALL NOT!' rang through the room, as little Ebby, so exclaiming at the top of his voice, rushed with kindling face to the spot from among all the boys—some of them twice his age.

But even while the words passed his lips, the heavy fall was heard, and the sound seemed to travel through his listening form and face, as, with a strange look of anguish in one so young, he stood still, threw up his arms, and burst into an uncontrollable passion of tears.

With a coarse laugh at this, the usher led him back by his ear to the form; and there he sat, long after his sobbing had subsided, like one dazed and stunned."

From an account written in 1879 by Ebenezer's brother, Sumner Jones.

The lumber of a London-going dray,
The still-new stucco on the London clay,
Hot summer silence over Holloway.

Dissenting chapels, tea-bowers, lovers' lairs,
Neat new-built villas, ample Grecian squares,
Remaining orchards ripening Windsor pears.

Hot silence where the older mansions hide
On Highgate Hill's thick elm-encrusted side,
And Pancras, Hornsey, Islington divide.

June's hottest silence where the hard rays strike
Yon hill-foot house, window and wall alike,
School of the Reverend Mr. Bickerdike,

For sons of Saints, blest with this world's possessions
(Seceders from the Protestant Secessions),
Good grounding in the more genteel professions.

A lurcher dog, which draymen kick and pass
Tongue lolling, thirsty over shadeless grass,
Leapt up the playground ladder to the class.

The godly usher left his godly seat,
His skin was prickly in the ungodly heat,
The dog lay panting at his godly feet.

The milkman on the road stood staring in.
The playground nettles nodded "Now begin"—
And Evil waited, quivering, for sin.

He lifted it and not a word he spoke,
His big hand tightened. Could he make it choke?
He trembled, sweated, and his temper broke.

"YOU SHALL NOT!" clear across to Highgate Hill
A boy's voice sounded. Creaking forms were still.
The cat jumped slowly from the window sill.

"YOU SHALL NOT!" flat against the summer sun,
Hard as the hard sky frowning over one,
Gloat, little boys! enjoy the coming fun!

"GOD DAMNS A CUR. I AM, I AM HIS WORD!"
He flung it, flung it and it never stirred,
"You shall not!—shall not!" ringing on unheard.

Blind desolation! bleeding, burning rod!
Big, bull-necked Minister of Calvin's God!
Exulting milkman, redfaced, shameless clod,

Look on and jeer! Not Satan's thunder-quake
Can cause the mighty walls of Heaven to shake
As now they do, to hear a boy's heart break.

4

POEMS OF HOLIDAYS

From SUMMONED BY BELLS

Come, Hygiene, goddess of the growing boy,
I here salute thee in Sanatogen!
Anaemic girls need Virol, but for me
Be Scott's Emulsion, rusks, and Mellin's Food,
Cod-liver oil and malt, and for my neck
Wright's Coal Tar Soap, Euthymol for my teeth.
Come, friends of Hygiene, Electricity
And those young twins, Free Thought and clean Fresh Air:
Attend the long express from Waterloo
That takes us down to Cornwall. Tea-time shows
The small fields waiting, every blackthorn hedge
Straining inland before the south-west gale.

The emptying train, wind in the ventilators,
Puffs out to Egloskerry to Tresméer
Through minty meadows, under bearded trees
And hills upon whose sides the clinging farms
Hold Bible Christians. Can it really be
That this same carriage came from Waterloo?
On Wadebridge station what a breath of sea
Scented the Camel valley! Cornish air,
Soft Cornish rains, and silence after steam . . .
As out of Derry's stable came the brake
To drag us up those long, familiar hills,
Past haunted woods and oil-lit farms and on
To far Trebetherick by the sounding sea.

Oh what a host of questions in me rose:
Were spring tides here or neap? And who was down?
Had Mr. Rosevear built himself a house?
Was there another wreck upon Doom Bar?
The carriage lamps lit up the pennywort
And fennel in the hedges of the lane;
Here slugs were crawling over slabs of slate;
Then, safe in bed, I watched the long-legg'd fly
With red transparent body tap the walls

And fizzle in the candle flame and drag
Its poisonous-looking abdomen away
To somewhere out of sight and out of mind,
While through the open window came the roar
Of full Atlantic rollers on the beach.

Then before breakfast down toward the sea
I ran alone, monarch of miles of sand,
Its shining stretches satin-smooth and vein'd.
I felt beneath bare feet the lugworm casts
And walked where only gulls and oyster-catchers
Had stepped before me to the water's edge.
The morning tide flowed in to welcome me,
The fan-shaped scallop shells, the backs of crabs,
The bits of driftwood worn to reptile shapes,
The heaps of bladder-wrack the tide had left
(Which, lifted up, sent sandhoppers to leap
In hundreds round me) answered "Welcome back!"

Along the links and under cold Bray Hill
Fresh water pattered from an iris marsh
And drowned the golf-balls on its stealthy way
Over the slates in which the elvers hid,
And spread across the beach. I used to stand,
A speculative water engineer—
Here I would plan a dam and there a sluice
And thus divert the stream, creating lakes,
A chain of locks descending to the sea.
Inland I saw, above the tamarisks,
From various villas morning breakfast smoke
Which warned me then of mine; so up the lane
I wandered home contented, full of plans,
Pulling a length of pink convolvulus
Whose blossoms, almost as I picked them, died.

Bright as the morning sea those early days!
Though there were tears, and sand thrown in my eyes.
And punishments and smells of mackintosh,

Long barefoot climbs to fetch the morning milk,
Terrors from hissing geese and angry shouts,
Slammed doors and waitings and a sense of dread,
Still warm as shallow sea-pools in the sun
And welcoming to me the girls and boys.

Wet rocks on which our bathing-dresses dried;
Small coves, deserted in our later years
For more adventurous inlets down the coast:
Paralysis when climbing up the cliff—
Too steep to reach the top, too far to fall,
Tumbling to death in seething surf below,
A ledge just wide enough to lodge one's foot,
A sea-pink clump the only thing to clutch,
Cold wave-worn slate so mercilessly smooth
And no one near and evening coming on—
Till Ralph arrived: "Now put your left foot here.
Give us your hand" . . . and back across the years
I swing to safety with old friends again.
Small seem they now, those once tremendous cliffs,
Diminished now those joy-enclosing bays.

* * *

SEASIDE GOLF

How straight it flew, how long it flew,
  It clear'd the rutty track
And soaring, disappeared from view
  Beyond the bunker's back—
A glorious, sailing, bounding drive
That made me glad I was alive.

And down the fairway, far along
  It glowed a lonely white;
I played an iron sure and strong
  And clipp'd it out of sight,
And spite of grassy banks between
I knew I'd find it on the green.

And so I did. It lay content
   Two paces from the pin;
A steady putt and then it went
   Oh, most securely in.
The very turf rejoiced to see
That quite unprecedented three.

Ah! seaweed smells from sandy caves
   And thyme and mist in whiffs,
In-coming tide, Atlantic waves
   Slapping the sunny cliffs,
Lark song and sea sounds in the air
And splendour, splendour everywhere.

TREBETHERICK

We used to picnic where the thrift
   Grew deep and tufted to the edge;
We saw the yellow foam-flakes drift
   In trembling sponges on the ledge
Below us, till the wind would lift
   Them up the cliff and o'er the hedge.
Sand in the sandwiches, wasps in the tea,
Sun on our bathing-dresses heavy with the wet,
Squelch of the bladder-wrack waiting for the sea,
Fleas round the tamarisk, an early cigarette.

From where the coastguard houses stood
   One used to see, below the hill,
The lichened branches of a wood
   In summer silver-cool and still;
And there the Shade of Evil could
   Stretch out at us from Shilla Mill.
Thick with sloe and blackberry, uneven in the light,
Lonely ran the hedge, the heavy meadow was remote,
The oldest part of Cornwall was the wood as black as night,
And the pheasant and the rabbit lay torn open at the throat.

But when a storm was at its height,
   And feathery slate was black in rain,
And tamarisks were hung with light
   And golden sand was brown again,
Spring tide and blizzard would unite
   And sea came flooding up the lane.
Waves full of treasure then were roaring up the beach,
Ropes round our mackintoshes, waders warm and dry,
We waited for the wreckage to come swirling into reach,
Ralph, Vasey, Alastair, Biddy, John and I.

Then roller into roller curled
   And thundered down the rocky bay,
And we were in a water-world
   Of rain and blizzard, sea and spray,
And one against the other hurled
   We struggled round to Greenaway.
Blesséd be St. Enodoc, blesséd be the wave,
Blesséd be the springy turf, we pray, pray to thee,
Ask for our children all the happy days you gave
To Ralph, Vasey, Alastair, Biddy, John and me.

EAST ANGLIAN BATHE

Oh when the early morning at the seaside
   Took us with hurrying steps from Horsey Mere
To see the whistling bent-grass on the leeside
   And then the tumbled breaker-line appear,
On high, the clouds with mighty adumbration
   Sailed over us to seaward fast and clear
And jellyfish in quivering isolation
   Lay silted in the dry sand of the breeze
And we, along the table-land of beach blown
   Went gooseflesh from our shoulders to our knees
And ran to catch the football, each to each thrown,
   In the soft and swirling music of the seas.

There splashed about our ankles as we waded
  Those intersecting wavelets morning-cold,
And sudden dark a patch of sea was shaded,
  And sudden light, another patch would hold
The warmth of whirling atoms in a sun-shot
  And underwater sandstorm green and gold.
So in we dived and louder than a gunshot
  Sea-water broke in fountains down the ear.
How cold the bathe, how chattering cold the drying,
  How welcoming the inland reeds appear,
The wood-smoke and the breakfast and the frying,
  And your warm freshwater ripples, Horsey Mere.

BESIDE THE SEASIDE

Green Shutters, shut your shutters! Windyridge,
Let winds unnoticed whistle round your hill!
High Dormers, draw your curtains! Slam the door,
And pack the family in the Morris eight.
Lock up the garage. Put her in reverse,
Back out with care, now, forward, off—away!
The richer people living farther out
O'ertake us in their Rovers. We, in turn,
Pass poorer families hurrying on foot
Towards the station. Very soon the town
Will echo to the groan of empty trams
And sweetshops advertise Ice Cream in vain.

Solihull, Headingley and Golders Green,
Preston and Swindon, Manchester and Leeds,
Braintree and Bocking, hear the sea! the sea!
The smack of breakers upon windy rocks,
Spray blowing backwards from their curling walls
Of green translucent water. England leaves
Her centre for her tide-line. Father's toes,
Though now encased in coloured socks and shoes

And pressing the accelerator hard,
Ache for the feel of sand and little shrimps
To tickle in between them. Mother vows
To be more patient with the family;
Just for its sake she will be young again.
And, at that moment, Jennifer is sick
(Over-excitement must have brought it on,
The hurried breakfast and the early start)
And Michael's rather pale, and as for Anne . . .
"Please stop a moment, Hubert, anywhere."

So evening sunlight shows us Sandy Cove
The same as last year and the year before.
Still on the brick front of the Baptist Church
SIX-THIRTY. PREACHER:—*Mr. Pentecost—*
All visitors are welcomed. Still the quartz
Glitters along the tops of garden walls.
Those macrocarpa still survive the gales
They must have had last winter. Still the shops
Remain unaltered on the Esplanade—
The Circulating Library, the Stores,
Jill's Pantry, Cynthia's Ditty Box (Antiques),
Trecarrow (Maps and Souvenirs and Guides).
Still on the terrace of the big hotel
Pale pink hydrangeas turn a rusty brown
Where sea winds catch them, and yet do not die.

The bumpy lane between the tamarisks,
The escallonia hedge, and still it's there—
Our lodging-house, ten minutes from the shore.
Still unprepared to make a picnic lunch
Except by notice on the previous day.
Still nowhere for the children when it's wet
Except that smelly, overcrowded lounge.
And still no garage for the motor-car.
Still on the bedroom wall, the list of rules:
Don't waste the water. It is pumped by hand.

Don't throw old blades into the W.C.
Don't keep the bathroom long and don't be late
For meals and don't hang swim-suits out on sills
(*A line has been provided at the back*).
Don't empty children's sand-shoes in the hall.
Don't this, Don't that. Ah, still the same, the same
As it was last year and the year before—
But rather more expensive, now, of course.
"Anne, Jennifer and Michael—run along
Down to the sands and find yourselves some friends
While Dad and I unpack." The sea! the sea!

On a secluded corner of the beach
A game of rounders has been organised
By Mr. Pedder, schoolmaster and friend
Of boys and girls—particularly girls.
And here it was the tragedy began,
That life-long tragedy to Jennifer
Which ate into her soul and made her take
To secretarial work in later life
In a department of the Board of Trade.
See boys and girls assembled for the game.
Reflected in the rock pools, freckled legs
Hop, skip and jump in coltish ecstasy.
Ah! parted lips and little pearly teeth,
Wide eyes, snub noses, shorts, divided skirts!
And last year's queen of them was Jennifer.
The snubbiest, cheekiest, lissomest of all.
One smile from her sent Mr. Pedder back
Contented to his lodgings. She could wave
Her little finger and the elder boys
Came at her bidding. Even tiny Ruth,
Old Lady D'Erncourt's grandchild, pet of all,
Would bring her shells as timid offerings.

So now with Anne and Michael see her stand,
Our Jennifer, our own, our last year's queen,
For this year's *début* fully confident.

"Get in your places." Heard above the waves
Are Mr. Pedder's organising shouts.
"Come on. Look sharp. The tide is coming in!"
"He hasn't seen me yet," thinks Jennifer.
"Line up your team behind you, Christabel!"
On the wet sea-sand waiting to be seen
She stands with Anne and Michael. Let him turn
And then he'll see me. Let him only turn.
Smack went the tennis ball. The bare feet ran.
And smack again. "He's out! Well caught, Delphine!"
Shrieks, cartwheels, tumbling joyance of the waves.
Oh Mr. Pedder, look! Oh here I am!
And there the three of them forlornly stood.
"You ask him, Jennifer." "No—Michael?—Anne?"
"I'd rather not." "Fains I." "It's up to you."
"Oh, very well, then." Timidly she goes,
Timid and proud, for the last time a child.
"Can *we* play, Mr. Pedder?" But his eyes
Are out to where, among the tousled heads,
He sees the golden curls of Christabel.
"Can *we* play, Mr. Pedder?" So he turns.
"*Who* have we here?" The jolly, jolly voice,
The same but not the same. "*Who* have we here?
The Rawlings children! Yes, of course, you may,
Join that side, children, under Christabel."
No friendly wallop on the B.T.M.
No loving arm-squeeze and no special look.
Oh darting heart-burn, *under Christabel!*

So all those holidays the bitter truth
Sank into Jennifer. No longer queen,
She had outgrown her strength, as Mummy said,
And Mummy made her wear these spectacles.
Because of Mummy she had lost her looks.
Had lost her looks? Still she was Jennifer.
The sands were still the same, the rocks the same,
The seaweed-waving pools, the bathing-cove,

The outline of the cliffs, the times of tide.
And I'm the same, of course I'm always ME.
But all that August those terrific waves
Thundered defeat along the rocky coast,
And ginger-beery surf hissed 'Christabel!'

Enough of tragedy! Let wail of gulls,
The sunbows in the breakers and the breeze
Which blows the sand into the sandwiches,
Let castles crumbling in the rise of tide,
Let cool dank caves and dark interstices
Where, underneath the squelching bladder-wrack,
Lurk stinging fin and sharp, marauding claw
Ready to pierce the rope-soled bathing-shoe,
Let darting prawn and helpless jelly-fish
Spell joy or misery to youth. For we,
We older ones, have thoughts of higher things.
Whether we like to sit with Penguin books
In sheltered alcoves farther up the cliff,
Or to eat winkles on the Esplanade,
Or to play golf along the crowded course,
Or on a twopenny borough council chair
To doze away the strains of *Humoresque*,
Adapted for the cornet and the drums
By the conductor of the Silver Band,
Whether we own a tandem or a Rolls,
Whether we Rudge it or we trudge it, still
A single topic occupies our minds.
'Tis hinted at or boldly blazoned in
Our accents, clothes and ways of eating fish,
And being introduced and taking leave,
'Farewell', 'So long', 'Bunghosky', 'Cheeribye'—
That topic all-absorbing, as it was,
Is now and ever shall be, to us—CLASS.

Mr. and Mrs. Stephen Grosvenor-Smith
(He manages a Bank in Nottingham)

Have come to Sandy Cove for thirty years
And now they think the place is going down.
"Not what it was, I'm very much afraid.
Look at that little mite with *Attaboy*
Printed across her paper sailor hat.
Disgusting, isn't it? Who *can* they be,
Her parents, to allow such forwardness?"

The Browns, who thus are commented upon,
Have certainly done very well indeed.
The elder children bringing money in,
Father still working; with allowances
For this and that and little income-tax,
They probably earn seven times as much
As poor old Grosvenor-Smith. But who will grudge
Them this, their wild, spontaneous holiday?
The morning paddle, then the mystery tour
By motor-coach inland this afternoon.
For that old mother what a happy time!
At last past bearing children, she can sit
Reposeful on a crowded bit of beach.
A week of idleness, the salty winds
Play in her greying hair; the summer sun
Puts back her freckles so that Alfred Brown
Remembers courting days in Gospel Oak
And takes her to the Flannel Dance to-night.
But all the same they think the place 'Stuck up'
And Blackpool, next year—if there *is* a next.

And all the time the waves, the waves, the waves
Chase, intersect and flatten on the sand
As they have done for centuries, as they will
For centuries to come, when not a soul
Is left to picnic on the blazing rocks,
When England is not England, when mankind
Has blown himself to pieces. Still the sea,

Consolingly disastrous, will return
While the strange starfish, hugely magnified.
Waits in the jewelled basin of a pool.

HUNTER TRIALS

It's awf'lly bad luck on Diana,
  Her ponies have swallowed their bits;
She fished down their throats with a spanner
  And frightened them all into fits.

So now she's attempting to borrow.
  Do lend her some bits, Mummy, *do*;
I'll lend her my own for to-morrow,
  But to-day *I*'ll be wanting them too.

Just look at Prunella on Guzzle,
  The wizardest pony on earth;
Why doesn't she slacken his muzzle
  And tighten the breech in his girth?

I say, Mummy, there's Mrs. Geyser
  And doesn't she look pretty sick?
I bet it's because Mona Lisa
  Was hit on the hock with a brick.

Miss Blewitt says Monica threw it,
  But Monica says it was Joan,
And Joan's very thick with Miss Blewitt,
  So Monica's sulking alone.

And Margaret failed in her paces,
  Her withers got tied in a noose,
So her coronets caught in the traces
  And now all her fetlocks are loose.

Oh, it's me now. I'm terribly nervous.
  I wonder if Smudges will shy.
She's practically certain to swerve as
  Her Pelham is over one eye.

* * * * *

Oh wasn't it naughty of Smudges?
  Oh, Mummy, I'm sick with disgust
She threw me in front of the Judges,
  And my silly old collarbone's bust.

5

POEMS OF PEOPLE

From SUMMONED BY BELLS

PERCIVAL MANDEVILLE, the perfect boy,
Was all a schoolmaster could wish to see—
Upright and honourable, good at games,
Well-built, blue-eyed; a sense of leadership
Lifted him head and shoulders from the crowd.
His work was good. His written answers, made
In a round, tidy and decided hand,
Pleased the examiners. His open smile
Enchanted others. He could also frown
On anything unsporting, mean or base,
Unworthy of the spirit of the school
And what it stood for. Oh the dreadful hour
When once upon a time he frowned on me!

Just what had happened I cannot recall—
Maybe some bullying in the dormitory;
But well I recollect his warning words:
"I'll fight you, Betjeman, you swine, for that,
Behind the bike shed before morning school."
So all the previous night I spewed with fear.
I could not box: I greatly dreaded pain.
A recollection of the winding punch
Jack Drayton once delivered, blows and boots
Upon the bum at Highgate Junior School,
All multiplied by X from Mandeville,
Emptied my bladder. Silent in the dorm
I cleaned my teeth and clambered into bed.
Thin seemed pyjamas and inadequate
The regulation blankets once so warm.
"What's up?" "Oh, nothing." I expect they knew . . .

And, in the morning, cornflakes, bread and tea,
Cook's Farm Eggs and a spoon of marmalade,
Which heralded the North and Hillard hours
Of Latin composition, brought the post.

Breakfast and letters! Then it was a flash
Of hope, escape and inspiration came:
Invent a letter of bad news from home.
I hung my head and tried to look as though,
By keeping such a brave stiff upper lip
And just not blubbing, I was noble too.
I sought out Mandeville. "I say," I said,
"I'm frightfully sorry I can't fight today.
I've just received some rotten news from home:
My mater's very ill." No need for more—
His arm was round my shoulder comforting:
"All right, old chap. Of course I understand."

* * *

THE OLYMPIC GIRL

The sort of girl I like to see
Smiles down from her great height at me.
She stands in strong, athletic pose
And wrinkles her *retroussé* nose.
Is it distaste that makes her frown,
So furious and freckled, down
On an unhealthy worm like me?
Or am I what she likes to see?
I do not know, though much I care.
εἴθε γενοίμην . . . would I were
(Forgive me, shade of Rupert Brooke)
An object fit to claim her look.

Oh! would I were her racket press'd
With hard excitement to her breast
And swished into the sunlit air
Arm-high above her tousled hair,
And banged against the bounding ball
"Oh! Plung!" my tauten'd strings would call
"Oh! Plung! my darling, break my strings
For you I will do brilliant things."

And when the match is over, I
Would flop beside you, hear you sigh;
And then, with what supreme caress,
You'd tuck me up into my press.
Fair tigress of the tennis courts,
So short in sleeve and strong in shorts,
Little, alas, to you I mean,
For I am bald and old and green.

HOW TO GET ON IN SOCIETY

Phone for the fish-knives, Norman
  As Cook is a little unnerved;
You kiddies have crumpled the serviettes
  And I must have things daintily served.

Are the requisites all in the toilet?
  The frills round the cutlets can wait
Till the girl has replenished the cruets
  And switched on the logs in the grate.

It's ever so close in the lounge, dear,
  But the vestibule's comfy for tea
And Howard is out riding on horseback
  So do come and take some with me.

Now here is a fork for your pastries
  And do use the couch for your feet;
I know what I wanted to ask you—
  Is trifle sufficient for sweet?

Milk and then just as it comes dear?
  I'm afraid the preserve's full of stones;
Beg pardon, I'm soiling the doileys
  With afternoon tea-cakes and scones.

POT POURRI FROM A SURREY GARDEN

Miles of pram in the wind and Pam in the gorse track,
    Coco-nut smell of the broom, and a packet of Weights
Press'd in the sand. The thud of a hoof on a horse-track—
        A horse-riding horse for a horse-track—
        Conifer county of Surrey approached
    Through remarkable wrought-iron gates.

Over your boundary now, I wash my face in a bird-bath,
    Then which path shall I take? that over there by the pram?
Down by the pond! or—yes, I will take the slippery third path,
        Trodden away with gym shoes,
        Beautiful fir-dry alley that leads
    To the bountiful body of Pam.

Pam, I adore you, Pam, you great big mountainous sports girl,
    Whizzing them over the net, full of the strength of five:
That old Malvernian brother, you zephyr and khaki shorts girl,
        Although he's playing for Woking,
        Can't stand up
    To your wonderful backhand drive.

See the strength of her arm, as firm and hairy as Hendren's;
    See the size of her thighs, the pout of her lips as, cross,
And full of a pent-up strength, she swipes at the rhododendrons,
        Lucky the rhododendrons,
        And flings her arrogant love-lock
    Back with a petulant toss.

Over the redolent pinewoods, in at the bathroom casement,
    One fine Saturday, Windlesham bells shall call:
Up the Butterfield aisle rich with Gothic enlacement,
        Licensed now for embracement,
        Pam and I, as the organ
    Thunders over you all.

IN THE PUBLIC GARDENS

In the Public Gardens,
    To the airs of Strauss,
Eingang we're in love again
    When *ausgang* we were *aus*.

The waltz was played, the songs were sung,
    The night resolved our fears;
From bunchy boughs the lime trees hung
    Their gold electroliers.

Among the loud Americans
    Zwei Engländer were we,
You so white and frail and pale
    And me so deeply me.

I bought for you a dark-red rose,
    I saw your grey-green eyes,
As high above the floodlights,
    The true moon sailed the skies.

In the Public Gardens,
    Ended things begin;
Ausgang we were out of love
    Und eingang we are in.

A SUBALTERN'S LOVE-SONG

Miss J. Hunter Dunn, Miss J. Hunter Dunn,
Furnish'd and burnish'd by Aldershot sun,
What strenuous singles we played after tea,
We in the tournament—you against me!

Love-thirty, love-forty, oh! weakness of joy,
The speed of a swallow, the grace of a boy,
With carefullest carelessness, gaily you won,
I am weak from your loveliness, Joan Hunter Dunn.

Miss Joan Hunter Dunn, Miss Joan Hunter Dunn,
How mad I am, sad I am, glad that you won.
The warm-handled racket is back in its press,
But my shock-headed victor, she loves me no less.

Her father's euonymus shines as we walk,
And swing past the summer-house, buried in talk,
And cool the verandah that welcomes us in
To the six-o'clock news and a lime-juice and gin.

The scent of the conifers, sound of the bath,
The view from my bedroom of moss-dappled path,
As I struggle with double-end evening tie,
For we dance at the Golf Club, my victor and I.

On the floor of her bedroom lie blazer and shorts
And the cream-coloured walls are be-trophied with sports,
And westering, questioning settles the sun
On your low-leaded window, Miss Joan Hunter Dunn.

The Hillman is waiting, the light's in the hall,
The pictures of Egypt are bright on the wall,
My sweet, I am standing beside the oak stair
And there on the landing's the light on your hair.

By roads 'not adopted', by woodlanded ways,
She drove to the club in the late summer haze,
Into nine-o'clock Camberley, heavy with bells
And mushroomy, pine-woody, evergreen smells.

Miss Joan Hunter Dunn, Miss Joan Hunter Dunn,
I can hear from the car-park the dance has begun.
Oh! full Surrey twilight! importunate band!
Oh! strongly adorable tennis-girl's hand!

Around us are Rovers and Austins afar,
Above us, the intimate roof of the car,
And here on my right is the girl of my choice,
With the tilt of her nose and the chime of her voice,

And the scent of her wrap, and the words never said,
And the ominous, ominous dancing ahead.
We sat in the car park till twenty to one
And now I'm engaged to Miss Joan Hunter Dunn.

THE OLD LIBERALS

Pale green of the *English Hymnal*! Yattendon hymns
  Played on the *hautbois* by a lady dress'd in blue
  Her white-hair'd father accompanying her thereto
On tenor or bass-recorder. Daylight swims
  On sectional bookcase, delicate cup and plate
  And William de Morgan tiles around the grate
And many the silver birches the pearly light shines through.

I think such a running together of woodwind sound,
  Such painstaking piping high on a Berkshire hill,
  Is sad as an English autumn heavy and still,
Sad as a country silence, tractor-drowned;

For deep in the hearts of the man and the woman playing
  The rose of a world that was not has withered away.
Where are the wains with garlanded swathes a-swaying?
Where are the swains to wend through the lanes a-maying?
  Where are the blithe and jocund to ted the hay?
  Where are the free folk of England? Where are they?

Ask of the Abingdon bus with full load creeping
   Down into denser suburbs. The birch lets go
   But one brown leaf upon browner bracken below.
Ask of the cinema manager. Night airs die
To still, ripe scent of the fungus and wet woods weeping.
   Ask at the fish and chips in the Market Square.
   Here amid firs and a final sunset flare
Recorder and *hautbois* only moan at a mouldering sky.

LORD COZENS HARDY

Oh Lord Cozens Hardy
   Your mausoleum is cold,
The dry brown grass is brittle
   And frozen hard the mould
And where those Grecian columns rise
   So white among the dark
Of yew trees and of hollies in
   That corner of the park
By Norfolk oaks surrounded
   Whose branches seem to talk,
I know, Lord Cozens Hardy,
   I would not like to walk.

And even in the summer,
   On a bright East-Anglian day
When round your Doric portico
   Your children's children play
There's a something in the stillness
   And our waiting eyes are drawn
From the butler and the footman
   Bringing tea out on the lawn,
From the little silver spirit lamp
   That burns so blue and still,
To the half-seen mausoleum
   In the oak trees on the hill.

But when, Lord Cozens Hardy,
  November stars are bright,
And the King's Head Inn at Letheringsett
  Is shutting for the night,
The villagers have told me
  That they do not like to pass
Near your curious mausoleum
  Moon-shadowed on the grass
For fear of seeing walking
  In the season of All Souls
That first Lord Cozens Hardy,
  The Master of the Rolls.

EXCHANGE OF LIVINGS

Lines suggested by an advertisement in a
Broad Church newspaper

The church was locked, so I went to the incumbent
the incumbent enjoying a supine incumbency—
a tennis court, a summerhouse, deckchairs by the walnut tree
and only the hum of the bees in the rockery.
"May I have the keys of the church, your incumbency?"
"Yes, my dear sir, as a moderate churchman,
I am willing to exchange: light Sunday duty:
                nice district: pop 149: eight hundred per annum:
no extremes: A and M: bicyclist essential:
                                        same income expected."

"I think I'm the man that you want, your incumbency.
Here's my address when I'm not on my bicycle,
                poking about for recumbent stone effigies—
14, Mount Ephraim, Cheltenham, Glos:
Rector St. George-in-the-Rolling Pins, Cripplegate:
non resident pop in the City of London:
eight fifty per annum (but verger an asset):
willing to exchange (no extremes) for incumbency,
similar income, but closer to residence."

DIARY OF A CHURCH MOUSE

Here among long-discarded cassocks,
Damp stools, and half-split open hassocks,
Here where the Vicar never looks
I nibble through old service books.
Lean and alone I spend my days
Behind this Church of England baize.
I share my dark forgotten room
With two oil-lamps and half a broom.
The cleaner never bothers me,
So here I eat my frugal tea.
My bread is sawdust mixed with straw;
My jam is polish for the floor.

Christmas and Easter may be feasts
For congregations and for priests,
And so may Whitsun. All the same,
They do not fill my meagre frame.
For me the only feast at all
Is Autumn's Harvest Festival,
When I can satisfy my want
With ears of corn around the font.
I climb the eagle's brazen head
To burrow through a loaf of bread.
I scramble up the pulpit stair
And gnaw the marrows hanging there.

It is enjoyable to taste
These items ere they go to waste,
But how annoying when one finds
That other mice with pagan minds
Come into church my food to share
Who have no proper business there.
Two field mice who have no desire
To be baptized, invade the choir.

A large and most unfriendly rat
Comes in to see what we are at.
He says he thinks there is no God
And yet he comes . . . it's rather odd.
This year he stole a sheaf of wheat
(It screened our special preacher's seat),
And prosperous mice from fields away
Came in to hear the organ play,
And under cover of its notes
Ate through the altar's sheaf of oats.
A Low Church mouse, who thinks that I
Am too papistical, and High,
Yet somehow doesn't think it wrong
To munch through Harvest Evensong,
While I, who starve the whole year through,
Must share my food with rodents who
Except at this time of the year
Not once inside the church appear.

Within the human world I know
Such goings-on could not be so,
For human beings only do
What their religion tells them to.
They read the Bible every day
And always, night and morning, pray,
And just like me, the good church mouse,
Worship each week in God's own house.

But all the same it's strange to me
How very full the church can be
With people I don't see at all
Except at Harvest Festival.

6

DISCOVERING ARCHITECTURE

From SUMMONED BY BELLS

ONE lucky afternoon in Chaundy's shop
I bought a book with tipped-in colour plates—
'City of Dreaming Spires' or some such name—
Soft late-Victorian water-colours framed
Against brown paper pages. Thus it was
'Sunset in Worcester Gardens' meant for me
Such beauty in that black and shallow pool
That even to-day, when from the ilex tree
I see its shining length, I fail to hear
The all-too-near and omnipresent train.
The Founder's Tower in Magdalen still seems drowned
In red Virginia creeper, and The High
Has but one horse-tram down its famous length,
While a gowned Doctor of Divinity
Enters the porch of Univ.; Christ Church stairs
(A single column supporting the intricate roof),
Wallflowers upon the ruined city wall,
Wistaria-mantled buildings in St. John's—
All that was crumbling, picturesque and quaint
Informed my taste and sent me biking off,
Escaped from games, for Architecture bound.

Can words express the unexampled thrill
I first enjoyed in Norm., E.E. and Dec.?
Norm., crude and round and strong and primitive,
E.E., so lofty, pointed, fine and pure,
And Dec. the high perfection of it all,
Flowingly curvilinear, from which
The Perp. showed such a 'lamentable decline'.
Who knew what undiscovered glories hung
Waiting in locked-up churches—vaulting shafts,
Pillar-piscinas, floreated caps.,
Squints, squinches, low side windows, quoins and groins—
Till I had roused the Vicar, found the key,
And made a quick inspection of the church?
Then, full of my discovery returned,
Hot from my bicycle to Gerald Haynes.

Much do I owe this formidable man
(Harrow and Keble): from his shambling height
Over his spectacles he nodded down.
We called him 'Tortoise'. From his lower lip
Invariably hung a cigarette.
A gym-shoe in his hand, he stood about
Waiting for misdemeanours—then he'd pounce:
"Who's talking here?" The dormitory quailed.
"Who's talking?" Then, though innocent myself,
A schoolboy hero to the dorm at last,
Bravely I answered, "Please, sir, it was me."
"All right. Bend over." A resounding three
From the strong gym-shoe brought a gulp of pain.
"I liked the way you took that beating, John.
Reckon yourself henceforth a gentleman."

Were those the words that made me follow him,
Waiting for hours in churches while he fixed
His huge plate camera up and, a black cloth
Over his bald head, photographed the font?
Was that the reason why the pale grey slides
Of tympana, scratch dials and Norfolk screens
So pleased me at his lectures? I think not:
Rather his kindness and his power to share
Joys of his own, churches and botany,
With those of us whose tastes he could inform.
He motor-bicycled his life away,
Looking for orchids in the Wytham Woods,
And Early English in Northamptonshire.
He was the giver: ours it was to take.

The bindweed hung in leafy loops
  O'er half a hundred hawthorn caves,
For Godstow bound, the white road wound
  In swirls of dust and narrow shaves,
And we were biking, Red Sea troops,
  Between the high cow-parsley waves.

Port Meadow's level green grew near
  With Wytham Woods and Cumnor Hurst:
I clicked my Sturmey-Archer gear
  And pedalled till I nearly burst—
And, king of speed, attained the lead
  And got to gushing Godstow first.

The skiffs were moored above the lock,
  They bumped each other side to side:
I boarded one and made her rock—
  "Shut up, you fool," a master cried.
By reed and rush and alder-bush
  See soon our long procession glide.

There is a world of water weed
  Seen only from a shallow boat:
Deep forests of the bladed reed
  Whose wolves are rats of slimy coat,
Whose yellow lily-blossoms need
  Broad leaves to keep themselves afloat.

A heaving world, half-land, half-flood;
  It rose and sank as ripples rolled,
The hideous larva from the mud
  Clung to a reed with patient hold,
Waiting to break its sheath and make
  An aeroplane of green and gold.

The picnic and the orchid hunt,
  On Oxey mead the rounders played,
The belly-floppers from the punt,
  The echoes that our shouting made:
The rowing back, relaxed and slack,
  The shipping oars in Godstow shade . . .

Once more we biked beside the hedge—
  And darker seemed the hawthorn caves
And lonelier looked the water's edge,
  And we were sad returning slaves
To bell and rule and smell of school,
  Beyond the high cow-parsley waves.

* * *

HYMN

The Church's Restoration
  In eighteen-eighty-three
Has left for contemplation
  Not what there used to be.
How well the ancient woodwork
  Looks round the Rect'ry hall,
Memorial of the good work
  Of him who plann'd it all.

He who took down the pew-ends
  And sold them anywhere
But kindly spared a few ends
  Work'd up into a chair.
O worthy persecution
  Of dust! O hue divine!
O cheerful substitution,
  Thou varnishéd pitch-pine!

Church furnishing! Church furnishing!
  Sing art and crafty praise!
He gave the brass for burnishing,
  He gave the thick red baize,
He gave the new addition,
  Pull'd down the dull old aisle,
—To pave the sweet transition
  He gave th' encaustic tile.

Of marble brown and veinéd
  He did the pulpit make;
He order'd windows stainéd
  Light red and crimson lake.
Sing on, with hymns uproarious,
  Ye humble and aloof,
Look up! and oh how glorious
  He has restored the roof!

AN ARCHÆOLOGICAL PICNIC

In this high pasturage, this Blunden time,
 With Lady's Finger, Smokewort, Lovers' Loss,
And lin-lan-lone, a Tennysonian chime
 Stirring the sorrel and the gold-starred moss,
 Cool is the chancel, bright the altar cross.

Drink, Mary, drink your fizzy lemonade
 And leave the king-cups; take your grey felt hat;
Here, where the low-side window lends a shade,
 There, where the key lies underneath the mat,
 The rude forefathers of the hamlet sat.

Sweet smell of cerements and of cold wet stones,
 Hassock and cassock, paraffin and pew;
Green is a light which that sublime Burne-Jones
 White-hot and wondering from the glass-kiln drew,
 Gleams and re-gleams this Trans arcade anew.

So stand you waiting, freckled innocence!
 For me the squinch and squint and Trans arcade;
For you, where meadow grass is evidence,
 With flattened pattern, of our picnic made,
 One bottle more of fizzy lemonade.

SUNDAY MORNING, KING'S CAMBRIDGE

File into yellow candle light, fair choristers of King's
 Lost in the shadowy silence of canopied Renaissance stalls
In blazing glass above the dark glow skies and thrones and wings
 Blue, ruby, gold and green between the whiteness of the walls
And with what rich precision the stonework soars and springs
 To fountain out a spreading vault—a shower that never falls.

The white of windy Cambridge courts, the cobbles brown and dry,
  The gold of plaster Gothic with ivy overgrown,
The apple-red, the silver fronts, the wide green flats and high,
  The yellowing elm-trees circled out on islands of their own—
Oh, here behold all colours change that catch the flying sky
  To waves of pearly light that heave along the shafted stone.

In far East Anglian churches, the clasped hands lying long
  Recumbent on sepulchral slabs or effigied in brass
Buttress with prayer this vaulted roof so white and light and strong
  And countless congregations as the generations pass
Join choir and great crowned organ case, in centuries of song
  To praise Eternity contained in Time and coloured glass.

THE TOWN CLERK'S VIEWS

"Yes, the Town Clerk will see you." In I went.
He was, like all Town Clerks, from north of Trent;
A man with bye-laws busy in his head
Whose Mayor and Council followed where he led.
His most capacious brain will make us cower,
His only weakness is a lust for power—
And that is not a weakness, people think,
When unaccompanied by bribes or drink.
So let us hear this cool careerist tell
His plans to turn our country into hell.

"I cannot say how shock'd I am to see
The *variations* in our scenery.
Just take for instance, at a casual glance,
Our muddled coastline opposite to France:
Dickensian houses by the Channel tides
With old hipp'd roofs and weather-boarded sides.
I blush to think one corner of our isle
Lacks concrete villas in the modern style.

Straight lines of hops in pale brown earth of Kent,
Yeomen's square houses once, no doubt, content
With willow-bordered horse-pond, oast-house, shed,
Wide orchard, garden walls of browny-red—
All useless now, but what fine sites they'd be
For workers' flats and some light industry.

"Those lumpy church towers, unadorned with spires,
And wavy roofs that burn like smouldering fires
In sharp spring sunlight over ashen flint
Are out of date as some old aquatint.
Then glance below the line of Sussex downs
To stucco terraces of seaside towns
Turn'd into flats and residential clubs
Above the wind-slashed Corporation shrubs.
Such Georgian relics should by now, I feel,
Be all rebuilt in glass and polished steel.

"Bournemouth is looking up. I'm glad to say
That modernistic there has come to stay.
I walk the asphalt paths of Branksome Chine
In resin-scented air like strong Greek wine
And dream of cliffs of flats along those heights,
Floodlit at night with green electric lights.
But as for Dorset's flint and Purbeck stone,
Its old thatched farms in dips of down alone—
It should be merged with Hants and made to be
A self-contained and plann'd community.
Like Flint and Rutland, it is much too small
And has no reason to exist at all.

"Of Devon one can hardly say the same,
But South-West Area One's a better name
For those red sandstone cliffs that stain the sea
By mid-Victoria's Italy—Torquay.
And South-West Area Two could well include
The whole of Cornwall from Land's End to Bude.

Need I retrace my steps through other shires?
Pinnacled Somerset? Northampton's spires?
Burford's broad High Street is descending still
Stone-roofed and golden-walled her elmy hill
To meet the river Windrush. What a shame
Her houses are not brick and all the same.

"Oxford is growing up to date at last.
Cambridge, I fear, is living in the past.
She needs more factories, not useless things
Like that great chapel which they keep at King's.
As for remote East Anglia, he who searches
Finds only thatch and vast, redundant churches.

"But that's the dark side. I can safely say
A beauteous England's really on the way.
Already our hotels are pretty good
For those who're fond of *very simple food*—
Cod and two veg., free pepper, salt and mustard,
Followed by nice hard plums and lumpy custard,
A pint of bitter beer for one-and-four,
Then coffee in the lounge a shilling more.
In a few years this country will be looking
As uniform and tasty as its cooking.
Hamlets which fail to pass the planners' test
Will be demolished. We'll rebuild the rest
To look like Welwyn mixed with Middle West.

"All fields we'll turn to sports grounds, lit at night
From concrete standards by fluorescent light:
And over all the land, instead of trees,
Clean poles and wire will whisper in the breeze.
We'll keep one ancient village just to show
What England once was when the times were slow—
Broadway for me. But here I know I must
Ask the opinion of our National Trust.
And ev'ry old cathedral that you enter
By then will be an Area Culture Centre.

Instead of nonsense about Death and Heaven
Lectures on civic duty will be given;
Eurhythmic classes dancing round the spire,
And economics courses in the choir.
So don't encourage tourists. Stay your hand
Until we've really got the country plann'd."

7

POEMS OF PLACES

From SUMMONED BY BELLS

WHEN I returned from school I found we'd moved:
"53 Church Street. Yes, the slummy end"—
A little laugh accompanied the joke,
For we were Chelsea now and we had friends
Whose friends had friends who knew Augustus John:
We liked bold colour schemes—orange and black—
And clever daring plays about divorce
At the St. Martin's. Oh, our lives were changed!
Ladies with pearls and hyphenated names
Supplanted simpler aunts from Muswell Hill:
A brand-new car and brand-new chauffeur came
To carry off my father to the Works.
Old Hannah Wallis left:
For years she'd listened to me reading verse;
Tons, if you added them, of buttered toast
Had she and I consumed through all the days
In happy Highgate. Now her dear old face,
Black bonnet, sniffs and comfortable self
Were gone to Tottenham where her daughter lived.

What is it first breeds insecurity?
Perhaps a change of house? I missed the climb
By garden walls and fences where a stick,
Dragged on the palings, clattered to my steps.
I missed the smell of trodden leaves and grass,
Millfield and Merton Lanes and sheep-worn tracks
Under the hawthorns west of Highgate ponds.
I missed the trams, the few North London trains,
The frequent Underground to Kentish Town.
Here in a district only served by bus,
Here on an urban level by the Thames—
I never really liked the Chelsea house.
"It's simply sweet, Bess," visitors exclaimed,
Depositing their wraps and settling down
To a nice rubber. "So artistic, too."
To me the house was poky, dark and cramped,

Haunted by quarrels and the ground-floor ghost.
I'd slam behind me our green garden door—
Well do I recollect that bounding thrill!—
And hare to Cheyne Gardens—free! free! free!—
By Lawrence Street and Upper Cheyne Row,
Safe to the tall red house of Ronnie Wright.

Great was my joy with London at my feet—
All London mine, five shillings in my hand
And not expected back till after tea!
Great was our joy, Ronald Hughes Wright's and mine,
To travel by the Underground all day
Between the rush hours, so that very soon
There was no station, north to Finsbury Park,
To Barking eastwards, Clapham Common south,
No temporary platform in the west
Among the Actons and the Ealings, where
We had not once alighted. Metroland
Beckoned us out to lanes in beechy Bucks—
Goldschmidt and Howland (in a wooden hut
Beside the station): 'Most attractive sites
Ripe for development'; 'Charrington's for coal';
And not far off the neo-Tudor shops.
We knew the different railways by their smells.
The City and South reeked like a changing-room;
Its orange engines and old rolling stock,
Its narrow platforms, undulating tracks,
Seemed even then historic. Next in age,
The Central London, with its cut-glass shades
On draughty stations, had an ozone smell—
Not seaweed-scented ozone from the sea
But something chemical from Birmingham.
When, in a pause between the stations, quiet
Descended on the carriage we would talk
Loud gibberish in angry argument,
Pretending to be foreign.

* * * * *

All silvery on frosty Sunday nights
Were City steeples white against the stars.
And narrowly the chasms wound between
Italianate counting-houses, Roman banks,
To this church and to that. Huge office-doors,
Their granite thresholds worn by weekday feet
(Now far away in slippered ease at Penge),
Stood locked. St. Botolph this, St. Mary that
Alone shone out resplendent in the dark.
I used to stand by intersecting lanes
Among the silent offices, and wait,
Choosing which bell to follow: not a peal,
For that meant somewhere active; not St. Paul's,
For that was too well-known. I liked things dim—
Some lazy Rector living in Bexhill
Who most unwillingly on Sunday came
To take the statutory services.

A single bell would tinkle down a lane:
My echoing steps would track the source of sound—
A cassocked verger, bell-rope in his hands,
Called me to high box pews, to cedar wood
(Like incense where no incense ever burned),
To ticking gallery-clock, and charity bench,
And free seats for the poor, and altar-piece—
Gilded Commandment boards—and sword-rests made
For long-discarded aldermanic pomp.
A hidden organist sent reedy notes
To flute around the plasterwork. I stood,
And from the sea of pews a single head
With cherries nodding on a black straw hat
Rose in a neighbouring pew. The caretaker?
Or the sole resident parishioner?
And so once more, as for three hundred years,
This carven wood, these grey memorial'd walls

Heard once again the Book of Common Prayer,
While somewhere at the back the verger, now
Turned Parish Clerk, would rumble out "Amen."

* * *

SOUTH LONDON SKETCH, 1844

Lavender Sweep is drowned in Wandsworth,
  Drowned in jessamine up to the neck,
Beetles sway upon bending grass leagues
  Shoulder-level to Tooting Bec.
Rich as Middlesex, rich in signboards,
  Lie the lover-trod lanes between,
Red Man, Green Man, Horse and Waggoner,
  Elms and sycamores round a green.
Burst, good June, with a rush this morning,
  Bindweed weave me an emerald rope,
Sun, shine bright on the blossoming trellises,
  June and lavender, bring me hope.

WESTGATE-ON-SEA

Hark, I hear the bells of Westgate,
  I will tell you what they sigh,
Where those minarets and steeples
  Prick the open Thanet sky.

Happy bells of eighteen-ninety,
  Bursting from your freestone tower!
Recalling laurel, shrubs and privet,
  Red geraniums in flower,

Feet that scamper on the asphalt
  Through the Borough Council grass,
Till they hide inside the shelter
  Bright with ironwork and glass,

Striving chains of ordered children
  Purple by the sea-breeze made,
Striving on to prunes and suet
  Past the shops on the Parade.

Some with wire around their glasses,
  Some with wire across their teeth,
Writhing frames for running noses
  And the drooping lip beneath.

Church of England bells of Westgate!
  On this balcony I stand,
White the woodwork wriggles round me,
  Clock towers rise on either hand.

For me in my timber arbour
  You have one more message yet,
"Plimsolls, plimsolls in the summer,
  Oh goloshes in the wet!"

MARGATE, 1940

From out the Queen's Highcliffe for weeks at a stretch
I watched how the mower evaded the vetch,
So that over the putting-course rashes were seen
Of pink and of yellow among the burnt green.

How restful to putt, when the strains of a band
Announced a *thé dansant* was on at the Grand,
While over the privet, comminglingly clear,
I heard lesser 'Co-Optimists' down by the pier.

How lightly municipal, meltingly tarr'd,
Were the walks through the Lawns by the Queen's Promenade
As soft over Cliftonville languished the light
Down Harold Road, Norfolk Road, into the night.

Oh! then what a pleasure to see the ground floor
With tables for two laid as tables for four,
And bottles of sauce and Kia-Ora[1] and squash
Awaiting their owners who'd gone up to wash——

Who had gone up to wash the ozone from their skins
The sand from their legs and the Rock from their chins,
To prepare for an evening of dancing and cards
And forget the sea-breeze on the dry promenades.

From third floor and fourth floor the children looked down
Upon ribbons of light in the salt-scented town;
And drowning the trams roared the sound of the sea
As it washed in the shingle the scraps of their tea.

*　　*　　*　　*　　*

Beside the Queen's Highcliffe now rank grows the vetch,
Now dark is the terrace, a storm-battered stretch;
And I think, as the fairy-lit sights I recall,
It is those we are fighting for, foremost of all.

[1] Pronounced Kee-ora.

HENLEY-ON-THAMES

I see the winding water make
A short and then a shorter lake
　　As here stand I,
　　And house-boat high,
Survey the Upper Thames.
　By sun the mud is amber-dyed
　In ripples slow and flat and wide,
　That flap against the house-boat side
And flop away in gems.

In mud and elder-scented shade
A reach away the breach is made
　　By dive and shout
　　That circles out

To Henley tower and town;
 And "Boats for Hire" the rafters ring,
 And pink on white the roses cling,
 And red the bright geraniums swing
In baskets dangling down.

When shall I see the Thames again?
The prow-promoted gems again,
  As beefy ATS
  Without their hats
Come shooting through the bridge?
 And "cheerioh" and "cheeri-bye"
 Across the waste of waters die,
 And low the mists of evening lie
And lightly skims the midge.

WANTAGE BELLS

Now with the bells through the apple bloom
  Sunday-ly sounding
And the prayers of the nuns in their chapel gloom
  Us all surrounding,
 Where the brook flows
 Brick walls of rose
Send on the motionless meadow the bell notes rebounding.

Wall flowers are bright in their beds
  And their scent all pervading,
Withered are primroses heads
  And the hyacinth fading
 But flowers by the score
 Multitudes more
Weed flowers and seed flowers and mead flowers our paths
are invading.

Where are the words to express
Such a reckless bestowing?
The voices of birds utter less
Than the thanks we are owing,
Bell notes alone
Ring praise of their own
As clear as the weed-waving brook and as evenly flowing.

UPPER LAMBOURN

Up the ash-tree climbs the ivy,
Up the ivy climbs the sun,
With a twenty-thousand pattering
Has a valley breeze begun,
Feathery ash, neglected elder,
Shift the shade and make it run—

Shift the shade toward the nettles,
And the nettles set it free
To streak the stained Carrara headstone
Where, in nineteen-twenty-three,
He who trained a hundred winners
Paid the Final Entrance Fee.

Leathery limbs of Upper Lambourn,
Leathery skin from sun and wind,
Leathery breeches, spreading stables,
Shining saddles left behind—
To the down the string of horses
Moving out of sight and mind.

Feathery ash in leathery Lambourn
Waves above the sarsen stone,
And Edwardian plantations
So coniferously moan
As to make the swelling downland,
Far-surrounding, seem their own.

HERTFORDSHIRE

I had forgotten Hertfordshire,
  The large unwelcome fields of roots
Where with my knickerbockered sire
  I trudged in syndicated shoots;

And that unlucky day when I
  Fired by mistake into the ground
Under a Lionel Edwards sky
  And felt disapprobation round.

The slow drive home by motor-car,
  A heavy Rover Landaulette,
Through Welwyn, Hatfield, Potters Bar,
  Tweed and cigar smoke, gloom and wet:

"How many times must I explain
  The way a boy should hold a gun?"
I recollect my father's pain
  At such a milksop for a son.

And now I see these fields once more
  Clothed, thank the Lord, in summer green,
Pale corn waves rippling to a shore
  The shadowy cliffs of elm between,

Colour-washed cottages reed-thatched
  And weather-boarded water mills,
Flint churches, brick and plaster patched,
  On mildly undistinguished hills—

They still are there. But now the shire
  Suffers a devastating change,
Its gentle landscape strung with wire,
  Old places looking ill and strange.

One can't be sure where London ends,
  New towns have filled the fields of root
Where father and his business friends
  Drove in the Landaulette to shoot;

Tall concrete standards line the lane,
  Brick boxes glitter in the sun:
Far more would these have caused him pain
  Than my mishandling of a gun.

NORFOLK

How did the Devil come? When first attack?
  These Norfolk lanes recall lost innocence,
The years fall off and find me walking back
  Dragging a stick along the wooden fence
Down this same path, where, forty years ago,
My father strolled behind me, calm and slow.

I used to fill my hand with sorrel seeds
  And shower him with them from the tops of stiles,
I used to butt my head into his tweeds
  To make him hurry down those languorous miles
Of ash and alder-shaded lanes, till here
Our moorings and the masthead would appear.

There after supper lit by lantern light
  Warm in the cabin I could lie secure
And hear against the polished sides at night
  The lap lap lapping of the weedy Bure,
A whispering and watery Norfolk sound
Telling of all the moonlit reeds around.

How did the Devil come? When first attack?
  The church is just the same, though now I know
Fowler of Louth restored it. Time, bring back
  The rapturous ignorance of long ago,
The peace, before the dreadful daylight starts,
Of unkept promises and broken hearts.

LAKE DISTRICT

'On their way back they found the girls at Easedale, sitting beside the cottage where they sell ginger beer in August.' (*Peer and Heiress*, by Walter Besant.)

I pass the cruet and I see the lake
  Running with light, beyond the garden pine,
  That lake whose waters make me dream her mine.
Up to the top board mounting for my sake,
For me she breathes, for me each soft intake,
  For me the plunge, the lake and limbs combine.
  I pledge her in non-alcoholic wine
And give the H.P. Sauce another shake.

Spirit of Grasmere, bells of Ambleside,
  Sing you and ring you, water bells, for me;
    You water-colour waterfalls may froth.
Long hiking holidays will yet provide
  Long stony lanes and back at six to tea
    And Heinz's ketchup on the tablecloth.

ESSEX

'The vagrant visitor erstwhile,'
  My colour-plate book says to me,
'Could wend by hedgerow-side and stile,
  From Benfleet down to Leigh-on-Sea.'

And as I turn the colour-plates
  Edwardian Essex opens wide,
Mirrored in ponds and seen through gates,
  Sweet uneventful countryside.

Like streams the little by-roads run
  Through oats and barley round a hill
To where blue willows catch the sun
  By some white weather-boarded mill.

'A summer Idyll Matching Tye'
   'At Havering-atte-Bower, the Stocks'
And cobbled pathways lead the eye
   To cottage doors and hollyhocks.

Far Essex,—fifty miles away
   The level wastes of sucking mud
Where distant barges high with hay
   Come sailing in upon the flood.

Near Essex of the River Lea
   And anglers out with hook and worm
And Epping Forest glades where we
   Had beanfeasts with my father's firm.

At huge and convoluted pubs
   They used to set us down from brakes
In that half-land of football clubs
   Which London near the Forest makes.

The deepest Essex few explore
   Where steepest thatch is sunk in flowers
And out of elm and sycamore
   Rise flinty fifteenth-century towers.

I see the little branch line go
   By white farms roofed in red and brown,
The old Great Eastern winding slow
   To some forgotten country town.

Now yarrow chokes the railway track,
   Brambles obliterate the stile,
No motor coach can take me back
   To that Edwardian 'erstwhile'.

HARROW-ON-THE-HILL

When melancholy Autumn comes to Wembley
  And electric trains are lighted after tea
The poplars near the Stadium are trembly
  With their tap and tap and whispering to me,
    Like the sound of little breakers
    Spreading out along the surf-line
When the estuary's filling
    With the sea.

Then Harrow-on-the-Hill's a rocky island
  And Harrow churchyard full of sailors' graves
And the constant click and kissing of the trolley buses hissing
  Is the level to the Wealdstone turned to waves
    And the rumble of the railway
    Is the thunder of the rollers
As they gather up for plunging
    Into caves.

There's a storm cloud to the westward over Kenton,
  There's a line of harbour lights at Perivale,
Is it rounding rough Pentire in a flood of sunset fire
  The little fleet of trawlers under sail?
    Can those boats be only roof tops
    As they stream along the skyline
In a race for port and Padstow
    With the gale?

A LINCOLNSHIRE TALE

Kirkby with Muckby-cum-Sparrowby-cum-Spinx
Is down a long lane in the county of Lincs,
And often on Wednesdays, well-harnessed and spruce,
I would drive into Wiss over Winderby Sluice.

A whacking great sunset bathed level and drain
From Kirkby with Muckby to Beckby-on-Bain,
And I saw, as I journeyed, my marketing done
Old Caistorby tower take the last of the sun.

The night air grew nippy. An autumn mist roll'd
(In a scent of dead cabbages) down from the wold,
In the ocean of silence that flooded me round
The crunch of the wheels was a comforting sound.

The lane lengthened narrowly into the night
With the Bain on its left bank, the drain on its right,
And feebly the carriage-lamps glimmered ahead
When all of a sudden *the pony fell dead.*

The remoteness was awful, the stillness intense,
Of invisible fenland, around and immense;
And out of the dark, with a roar and a swell,
Swung, hollowly thundering, Speckleby bell.

Though myself the Archdeacon for many a year,
I had not summoned courage for visiting here;
Our incumbents were mostly eccentric or sad
But—*the Speckleby Rector was said to be mad.*

Oh cold was the ev'ning and tall was the tower
And strangely compelling the tenor bell's power!
As loud on the reed-beds and strong through the dark
It toll'd from the church in the tenantless park.

The mansion was ruined, the empty demesne
Was slowly reverting to marshland again—
Marsh where the village was, grass in the Hall,
And the church and the Rectory waiting to fall.

And even in springtime with kingcups about
And stumps of old oak-trees attempting to sprout,
'Twas a sinister place, neither fenland nor wold,
And doubly forbidding in darkness and cold.

And down swung the tenor, a beacon of sound,
Over listening acres of waterlogged ground
I stood by the tombs to see pass and repass
The gleam of a taper, through clear leaded glass,

And such lighting of lights in the thunderous roar
That heart summoned courage to hand at the door;
I grated it open on scents I knew well,
The dry smell of damp rot, the hassocky smell.

What a forest of woodwork in ochres and grains
Unevenly doubled in diamonded panes,
And over the plaster, so textured with time,
Sweet discoloration of umber and lime.

The candles ensconced on each high panelled pew
Brought the caverns of brass-studded baize into view,
But the roof and its rafters were lost to the sight
As they soared to the dark of the Lincolnshire night:

And high from the chancel arch paused to look down
A sign-painter's beasts in their fight for the Crown,
While massive, impressive, and still as the grave
A three-decker pulpit frowned over the nave.

Shall I ever forget what a stillness was there
When the bell ceased its tolling and thinned on the air?
Then an opening door showed a long pair of hands
And the Rector himself in his gown and his bands.

* * * * *

Such a fell Visitation I shall not forget,
Such a rush through the dark, that I rush through it yet,
And I pray, as the bells ring o'er fenland and hill,
That the Speckleby acres be tenantless still.

8

LATER SCHOOL

From SUMMONED BY BELLS

LUXURIATING backwards in the bath,
I swish the warmer water round my legs
Towards my shoulders, and the waves of heat
Bring those five years of Marlborough through to me,
In comfortable retrospect: 'Thank God
I'll never have to go through them again.'
As with my toes I reach towards the tap
And turn it to a trickle, stealing warm
About my tender person, comes a voice,
An inner voice that calls, 'Be fair! be fair!
It was not quite as awful as you think.'
In steam like this the changing-room was bathed;
Pink bodies splashed hot water on themselves
After the wonderful release from games,
When Atherton would lead the songs we sang.
I see the tall Memorial Reading Room,
Which smelt of boots and socks and water-pipes,
Its deaf invigilator on his throne—
"*Do you tickle your arse with a feather, Mr. Purdick?*"
"*What?*"
"*Particularly nasty weather, Mr. Purdick!*"
"*Oh.*"

And, as the water cools, the Marlborough terms
Form into seasons. Winter starts us off,
Lasting two years, for we were new boys twice—
Once in a junior, then a senior house.
Spring has its love and summer has its art:
It is the winter that remains with me,
Black as our college suits, as cold and thin.

Doom! Shivering doom! Clutching a leather grip
Containing things for the first night of term—
House-slippers, sponge-bag, pyjams, Common Prayer,
My health certificate, photographs of home
(Where were my bike, my playbox and my trunk?)—

I walked with strangers down the hill to school.
The town's first gaslights twinkled in the cold.
Deserted by the coaches, poorly served
By railway, Marlborough was a lonely place;
The old Bath Road, in chalky whiteness, raised
Occasional clouds of dust as motors passed.

* * * * *

There was a building known as Upper School
(Abolished now, thank God, and all its ways),
An eighteen-fifty warehouse smelling strong
Of bat-oil, biscuits, sweat and rotten fruit.
The corporate life of which the bishop spoke,
At any rate among the junior boys,
Went on within its echoing whitewashed walls.

Great were the ranks and privileges there:
Four captains ruled, selected for their brawn
And skill at games; and how we reverenced them!
Twelve friends they chose as brawny as themselves.
'Big Fire' we called them; lording it they sat
In huge armchairs beside the warming flames
Or played at indoor hockey in the space
Reserved for them. The rest of us would sit
Crowded on benches round another grate.

Before the master came for evening prep
The captains entered at official pace
And, walking down the alley-way of desks,
Beat on their level lids with supple canes.
This was the sign for new boys to arise,
To pick up paper, apple-cores and darts
And fill huge baskets with the muck they found;
Then, wiping hands upon grey handkerchiefs
And trousers, settle down to Latin prose.

Upper School captains had the power to beat:
Maximum six strokes, usually three.
My frequent crime was far too many books,
So that my desk lid would not shut at all:
"Come to Big Fire then, Betjeman, after prep."
I tried to concentrate on delicate points—
Ut, whether final or consecutive?
(Oh happy private-school days when I knew!)—
While all the time I thought of pain to come.
Swift after prep all raced towards 'Big Fire',
Giving the captain space to swing his cane:
"*One*," they would shout and downward came the blow;
"*Two*" (rather louder); then, exultant, "*Three!*"
And some in ecstasy would bellow "*Four*."
These casual beatings brought us no disgrace,
Rather a kind of glory. In the dorm,
Comparing bruises, other boys could show
Far worse ones that the beaks and prefects made.

No, Upper School's most terrible disgrace
Involved a very different sort of pain.
Our discontents and enmities arose
Somewhere about the seventh week of term:
The holidays too far off to count the days
Till our release, the weeks behind, a blank.
"Haven't you heard?" said D. C. Wilkinson.
"Angus is to be basketed tonight."
Why Angus . . . ? Never mind. The victim's found.
Perhaps he sported coloured socks too soon,
Perhaps he smarmed his hair with scented oil,
Perhaps he was 'immoral' or a thief.
We did not mind the cause: for Angus now
The game was up. His friends deserted him,
And after his disgrace they'd stay away
For fear of being basketed themselves.
"*By* the boys, *for* the boys. The boys know best.

Leave it to them to pick the rotters out
With that rough justice decent schoolboys know."
And at the end of term the victim left—
Never to wear an Old Marlburian tie

In quieter tones we asked in Hall that night
Neighbours to pass the marge; the piles of bread
Lay in uneaten slices with the jam.
Too thrilled to eat we raced across the court
Under the frosty stars to Upper School.
Elaborately easy at his desk
Sat Angus, glancing through *The Autocar*.
Fellows walked past him trying to make it look
As if they didn't know his coming fate,
Though the boy's body called "Unclean! Unclean!"
And all of us felt goody-goody-good,
Nice wholesome boys who never sinned at all.
At ten to seven 'Big Fire' came marching in
Unsmiling, while the captains stayed outside
(For this was 'unofficial'). Twelve to one:
What chance had Angus? They surrounded him,
Pulled off his coat and trousers, socks and shoes
And, wretched in his shirt, they hoisted him
Into the huge waste-paper basket; then
Poured ink and treacle on his head. With ropes
They strung the basket up among the beams,
And as he soared I only saw his eyes
Look through the slats at us who watched below.

Seven. "It's prep." They let the basket down
And Angus struggled out. "Left! Right! Left! Right!"
We stamped and called as, stained and pale, he strode
Down the long alley-way between the desks,
Holding his trousers, coat and pointed shoes.
"You're for it next," said H. J. Anderson.

"I'm not." "You are. I've heard." So all that term
And three terms afterwards I crept about,
Avoiding public gaze. I kept my books
Down in the basement where the boot-hole was
And by its fishtail gas-jet nursed my fear.

9

GROWING UP

From SUMMONED BY BELLS

DEAR lanes of Cornwall! With a one-inch map,
A bicycle and well-worn *Little Guide*,
Those were the years I used to ride for miles
To far-off churches. One of them that year
So worked on me that, if my life was changed,
I owe it to St. Ervan and his priest
In their small hollow deep in sycamores.
The time was tea-time, calm free-wheeling time,
When from slashed tree-tops in the combe below
I heard a bell-note floating to the sun;
It gave significance to lichened stone
And large red admirals with outspread wings
Basking on buddleia. So, casting down
In the cool shade of interlacing boughs,
I found St. Ervan's partly ruined church.
Its bearded Rector, holding in one hand
A gong-stick, in the other hand a book,
Struck, while he read, a heavy-sounding bell,
Hung from an elm bough by the churchyard gate.
"Better come in. It's time for Evensong."

There wasn't much to see, there wasn't much
The *Little Guide* could say about the church.
Holy and small and heavily restored,
It held me for the length of Evensong,
Said rapidly among discoloured walls,
Impatient of my diffident response.
"Better come in and have a cup of tea."
The Rectory was large, uncarpeted;
Books and oil-lamps and papers were about;
The study's pale green walls were mapped with damp;
The pitch-pine doors and window-frames were cracked;
Loose noisy tiles along the passages
Led to a waste of barely furnished rooms:
Clearly the Rector lived here all alone.

He talked of poetry and Cornish saints;
He kept an apiary and a cow;
He asked me which church service I liked best—
I told him Evensong . . . "And I suppose
You think religion's mostly singing hymns
And feeling warm and comfortable inside?"
And he was right: most certainly I did.
"Borrow this book and come to tea again."
With Arthur Machen's *Secret Glory* stuffed
Into my blazer pocket, up the hill
On to St. Merryn, down to Padstow Quay
In time for the last ferry back to Rock,
I bicycled—and found Trebetherick
A worldly contrast with my afternoon.

I would not care to read that book again.
It so exactly mingled with the mood
Of those impressionable years, that now
I might be disillusioned. There were laughs
At public schools, at chapel services,
At masters who were still 'big boys at heart'—
While all the time the author's hero knew
A Secret Glory in the hills of Wales:
Caverns of light revealed the Holy Grail
Exhaling gold upon the mountain-tops;
At "Holy! Holy! Holy!" in the Mass
King Brychan's sainted children crowded round,
And past and present were enwrapped in one.

In quest of mystical experience
I knelt in darkness at St. Enodoc;
I visited our local Holy Well,
Whereto the native Cornish still resort
For cures for whooping-cough, and drop bent pins
Into its peaty water . . . Not a sign:
No mystical experience was vouchsafed:
The maidenhair just trembled in the wind

And everything looked as it always looked . . .
But somewhere, somewhere underneath the dunes,
Somewhere among the cairns or in the caves
The Celtic saints would come to me, the ledge
Of time we walk on, like a thin cliff-path
High in the mist, would show the precipice.

* * *

DISTANT VIEW OF A PROVINCIAL TOWN

Beside those spires so spick and span
  Against an unencumbered sky
The old Great Western Railway ran
  When someone different was I.

St. Aidan's with the prickly knobs
  And iron spikes and coloured tiles—
Where Auntie Maud devoutly bobs
  In those enriched vermilion aisles:

St. George's where the mattins bell
  But rarely drowned the trams for prayer—
No Popish sight or sound or smell
  Disturbed that gas-invaded air:

St. Mary's where the Rector preached
  In such a jolly friendly way
On cricket, football, things that reached
  The simple life of every day:

And that United Benefice
  With entrance permanently locked,
How Gothic, grey and sad it is
  Since Mr. Grogley was unfrocked!

The old Great Western Railway shakes
  The old Great Western Railway spins—
The old Great Western Railway makes
  Me very sorry for my sins.

CHRISTMAS

The bells of waiting Advent ring,
  The Tortoise stove is lit again
And lamp-oil light across the night
  Has caught the streaks of winter rain
In many a stained-glass window sheen
From Crimson Lake to Hooker's Green.

The holly in the windy hedge
  And round the Manor House the yew
Will soon be stripped to deck the ledge,
  The altar, font and arch and pew,
So that the villagers can say
"The church looks nice" on Christmas Day.

Provincial public houses blaze
  And Corporation tramcars clang,
On lighted tenements I gaze
  Where paper decorations hang,
And bunting in the red Town Hall
Says "Merry Christmas to you all."

And London shops on Christmas Eve
  Are strung with silver bells and flowers
As hurrying clerks the City leave
  To pigeon-haunted classic towers,
And marbled clouds go scudding by
The many-steepled London sky.

And girls in slacks remember Dad,
  And oafish louts remember Mum,
And sleepless children's hearts are glad,
  And Christmas-morning bells say "Come!"
Even to shining ones who dwell
Safe in the Dorchester Hotel.

And is it true? And is it true,
  This most tremendous tale of all,
Seen in a stained-glass window's hue,
  A Baby in an ox's stall?
The Maker of the stars and sea
Become a Child on earth for me?

And is it true? For if it is,
  No loving fingers tying strings
Around those tissued fripperies,
  The sweet and silly Christmas things
Bath salts and inexpensive scent
And hideous tie so kindly meant.

No love that in a family dwells,
  No carolling in frosty air,
Nor all the steeple-shaking bells
  Can with this single Truth compare—
That God was Man in Palestine
And lives to-day in Bread and Wine.

NOTES

1. POEMS OF CHILDHOOD

p. 9. SUMMONED BY BELLS

John Betjeman lived, as a child, in a house on Highgate West Hill. This is a steep hill that runs down from the village of Highgate—to the north of central London—to Parliament Hill Fields, then on to Kentish Town. To the left of this long, curving hill, as you go up it, lies Hampstead Heath and miles of woodland of the Kenwood estate. The Betjemans' house was also on the left of the hill, with its back to the Heath. Millfield and Merton Lanes run off the main road on to the Heath, Merton above the Betjemans' house, and Millfield below it.

hornbeams: trees of hard, tough wood, like beeches.

Middlesex: at that time Highgate was in the county of Middlesex.

Delaunay-Belleville: one of the first makes of motor-car.

Constable: John Constable (1776–1837) was one of the greatest realistic landscape painters of the nineteenth-century English countryside.

Keats: the poet John Keats (1795–1821) lived in Hampstead for some years—on the other side of the Heath from Highgate. The street where he lived is now called Keats' Grove.

Caenwood Towers: a beautiful house with a most impressive central tower built in 1870 on the edge of the Kenwood estate.

Grand Duke Michael's house: a house that John glimpsed behind a tree-shaded drive, near Caenwood Towers.

Holly Lodge: a house built high on the eastern side of Highgate West Hill that was the home of the Baroness Burdett-Coutts (1814–1906), a wealthy, generous woman, noted for her works of charity.

p. 9. John Betjeman's father worked in the family business in Islington. The firm made period furniture, silverware and all kinds of bric-à-brac, so the family was comfortably well off, but not wealthy. In those days—round about 1912—people were very conscious of social differences. The working classes, the middle classes, the upper classes and the aristocracy were all sharply divided from each other, and there were all kinds of sub-divisions within each class. Everyone was able to feel superior to someone else, but inferior to others. It was only in the working classes that things were different. There a unity of spirit and comradeship existed between the poor people who were all struggling against the same thing—want. John's father, a 'middle-class' businessman, living by trade, would be considered lower in status than someone from the upper classes whose money probably came from land, property or industry, or from a family fortune he had inherited.

John Betjeman soon became aware of these class differences as a small boy. He knew that financially his family were higher than the people next door, but lower than those in the grander houses up the hill, whose owners kept carriages and hosts of servants. This awareness of class differences stayed with him all his life and he grew up to be amused by the false and artificial barriers that people put up between each other, based only on income or family origins.

When John was told that the name Betjeman was German he was very upset. There was a good deal of anti-German feeling in Britain before the outbreak of the 1914–1918 war, and anything that could be accused of being German, however wrongly, was liable to be insulted or abused. The tide of national, patriotic feeling was at its height, and to be 'pure British' was the only way of being above reproach.

The name Betjeman was not German anyway; it was Dutch, but the neighbour's comments were enough to set John's mind wondering whether he was as safe and secure as he thought he was. Perhaps there was something strange about his family that made them outcasts and different from other people?

Burdett-Coutts estate: the grounds of Holly Lodge extended to the foot of the hill and formed the view from the front of the Betjemans' house. Now this parkland has become a huge, ugly housing estate.

brougham: a one-horsed, closed carriage.

p. 10. Although the seeds of a wrong and destructive idea had been sown in the little boy's mind, he loved his home and the beauties of the Highgate landscape about him, and, above all, Archibald, his toy bear.

nonconformist Chetwynd Road: one of the turnings off the main road with a Baptist chapel on the corner.

Kentish Town: a poor district of London at the end of Highgate Road, the road that Highgate West Hill becomes as it continues downwards.

Selfridge's: one of the biggest department stores in London.

Bon Marché: the name of a draper's shop with many branches where things were cheap and good.

Electric Palace: an early cinema that showed silent films.

eyrie: a bird's nest built high up, like that of an eagle. In this sense it is the Betjeman house, high up on the hill.

North London: the railway which ran across north London from Broad Street in the City, westwards to Richmond in Surrey.

Gospel Oak: a station near Kentish Town, on the North London Railway.

p. 10. Mrs. Betjeman, like many ladies of her day, would entertain visitors and have her 'at homes'. Every second Thursday of the month a number of her friends would arrive to play Auction Bridge. They took the game very seriously and often became quite heated, hurling acid remarks at one another. It was the custom then for small children to have to call 'Aunt' any female friend, as well as relative, of the family.

Votes for Women: this was a slogan much in use from about 1908 onwards when women began campaigning to be allowed a vote in the election of Members of Parliament. This was finally granted to them in 1928 after a long and hard struggle.

London Pride: a small, pink flower to be found in many town gardens.

p. 12. GROUP LIFE: LETCHWORTH

Another kind of childhood. In this poem a modern, over-enthusiastic mother is talking the kind of nonsense about her children that is so often exchanged over the garden fence, or outside the local super-market. She seems to have given some of her children exotic and wildly unsuitable names, too, like 'Aluréd' and 'Sympathy'.

weal: welfare.

Morris Dancers: Morris Dancing is a kind of English country dancing, dating from medieval times, for which traditional dress is worn.

ex-Service man: demobilized from the army, and probably wounded in the war. In this poem he is the lodger of the woman who is speaking.

kinderbank: a sand pit where children can play.

p. 13. FALSE SECURITY

This is an incident from John Betjeman's childhood in Highgate that shows again how people could be pre-occupied with social differences, even at the risk of deeply hurting a small child's feelings. John braves the winter darkness of West Hill, with its trees and hedges and imaginary ghosts, and struggles to the top. He is going to a party. When he gets there he feels the house to be warm and friendly, and the party wonderful. So is the little hostess who holds his hand. Then comes the horrible blow. When the guests are leaving he hears the mother tell one of them he is a 'common little boy'. His whole illusion is shattered and all his feelings of success and security wither at this awful accusation of social inferiority.

The Grove: a row of big houses at the top of the hill in Highgate Village.

Daniel Neal: a London shop specializing in children's wear, particularly shoes.

Heal: a London store, known for its furnishings and good quality materials.

p. 14. CROYDON

This is about the childhood of a boy of the 1870's—'Uncle Dick'—who was born in Croydon when it was a growing Victorian town of Surrey, surrounded by woodland, fields and unspoiled country.

Whitgift: the famous public school at Croydon.

spadgers: the cockney word for sparrows.

p. 14. INDOOR GAMES NEAR NEWBURY

Here is another children's party. The ending this time is happy, for Wendy, the hostess, has chosen the little boy as her special friend; and when he is taken home and put to bed, he is full of dreams and happiness about her.

Lagonda, *Hupmobile*, *Delage:* makes of motor-car.

Victrola: an early make of gramophone.

featly: nimbly.

2. DISCOVERING POETRY

p. 19. SUMMONED BY BELLS

The urge to write poetry came to John Betjeman when he was seven years old. He was bursting with ideas for things he wanted to write about, but had no ability to express them on paper. Two of the places he most wanted to write about were Highgate and the near-by heathland where he lived, and the sea coast near Trebetherick in north Cornwall where he spent his summer holidays. But however hard he tried, no inspiration came, and the verses he wrote filled him with shame when he was a little older. Yet he went on trying, whatever the discouragements. The two poems that follow in this section are what Betjeman wrote many years later on the two subjects that had meant so much to him as a child.

Cambridge comes a wind: John Betjeman's University was Oxford, and, because of the traditional rivalry between the two universities, he still feels the cold wind of criticism coming from Cambridge to disparage his achievements.

internal rhyming: the 'internal rhymes' of Shelley's 'Cloud' can be seen in the first and third lines:

I bring fresh showers for the thirsting flowers,
From the seas and the streams;
I bear light shade for the leaves when laid
In their noonday dreams.

Polzeath Bay: in north Cornwall, near Trebetherick.

St. Michael's church: on top of the hill in Highgate village. Its spire can be seen from many points of the heath.

parodies of A & M: Betjeman felt his poems to be feeble and rather ridiculous versions of *Hymns Ancient and Modern.*

Haslemere: a town in Surrey.

Allingham: William Allingham (1824–1889) was author of the famous poem 'The Fairies':

Up the airy mountain,
Down the rushy glen,
We daren't go a-hunting
For fear of little men . . .

rhymes A B, A B: the form of verse in which the first and third lines rhyme, so do the second and fourth.

thin St. Anne's: the church at the bottom of Highgate West Hill.

Fitzroy Park: the old carriage road from Highgate village to Fitzroy House. The Fitzroy estate is very near to that of Kenwood.

Holly Village: the cluster of spiky, gabled Victorian houses beside the Holly Lodge estate, near Highgate Cemetery.

Frank Bramley: (1857–1905) a late-Victorian painter whose famous picture 'The Hopeless Dawn' still hangs in the Tate Gallery in London.

Greenaway: a beach between Trebetherick and Polzeath Bay in north Cornwall.

p. 22. GREENAWAY

The poem describes the beach at Greenaway, washed by powerful and dangerous seas. John Betjeman knows it well and feels safe on its familiar stretch of shingle. Yet in a dream he has seen it from the sea, and has felt the unseen terrors beneath its beauty.

bladder-wrack: a common seaweed with bubble-like swellings in its fronds.

cowrie: a kind of sea-shell.

p. 23. PARLIAMENT HILL FIELDS

As Highgate West Hill becomes Highgate Road, and continues past Parliament Hill Fields down to Kentish Town, the district becomes dingy with factories, breweries, laundries and coal merchants' yards. In Betjeman's boyhood, horse-trams ran up and down this road and under the railway bridge of the old Great Eastern branch line to Gospel Oak. A journey back to Highgate West Hill from a shopping expedition in Kentish Town was like a journey into a different world; the one, industrial, poor and gloomy; and the other, light, airy and green.

Midland: the Midland Railway that used to run from St. Pancras to the North.

Cricklewood: a district in north-west London served by the Midland Railway, later the 'London, Midland and Scottish'.

Charrington, Sells, Dale and Co.: a firm of coal merchants with an office outside Kentish Town station. Their offices were often seen on London railway approach roads.

bobble-hanging plane: the fruit of the plane-tree that hangs down in little bobbles.

ashlar-speckled: uneven colouring of masonry made of large blocks of stone, smooth-faced and square-edged.

Eighteen-sixty Early English: Early English was the style of Gothic architecture that flourished between about 1180 and 1270. In the nineteenth century, churches were again built in the Gothic styles and this was called the 'Gothic Revival'.

3. POEMS OF EARLY SCHOOL

p. 27. SUMMONED BY BELLS

Peggy Purey-Cust was John Betjeman's first love. Peggy's golden hair and blue eyes made going to school a joy for him. He saw her as the heroine of all his favourite stories and once went to tea at her house. But he was never invited again and Peggy was always 'out' when he called. In fact she disappeared from the scene altogether, and going to school became a miserable business, especially when two bullies of boys beset his route. And, what was worse, the bullies changed schools when he did and they all went to Highgate Junior School together. He dreaded going back after holidays.

Byron House: an infant school in The Grove, Highgate Village.

blob-work: a kind of painting that was taught to small children.

spired St. Pancras: there is a splendid view across London from Highgate Village, and it would have been easy to see the spires of St. Pancras Station and the dome of St. Paul's Cathedral from Peggy's drawing-room.

Walter Crane: (1845–1915) an artist, illustrator and designer who, like William Morris, set a new fashion for interior decoration towards the end of the nineteenth century.

harbinger: one who goes ahead to announce the arrival of something or somebody.

Avernus: a hell-hole. Avernus is a lake in Campania, Italy, formed in an old volcanic crater with no natural outlet. It appears frequently in Greek and Roman history and was believed once to have been the entrance by which the Greek heroes Odysseus and Æneas descended into the infernal regions.

H. M. Brock: (1875–1960), an illustrator of books, especially school stories.

p. 28. AN INCIDENT IN THE EARLY LIFE OF EBENEZER JONES, POET, 1828

This poem is about another boy who went to school at Highgate, almost one hundred years before John Betjeman. He was Ebenezer Jones, who, after an unhappy boyhood in a strict, Methodist family, became a clerk in a city firm, working twelve hours daily. The dishonest practices that went on there upset him very much, and he managed to get away and become an accountant. He wanted to write poetry, and did write as much as time and rather poor health allowed him. A disastrous marriage and the poor reception by the critics of his book of poems, *Studies of Sensation and Event*, sent his health into further decline, but at the end of his life Dante Gabriel Rossetti revived public interest in his work, and people began to realize that Ebenezer Jones was, for all his unevenness, a poet of power and genius. *Studies of Sensation and Event* was re-issued, with the help of Ebenezer's brother Sumner, and Ebenezer wrote some new poems which show him at the height of his powers. Before he died he was acclaimed as a very considerable poet by many of his contemporaries. Today he is not widely known, but the best of his poems are still said by critics to rank among the finest of their kind in English literature.

School in Ebenezer's day was often harsh and brutal, and this incident of cruelty to a dog shows the kind of thing that could easily happen when a vicious, bullying master was out to keep his pupils in fear of him.

(Introduction)

dissenting minister: nonconformist clergyman, in this instance, a Calvinistic Methodist.

conning our tasks: learning our lessons.

lurcher dog: the lurcher is a cross-breed between a collie or sheep-dog and a greyhound.

choleric: bad-tempered.

usher: assistant schoolmaster.

(Poem)

dray: a heavy, horse-drawn cart.

stucco: plaster used for coating wall surfaces and for the moulding of architectural decorations.

Holloway: district to the south of Highgate.

Dissenting chapels: nonconformist chapels.

Grecian squares: many of the squares in that part of London are designed on spacious, classical lines, including Canonbury Square, where Ebenezer Jones was born.

Saints: in this sense 'Saints' are people who belong to one of the nonconformist religious sects. These sects were formed by people who had broken away from the Established Church, and then broken away from each other ('Seceders from the Protestant Secessions'). At the beginning of the nineteenth century many of these people were becoming wealthy through trade and industry, and this continued as the century went on.

godly usher: many of the people who professed a strict religious observance, and practised church-going with fanatical zeal, behaved in a very un-Christian way in their daily lives. So the 'godly usher' would have no twinges of conscience when punishing his class of terror-stricken little boys, or throwing a dog to its death down the stairs. He would feel that he was establishing law and order in the name of God, in fact he says so quite plainly: 'I am his word.'

Calvin's God: Calvin (1509–1564) was the great Swiss divine and reformer who developed the doctrines of earlier reformers and preached that man is born in sin through Adam's fall. He said that man, therefore, is depraved, corrupt and hateful to God, and his only hope of redemption is by faith in God, repentance and strict mortification of the flesh. Calvin also believed in 'election', which is the doctrine that some are predestined to damnation by God and others predestined to salvation. The 'godly usher' smugly thought he was 'saved' and could therefore do no wrong.

4. POEMS OF HOLIDAYS

p. 33. SUMMONED BY BELLS

Most of John Betjeman's early holidays were spent in north Cornwall. As a small boy, hygienically cared for and nourished with all the patent foods that were good for children, he would be taken on the familiar journey to Cornwall, travelling by the express train that left from Waterloo. Then would follow the drive to the village of Trebetherick in a horse-drawn carriage, and John would be excited and curious about all the people and things he remembered from times before.

On his first morning he would rush off to the beach before breakfast, and then would follow long days of bathing, climbing, visits to the farm and all the joys of the sea and country.

John Betjeman begins this section of *Summoned by Bells* in the style adopted by the great Greek poets at the beginning of one of their epics, or stories in blank verse. The Greeks would always begin by calling upon one of their gods for inspiration, and after invoking the god in grand and magnificent language, they would call upon some of the kindred gods as well. After that, the story proper would begin.

Lines 2–6 list some of the much advertised patent foods, tonics, soap and toothpaste that were said to be best for health and hygiene.

Free Thought, *Fresh Air:* in this sense, gods kindred to hygiene in the realms of health and well-being.

Egloskerry, *Tresméer:* two villages in Cornwall on the main railway line.

Bible Christians: the Bible Christians formed an offshoot of Methodism that was peculiar to Cornwall. They were simple people who held revival meetings and founded chapels of their own. They were not at all like Calvinists; they were much more like the Salvation Army.

Wadebridge: the small port and railway-town on the river Camel which is the nearest point to the coastal villages near Polzeath in north Cornwall.

Trebetherick: a village near Polzeath.

neap: point at which high tides, at first and third quarters of the moon, are at their lowest.

Doom Bar: a dangerous, sandy part of the estuary on which ships had often been wrecked.

pennywort: a plant with round, cup-shaped leaves that often grows in crevices of rocks and walls.

fennel: a wild herb.

lugworm: worms found in sand of the sea shore, used as bait for fishing.

oyster-catcher: a black-backed bird, about the size of the common gull, that lives in rocky, sandy shores, particularly on the west coast. It has a long, bright orange bill and eats small fish, shrimps and shell-fish.

sandhoppers: tiny, shell-covered animals that live on the sea shore.

elvers: baby eels.

tamarisks: feathery, evergreen shrubs with pink or white flowers.

convolvulus: a twining plant with a bell-like flower.

sea-pink: a common sea plant also called 'thrift'. It has a tough, strong root.

p. 35. SEASIDE GOLF

Golf links beside the sea can often fill the player with more zest and well-being than those inland, for there is the view, the sound of the sea and the smell of it. The only games John Betjeman really enjoys are golf and tennis, and this poem tells of the time when he was so inspired by sea breezes over a game of golf that he got his ball into the hole in only three strokes. Never had he done it before!

p. 36. TREBETHERICK

This poem describes Trebetherick in sunny, calm weather and in a storm. It ends with a prayer that the wonderful days of happiness the little boy John and his friends had there may be given in time to their children too.

lichen: a green, fungus-like moss that grows on trees and rocks.

Shilla Mill: a water mill up a wooded valley behind Polzeath.

St. Enodoc: an early Welsh saint of the Celtic Church which flourished in Cornwall in the sixth and seventh centuries. The little thirteenth-century church close by the sea was named after him. The church was once partially buried under the sand dunes, but was dug out again during the nineteenth century.

p. 37. EAST ANGLIAN BATHE

This is about another of John Betjeman's holidays, this time in Norfolk. Horsey Mere is a lake—one of the Norfolk 'Broads'—a little inland from the sea shore. The East Anglian coast is often very cold for bathing, especially in windy weather.

leeside: the sheltered side, away from the wind.

adumbration: casting shadows.

p. 38. BESIDE THE SEASIDE

A poem about a different kind of holiday—the organized family holiday that many people have when they go for their yearly fortnight to a 'popular resort'. Often they stay in a boarding house or have 'bed and breakfast' in a house where rooms are let. The wealthier people stay in hotels. Yet for all these people their particular piece of seaside—'Sandy Cove' in this poem—means everything. They have been going there for years and probably wouldn't think of going anywhere else. Its pleasures are known and familiar, and however expensive and over-crowded it becomes, hundreds of families will come flocking back every year.

The story of Jennifer and Mr. Pedder is sad but only too likely. Perhaps Jennifer took it too much to heart, for all through life people have wonderful moments of success and favouritism, and other less happy moments of failure when nobody seems to want them.

But while Jennifer's heart is breaking and the grown-ups worry about class differences—are they better or worse, richer or poorer than their fellow holiday-makers?—the sea, powerful and timeless, goes on washing the shore as it has for thousands of years.

Green Shutters, *Windyridge*, *High Dormers:* typical names of family houses in town and suburb.

quartz: rough, shiny stone that is often embedded on the tops of garden walls.

macrocarpa: a kind of cypress tree.

Esplanade: the promenade—the road along the sea front which usually contains shops and amusement arcades.

hydrangea: a well-known shrub with pink, blue or white flowers, often grown in tubs outside houses or on terraces.

escallonia: a shrub with a pink flower and shiny leaf.

lodging-house: seaside lodging-houses can often be uncomfortable and very dreary. In this one—typical of many—visitors have to keep to the landlady's rules and are expected to be out all day. The visitors' lounge is small enough and ugly enough to deter anyone from wanting to go into it, however hard it might be raining outside!

secretarial work: this reference to Jennifer's work with the Board of Trade in later life means that she didn't marry and have children of her own. She was so upset by Mr. Pedder's snub to her that she never got over it, and was suspicious of all young men from then on.

lissomest: the most supple and agile of all.

début: first appearance.

interstices: crevices or chinks in the rocks.

Humoresque: Dvořák's famous *Humoresque*, which is often played by bands in special arrangements for brass instruments—or 'silver bands' whose brass instruments appear to be made of silver.

Rudge: a make of bicycle.

Flannel Dance: a dance where people went in informal clothes such as flannel trousers and blazers.

the strange starfish: John Betjeman finds the starfish a most alarming creature because, unlike other living creatures he knows, it is so impersonal that it is almost one with the rocks on which it rests. It is mysterious and unaccountable.

p. 44. HUNTER TRIALS

A nonsense-poem about pony-loving girls who like to spend as much of their holidays as they can on horseback.

5. POEMS OF PEOPLE

p. 49. SUMMONED BY BELLS

Some of the best known of John Betjeman's poems are his verse portraits of people. From childhood he has always had heroes and heroines to look up to, and it is them he describes with such candour and shrewdness: the school prefect who was the kind of ideal boy that Betjeman felt he ought to be, but never could be; and, in later life, the strong, brawny sports girls who made him fall in love with them for their skill and vitality. (He always hated sports at school himself and was no good at games.)

The 'Percival Mandeville' extract from *Summoned by Bells* comes from the beginning of the chapter about going to private boarding school. The lie Betjeman told to get out of fighting reflects with great credit on Mandeville, who, strong and clever though he was, would never 'hit a chap when he was down'.

North and Hillard: a Latin text-book.

p. 50. THE OLYMPIC GIRL

Here is the kind of athletic, Amazon girl that makes Betjeman feel small and weak by comparison. He feels very unworthy of her, but wishes he were her tennis-racket, for then, at least, she would take some notice of him.

retroussé: turned up.

εἶθε γενοίμην: 'would I were'.

Rupert Brooke: (1887–1915). This refers to a quotation from Brooke's poem 'The Old Vicarage, Grantchester'. Grantchester is a village outside Cambridge, Brooke's university town.

εἶθε γενοίμην . . . would I were
In Grantchester, in Grantchester!

p. 51. HOW TO GET ON IN SOCIETY

A light-hearted verse portrait of a lady who is trying hard to acquire the kind of etiquette she believes will place her firmly in the 'upper classes' in the eyes of her friends and neighbours. In the 1920's and after, words like 'serviettes', 'toilet', 'lounge', 'doileys' became passwords of middle-class respectability.

p. 52. POT POURRI FROM A SURREY GARDEN

The rhythm of this poem is strong and free, unlike the more formal rhythms used in most of the other poems. Each line goes with a swing that depends for its pace and effect on the skilful use of words. This is the kind of poem that should be read and enjoyed for the atmosphere and meaning *suggested* by the words, rather than for the literal meaning of each word in turn.

Pam is another muscular, tennis-playing sports girl who lives in Surrey. Surrey is not quite country, not quite London; it is something in between. When the railway came to it at the end of the nineteenth century, it made it possible for people to travel from there each day to their work in London. John Betjeman sees Surrey as an uncountrified, littered county, with Victorian churches built in the developed areas, and well-appointed villas belonging to prosperous businessmen, dotted among the conifer trees.

Pot Pourri : a mixture or selection. There was a famous late Victorian book called *Pot Pourri from a Surrey Garden* by Mrs. C. W. Earle. It was written as a diary of everyday events and was dedicated to her sister Lady Constance Lytton. Apart from Mrs. Earle's reflections on life in general the book gave valuable advice on gardening and cooking as well as all kinds of household hints.

Weights: a brand of cigarette.

Malvernian: Malvern is a well-known public school in Worcestershire.

Woking: a Surrey town.

Hendren: a famous cricketer.

Gothic enlacement: Victorian Gothic arches cutting into one another.

Licensed: married.

p. 53. IN THE PUBLIC GARDENS

Another light-hearted poem about two English people having a gay time in Vienna. The simplicity of the rhythm and the delightful use of the words *Eingang* and *Ausgang* conjure up the whole Viennese mood of the poem and make it easy to remember.

Strauss: Johann Strauss (1825–1899), the famous composer of waltzes.

Eingang: way in.

Ausgang: way out.

electroliers: clusters of electric lamps like chandeliers.

Zwei Engländer: two English people.

p. 53. A SUBALTERN'S LOVE-SONG

Joan Hunter Dunn is perhaps the most famous of all Betjeman's heroines. Again the setting is Surrey with its villas and conifers, its prosperous middle-class families, their sports clubs and cars. This time it is a Subaltern, a junior officer training at Aldershot, the near-by Army centre, who sings his song of praise. He is in love with the beautiful tennis-girl, and by the end of the poem he has got himself engaged to her, so his rhapsody is not in vain.

euonymus: a kind of shrub.

'*not adopted*': these are roads that are the responsibility of the house-owners in them, not of the local council. Often they are unmade and little more than well-worn mud tracks.

Camberley: the Surrey town which contains the famous officers' training academy of Sandhurst.

ominous: foreshadowing disaster. The Subaltern was obviously not a good dancer and was afraid of what Miss Hunter Dunn would think of his clumsiness.

p. 55. THE OLD LIBERALS

A sympathetic portrait of two rather faded people who, in a previous generation, would have stood for all that was progressive in intellectual thinking and the arts. The scene is Boar's Hill, an early suburb of Oxford. These were the people who had reflected the influence of William Morris (1834–1896), an artist and thinker who was one of the great figures of his age. Morris was also a craftsman; he designed furniture, textiles and anything connected with interior decoration. He was a poet and, towards the end of his life, he became an active pioneer for Socialism. His followers, like this elderly gentleman and his daughter, led simple, creative lives, filling their homes with artistic things and believing that human beings would all be happier if they would do the same and resist the coming of the mechanized age with its threat of destruction to individual thinking. Now, after the passing of years, they make music together and look sadly at the ugliness and vulgarity of modern life around them and see how far it has drifted from the ideals in which they believed.

Pale green: green is the Liberal colour.

Yattendon hymns: *The Yattendon Hymnal* was compiled at the end of the nineteenth century by Robert Bridges and H. Ellis Wooldridge. Some of the hymns were translated from Latin and Greek for the first time. The book was famous in its day and many of the hymns have passed into common usage. The hymnal is still in use now at Yattendon in Berkshire, where Robert Bridges lived.

hautbois: the old way of spelling 'oboe', the woodwind instrument.

William de Morgan: (1839–1917). An artist and novelist, famous for the beautiful tiles he made to decorate the interiors of houses.

wains: waggons.

swains: country lads.

ted: spread out for drying.

p. 56. LORD COZENS HARDY

This is a poem about the ghost of the first Lord Cozens Hardy seen by Norfolk villagers at a certain time of the year. The village is Letheringsett, near Holt, in north Norfolk, where the present Lord Cozens Hardy still owns Letheringsett Hall. But the poem is not based on truth. There is no mausoleum, no ghost, and the legend is imaginary, inspired by John Betjeman's visit to the village, and the idea it gave him for a good story.

Doric: style of architecture based on the Greek. This portico would have large, Doric pillars.

All Souls: The feast of All Saints, or All Souls, on the first of November every year.

Master of the Rolls: a judge in the Court of Appeal who is also in charge of certain public records.

p. 57. EXCHANGE OF LIVINGS

The chief delight of this poem is its play on the word 'incumbent', an ungainly and rather comic word when repeated often enough within a few sentences. It means 'the holder of office', and here the office is that of vicar of the parish. One clergyman has answered the advertisement of another who wants to move to a different parish. The two clergymen meet and compare notes on their respective parishes to decide whether they will make a swap.

supine: lying down—probably lazing in a deck-chair with his feet up.

A and M: Hymns Ancient and Modern.

recumbent: lying down.

Rector . . . Cripplegate: he would be the kind of vicar that lived miles away from his parish and visited it on Sundays to take the statutory services. City of London churches have very few resident parishioners anyway. (See p. 123; note on *Summoned by Bells*, Poems of Places.)

p. 58. DIARY OF A CHURCH MOUSE

The church mouse is one of the most charming and lovable of all John Betjeman's characters. She has a simple but shrewd outlook on life, living humbly in a forgotten junk cupboard, and getting little to eat except once a year at Harvest Festival. But how unfair it is, she thinks, that rats and mice from all around, who are never seen near the church the rest of the year, should come at Harvest Festival and greedily eat the food they have no right to. Some, she knows, have no religion at all, and some are of quite different religions, yet that does not stop them coming to steal the Church of England's festival food.

The little mouse is quite sure that human beings wouldn't behave so badly. Yet on second thoughts, perhaps she's wrong? For who are all those people who fill the church on Harvest Festival Sunday whom she's never seen before? Are humans as bad as the animals and come to church only on the big festivals, but not on all the other Sundays of the year?

pagan: heathen.

papistical: following the Church of Rome.

6. DISCOVERING ARCHITECTURE

p. 63. SUMMONED BY BELLS

It was while he was at private boarding school—the Dragon School in Oxford—that John Betjeman began to take an interest in church architecture. He found a book that contained Victorian water-colour pictures of buildings, and that set him off on his bicycle in search of village churches. One of the masters at the school helped and encouraged him, and his enthusiasm grew as he learned more and more from what he observed.

The lyric poem about the school picnic and orchid hunt follows straight on and ends the chapter of *Summoned by Bells* that is about John Betjeman's private school days.

Chaundy's shop: a bookshop in Oxford that used to be in the Broad, but was pulled down when the New Bodleian Library was built on its site.

ilex tree: the evergreen oak tree that grows in Worcester College Gardens.

Magdalen: Magdalen College, Oxford, the college to which Betjeman went as an undergraduate later on.

The High: the main street in Oxford where many colleges stand. Said at one time to be one of the most beautiful streets in Europe.

Univ.: University College, Oxford.

Norm.: Norman architecture, dating from 1066 to about 1180.

E.E.: Early English, the first great style of Gothic architecture, from about 1180 to 1270.

Dec.: Decorated, the second style of Gothic architecture, from about 1270 to 1380.

Perp.: Perpendicular, the third style of Gothic architecture from 1380 to the Reformation in the sixteenth century.

vaulting shafts . . . groins: these are all architectural terms for parts of church construction.

Harrow and Keble: Gerald Haynes went to public school at Harrow and to university at Keble College, Oxford.

tympana . . . Norfolk screens: more architectural terms for parts of church construction.

bindweed: convolvulus, a climbing wild plant.

Red Sea troops: Moses led the children of Israel across the Red Sea to escape the Egyptian pursuers. The Lord caused the water to be divided so that it stood still, like a wall on either side of them, and they walked across on a path of dry land. (Exodus 14.)

Sturmey-Archer: the three-speed gear of the bicycle.

p. 66. HYMN

A fashion existed in the second half of the nineteenth century for 'restoring', or re-designing, ancient churches and building new ones in the medieval 'Gothic' style. The work was often paid for by wealthy industrialists and landowners. The rectors of the old churches invariably welcomed the new 'improvements'—this one did, particularly as some of the old carved wood-work was transferred to his own hall. This poem describes the changes that were made to many churches at the time. The 'he' is, of course, the architect who was responsible for it all.

encaustic tile: tile inlaid with coloured clays which are burnt in.

p. 67. AN ARCHÆOLOGICAL PICNIC

The poet and his friend Mary have packed their picnic lunch and bottles of lemonade and gone off in search of antiquities. They have their picnic in a field, then go into the village church, but Mary soon sees enough of the church and the boy sends her back to the field to drink more lemonade while he stays to examine the church's architecture more closely.

Blunden time: the poet Edmund Blunden (born 1896) was one of the poets who wrote about the First World War, having fought in it himself. Blunden is also known as a very fine pastoral poet. Particularly beautiful are the poems where he is describing his native Kent. So 'Blunden time' means a time of country quiet.

Lady's Finger, *Smokewort*, *Lovers' Loss:* wild plants that grow in fields and hedgerows.

Tennysonian chime: 'The mellow lin-lan-lone of evening bells' is a phrase Tennyson uses in the poem 'Far-Far-Away' to describe three bells ringing in a country church.

where the key lies . . .: the church porch where, in the Middle Ages all the business of the village was conducted. That is why public notices are always hung there to this day.

cerements: grave clothes.

Burne-Jones: Sir Edward Burne-Jones (1833–1898) was one of the great 'Pre-Raphaelite' artists of the nineteenth century who designed and made some of the loveliest of stained-glass windows in English churches.

Trans arcade: arches built in the Transitional style. This style came between the rounded arches of the Norman and the pointed arches of the Gothic.

squinch and squint: architectural terms for parts of church construction.

p. 67. SUNDAY MORNING, KING'S CAMBRIDGE

The chapel of King's College, Cambridge, is one of the most beautiful buildings in the country and is a major achievement of English medieval architecture. It was built between 1448 and 1515 in Perpendicular style. The choir of this chapel is equally famous, and every Christmas Eve it sings the Festival of Nine Lessons and Carols which is now always broadcast. This poem describes some of the interior of the chapel and Betjeman's reflections as the choir files in to begin morning service.

plaster Gothic: examples of early Victorian Gothic Revival plasterwork that can be seen on some of the Cambridge college buildings, e.g., Sidney Sussex College.

p. 68. THE TOWN CLERK'S VIEWS

Quite a different attitude to architecture is expressed here. John Betjeman feels that one of the disasters of the present age is the passion for pulling down relics of past beauties and achievements, and replacing them with ugly, shoddy, stream-lined things designed for utility. This is a rather bitter verse-portrait of the kind of official who holds the views Betjeman most dislikes, and is, unhappily, in a position to put them into operation. He is the kind of power-seeking little man who is responsible for turning 'our country into hell'.

hipp'd roof: roof with two different angles on one slope.

aquatint: a picture printed by a special process of engraving on copper. Particularly popular in the nineteenth century.

Branksome Chine: a valley in Bournemouth leading to the sea.

Torquay: this was a fashionable health and holiday resort in Devonshire much favoured by the wealthy in Victorian times.

Oxford: the industrial development in and around Oxford in recent years has caused distress to all who love and respect the town with its ancient colleges and beautiful buildings. This has not yet happened to Cambridge.

Welwyn: Welwyn Garden City in Hertfordshire was one of the first 'Garden Cities' built at the beginning of this century. It was a planned attempt to build a town which preserved the feel and appearance of the countryside.

Middle West: The Middle West is one great region in the U.S.A. with Chicago at its centre. John Betjeman is thinking of the unimaginative mass-produced architecture which has been fostered by swift industrial expansion.

Broadway: in Gloucestershire. This is already a Cotswold show village, visited by thousands of tourists every year.

Eurythmic: the practice of bodily movement to music.

7. POEMS OF PLACES

SUMMONED BY BELLS

p. 75.

Places have always been important to John Betjeman. This extract from *Summoned by Bells* tells what a wrench it was for him when his parents moved from Highgate to Chelsea. Their whole outlook on life seemed to change with the move—now they were prosperous and mixing with artistic, advanced-thinking people of a higher social standing, and John hated being uprooted. He missed the old haunts and couldn't get used to the new house. So he spent as much time away from it as possible, touring the London Underground with a friend, and visiting churches and old buildings. On Sundays his favourite churches were in the City where hardly a soul would be in attendance but the statutory services had to take place all the same.

In all Betjeman's poems, there is a great sense of 'place'. Whether he is writing about Miss Joan Hunter Dunn or Ebenezer Jones, the background is not merely indicated by a few general impressions; it is described in detail, with familiar objects, smells and noises. It is not surprising that in this section, 'Poems of Places', there are more poems than in any other of the book, for there is a very large number to choose from.

Augustus John: (1878–1961). A famous artist who lived in Chelsea for many years and was considered to live the model 'bohemian', free-thinking life. Art students liked to copy him, and wealthy or otherwise distinguished people liked to know him—or, better still, have their portraits painted by him.

divorce: in the 1920's it was considered very daring to bring into the open a subject which had hitherto been suppressed in all genteel society.

St. Martin's: the St. Martin's theatre in London.

urban level: same level as the rest of the town.

rubber: a term used in some card games. Here the game would have been bridge.

Cheyne Gardens: by the river Thames, on the Chelsea Embankment.

Metroland: the country round London which could be reached by the Metropolitan Railway which ran underground most of the time, but came into the open as it approached country districts.

neo-Tudor: modern buildings built in imitation Tudor style.

Penge: an outer London suburb.

Commandment boards: the painted boards behind the altar, found in seventeenth- and eighteenth-century churches.

aldermanic pomp: ceremony attached to the office of an alderman, a town councillor who is next in dignity to the mayor.

p. 78. SOUTH LONDON SKETCH, 1844

The Wandsworth of 1844 was part of London's countryside, with lanes and village inns. Today only Wandsworth and Clapham Commons are left of the original fields; the rest is covered with houses, and the great railway station of Clapham Junction stands near-by. But some of the lovely street names still tell of the Wandsworth of the past—Lavender Sweep, Sheepcote Lane, Mossbury Road, Longhedge Street, and many others.

p. 78. WESTGATE-ON-SEA

Westgate is a late Victorian suburb of Margate, on the Kent coast. It is rather more exclusive than Margate and has red brick houses in wide, winding, tree-lined roads. Many of these houses are small private schools.

p. 79. MARGATE, 1940

In 1940, during the first year of the Second World War, many people had left the big towns of the south-east coast. The children had been taken away to safer places, and no lights were permitted to show at night. This was called the 'black-out'. In Margate, John Betjeman looks from the balcony of the hotel he has known for years, into the blackness of the night, and remembers the Margate he knew when, at the height of the season, all the entertainments were in full swing and lights twinkled at night along the sea front.

thé dansant: a tea-time dance.

'Co-Optimists': a once-famous London concert party which dressed as Pierrots and had seaside imitators.

Cliftonville: the next town along the coast—really an extension of Margate.

p. 80. HENLEY-ON-THAMES

Another place recollected in wartime—Henley, the little Oxfordshire town on the river Thames, famous for its boating and annual regatta.

prow-promoted gems: the bubbles made by ripples of water that fall away from the prow of the boat as it goes along. (See verse 1, last line.)

beefy ATS: the women of the Auxiliary Territorial Service—the women's branch of the Army—were known as 'Ats'.

p. 81. WANTAGE BELLS

Wantage is the Berkshire town where John Betjeman lives. It lies at the foot of the downs, and, in summer, flowers seem to be everywhere—in cottage gardens, in hedgerows and along the banks of the stream. He feels no words can express human gratitude for such beauty: only the church bells can ring out eloquent thanks and praise.

p. 82. UPPER LAMBOURN

Over a high ridge of downs from Wantage lies the village of Lambourn, famous for its race-horse training stables. The horses are ridden to exercise on practice gallops on the downs, and strings of them come and go from the village throughout the early hours of the day.

twenty-thousand: like the noise of twenty thousand little feet.

Carrara headstone: headstone made of white marble from Carrara in Italy. It is often imported and used for gravestones.

he who trained . . . : one of the race-horse trainers.

sarsen stone: a sandstone boulder found on the chalk downs.

p. 83. HERTFORDSHIRE

This is a story of John Betjeman's youth. His father took him into Hertfordshire to try to teach him how to shoot, but it was no good. John simply couldn't hold a gun properly and finished up by shooting into the ground. His father was pained by his clumsiness, but how much more pain he would have suffered now, Betjeman thinks, if he could see what has happened to Hertfordshire since then. New towns, factories, and houses have blotted out the former countryside, and now it is only a continuation of London.

knickerbockered: knickerbockers were baggy trousers gathered in just below the knee worn by sporting gentlemen.

syndicated shoots: land owned or rented by several people, any of whom may go and shoot birds and other game there during the shooting season—autumn and winter.

Lionel Edwards: (born 1878). An artist who specializes in sporting and hunting pictures with the rainy, grey skies of the English winter.

Landaulette: a form of early motor-car of which half the body would be open to the sky.

Brick boxes: modern houses.

p. 84. **NORFOLK**

This part of Norfolk makes Betjeman remember his childhood and the time before he began to suffer the pains of growing up—like falling in love, and being let down and heart-broken. When did *that* all begin, he wonders? But here in Norfolk he used to have happy walks with his father, and return to their boat on the Broads where he would lie in his cabin at night and listen to the lap of the water against the sides. In those days he was carefree and innocent, and how wonderful it was!

Bure: a Norfolk river.

p. 85. **LAKE DISTRICT**

At a lakeside café the poet is sitting and watching the lake, day-dreaming about a girl who goes to the top diving-board (he likes to imagine she's doing it specially for him) and plunges into the water. Yet the atmosphere of poetry and romance that dwells in the Lake District is somehow counter-blasted by the presence of H.P. Sauce and Heinz's ketchup and suggestions of very *un*romantic trippers.

p. 85. **ESSEX**

This is another poem which looks back in time and sees a landscape of more beauty than is there today. A book of colour-plates shows John Betjeman the Essex of Edwardian days and reminds him of his own memories of the county when he was a boy.

Benfleet: a village a little way up the Thames Estuary from Southend.

Leigh-on-Sea: a town on the coast.

Matching Tye: an Essex village.

convoluted: twisted in design.

yarrow: a wild herb.

p. 87. **HARROW-ON-THE-HILL**

Betjeman looks from Harrow-on-the-Hill, a north-west London suburb, in the dusk of an autumn evening and imagines he can see the Cornish coastline in the distance with the waves of the sea breaking upon it. In the half-light he sees a storm blowing up and a fleet of little trawlers hurrying round the headland to get into port before the storm breaks.

Wembley: the suburb to the south-east of Harrow-on-the-Hill.

Stadium: Wembley sports stadium.

estuary: in this sense, the estuary of the river Camel in north Cornwall, near Trebetherick, where John Betjeman went for holidays as a child.

Wealdstone: a part of Harrow below the hill.

Kenton: the suburb to the east of Harrow-on-the-Hill.

Perivale: the suburb to the south.

Pentire: Pentire Head, in north Cornwall, at the estuary of the river Camel.

Padstow: in north Cornwall—a little port town on the Camel estuary.

p. 87. A LINCOLNSHIRE TALE

This tale with a ghostly theme is told by a Lincolnshire Archdeacon. The places in the poem are not real ones but as many Lincolnshire villages end in 'by', John Betjeman has made up his own names in Lincolnshire style. The Archdeacon travels in his carriage one evening down a long lane that leads past Speckleby Church and Rectory. He has never, in all his years of office, visited the Rector here, for he has heard of strange happenings and it is said that the Rector is mad. When the carriage reaches Speckleby Church, the Archdeacon's blood freezes for the pony suddenly falls dead and the church bell begins to toll. The manor house and park has long been deserted, but he gets out of the carriage and walks across the neglected grounds towards the church. The bell seems to draw him there against his will. As he stands by the tombstones, he sees the light of a moving taper shining from inside the church. At last he summons up courage to open the door. Inside, there is the smell of damp and decay and as he looks into the church, the bell stops tolling. Then he sees the Rector himself appear through a door and the sight so fills him with terror that he rushes away blindly into the night.

umber: dark, brownish-yellow pigment.

sign-painter's beasts: painted with the crude vigour of the old signboard of a village inn.

fell: terrible.

8. LATER SCHOOL

p. 93. SUMMONED BY BELLS

John Betjeman went to public school when he was thirteen. The school was Marlborough in Wiltshire, which, like all public schools, allowed the boys themselves to form their own rules and customs, and for junior boys the first few years could be very miserable. This whole section is devoted to an extract from *Summoned by Bells* that describes John's life at Marlborough, and relates an incident that shows how a boy could be punished for some minor crime by his older schoolfellows. Times have changed since those days, of course, and what happened then would not be allowed to happen now.

The *Summoned by Bells* chapter begins with Betjeman lying in the bath with the steam swirling round him, letting his mind go back forty years to the school changing room which used to be filled with steam like this. Then he goes on with his memories of public school.

bat oil: the oil used on cricket bats.

Ut: a Latin preposition.

beaks: masters.

in Hall: dining-hall.

9. GROWING UP

p. 101. SUMMONED BY BELLS

Still in pursuit of churches and architecture, John Betjeman comes eventually to the church of St. Ervan, Cornwall, where the Rector invites him to attend Evensong. During the service he sees all he wants to see of the church, but he doesn't go away immediately afterwards, for the Rector asks him in for a cup of tea. He talks to the boy about his religious beliefs and when he finds they are just as he suspected—'singing hymns and feeling warm and comfortable inside'—he lends him a book. John goes away and reads the book, and it sets him thinking about the deeper meaning of religion in a way that has never occurred to him before. He awakens to a different way of thinking, and from now on he is changed with this new realization; he is no longer a child. He is growing up and discovering his own beliefs.

St. Ervan: an early Cornish saint after whom the little thirteenth-century church is named.

red admirals: a kind of butterfly.

buddleia: a kind of shrub with lilac or yellow flowers.

apiary: place where bees are kept.

Rock: a village on the estuary of the river Camel opposite to Padstow.

Holy Grail: the cup from which Christ was believed to have drunk at the Last Supper, about which many legends have been told.

King Brychan: a Welsh king, many of whose children became priests and nuns in the Celtic Church and were later made into saints.

Celtic: this generally applies to Scots, Irish, Welsh and Cornish, but here it means only the Cornish Celts.

p. 103. DISTANT VIEW OF A PROVINCIAL TOWN

The awakening of religious belief and uneasy feeling of conscience are reflected in this poem. The provincial town is Reading, Berkshire, which is one of the main railway stations between London and the West Country. Betjeman sees the spires that rise above the town—he knows all the churches—and sees the Great Western Railway, and somehow the two things stir deep feelings in him and make him feel remorse for his sins.

Popish: tending towards Roman Catholicism.

United Benefice: a church that once had a vicar of its own, but is now under the care of another church and its vicar.

unfrocked: his ecclesiastical office was taken away from him.

p. 104. CHRISTMAS

This poem takes the theme of awakening religious belief even further. What is the meaning of Christmas? Do all the present-giving, the decorations, the feasting and carol-singing mean anything more than having a gay holiday? If they *do* mean something more, and the Baby born in a Bethlehem stable was the Son of God, come to save mankind, then the truth of this outshines all other truths, and man must live by it.

Advent: the four-week season before Christmas.

Tortoise stove: a make of metal stove used in churches.

Crimson Lake, *Hooker's Green:* names of colours.

classic towers: a poetic reference to some of the City churches.

shining ones: rich people.

Bread and Wine: the Church's sacrament of Holy Communion.

THE NOEL STREATFEILD CHRISTMAS HOLIDAY BOOK

Also available in the Target series:

THE NOEL STREATFEILD SUMMER HOLIDAY BOOK

in preparation:

THE NOEL STREATFEILD EASTER HOLIDAY BOOK

THE NOEL STREATFEILD CHRISTMAS HOLIDAY BOOK

A collection of stories and poems to while away the snowy days of Christmas. . .

Illustrated by Sara Silcock

Target Books is a division of Tandem Publishing Ltd.,
14 Gloucester Road, London SW7 4RD

A Howard & Wyndham Company

First published in Great Britain by J. M. Dent & Sons, Ltd., 1973

First published in this edition by Tandem Publishing Ltd., 1975

ISBN 0 426 10911 2

Printed in Great Britain by litho by The Anchor Press Ltd., and bound by Wm. Brendon & Son, Ltd., both of Tiptree, Essex

Contents

My Christmas Holidays NOEL STREATFEILD 7
Christmas Day in New Zealand MARGARET MAHY 9
St Francis, My Great Aunt Emily and You, or How to Make a Christmas Crib RUMER GODDEN 12
Last Bus for Christmas PATRICIA LYNCH 18
Coco the Clown NICOLAI POLIAKOFF 27
The Legend of the Christmas Rose SELMA LAGERLÖF 43
The Wild White Horses JOYCE STRANGER 54
The Prayer of the Donkey RUMER GODDEN 69
The Camel RUMER GODDEN 70
The Stowaway RICHARD G. ROBINSON 72
The Christmas Cherries CHRÉTIEN DE TROYES 82
A Shower of Snow HELEN CRESSWELL 91
The Lady of the Lake GODFRIED BOMANS 102
A Handful of Dates TAYEB SALIH 112
The Veiled Lodger SIR ARTHUR CONAN DOYLE 118
What Happened to Pauline, Petrova and Posy NOEL STREATFEILD 135
Miss Teazle and the White Elephants MARGARET J. BAKER 142
Christmas JOHN BETJEMAN 156
ACKNOWLEDGMENTS 159

My Christmas Holidays

I wonder which is the best of the school holidays. When I was your age I looked forward passionately to all three, but then I hated being at school. Oh, the joy of the last day of term! The moment when you cleared out your desk and dusted all the books, which we had to do, something, which I dare say you don't. Oh, the pleasure of stuffing all the bumph—drawings, essays your parents were supposed to enjoy reading—into your satchel, then shouting goodbyes, striding off for home. For me the striding was in the company of my sisters—one older than myself, one younger. For me—not for my sisters—there was a snag before joy could be unconfined. It was THE ENVELOPE. It lay white and crisp on top of the bumph in my satchel and without doubt was the bearer of bad news. It might just as well have had a black border.

Why is it—and this seems to have happened in all generations—that while the rest of the children in a family do well at school, one is a complete failure? It doesn't seem to have anything to do with brains, more often it would appear to be sheer cussedness.

In this book, which is one of three about holidays, you can picture me and my two sisters coming home for the start of the Christmas holidays. My sisters, radiantly happy—and why not? —for in their envelopes there would be no 'inattentive' or 'slovenly work' nor even 'could do better if she would try'. They had each a whole column of 'much improved', 'excellent' or 'shows real talent'.

Term after term I would loiter by every drain longing to

post my report down it, but I was always prevented by one of my sisters saying: 'It will do no good for if you haven't got it Daddy will suppose it's worse than it is.' Which was not true for no one could imagine my report worse than it was.

One Christmas holiday my report was so bad that it actually made my mother laugh. It was the result of an exam in which I got two out of a hundred. Surprised, I said without thinking, 'I wonder what I got two for?'

Fortunately the report reading took place the moment we got home. Usually this was followed for me by a 'talk' in Father's study. It was not of course a talk, it was a lecture which combined explaining to me what grief my bad work brought, not only to my school, to my parents but also to God. Father was a parson so I accepted this last as a matter of course, though marvelling why someone as busy as God should have time to grieve because of my bad report.

Then suddenly my talk was over, reports were forgotten and we fell head over heels into the magic of Christmas.

Everybody who keeps Christmas attempts to make each new Christmas as glorious as the last, carrying on customs from one year to the next. But before I write about the customs with which I grew up let's get a Christmassy feeling with some poetry. I have four poems about Christmas for you and I have chosen to start with 'Christmas Day in New Zealand' just because it is so different. Living where we do it's hard to imagine a Christmas without holly, mistletoe, robins and, if no snow, at least cold weather and grey skies. But of course Christmas is kept all over the world and so, for half the world it is summer. A summer Christmas Day probably means picnics, swimming and perhaps a barbecue in the evening. But some things we all share: presents, Christmas cards, probably a tree and, for most of us, it is the celebration of Christ's birth. So here is a carol in which you hear how, though the weather is different, the feeling is just the same as our own.

Christmas Day in New Zealand

Our Christmas Day is blue and gold,
And warm our Christmas Night.
Blue for the colour of Mary's cloak
Soft in the candle-light,
Gold for the glow of the Christmas Star
That shone serene and bright.

Warm for the love of the little babe
Safe in the oxen stall.
We know our Christmas by these signs
And yet around my wall
On Christmas cards the holly gleams
And snow flakes coldly fall,
And robins I have never seen
Pipe out a Christmas call.

Margaret Mahy

Christmas didn't begin as early when I was a child as it does now. Shops did not start to decorate before December and you never saw a Father Christmas until about two weeks before Christmas when, as now, you could meet him in toy shops where—in those days—for sixpence you could shake him by the hand and get a present. But of course it was what went on at home which made us feel Christmassy.

The first Christmas thing we had to do was make the Christmas decorations, they were never bought in shops in those days. We three girls and my brother would sit round the table in what we still called 'the nursery'. In the middle of the table was a large bowl of home-made paste and we each had a brush and a packet of brightly-coloured tissue paper strips which we, by hooking them through each other, turned into chains. You very seldom see paper chains now, so many pretty things are on the market to take their place. But I can promise you—and any of you who have made them will back me up—there is nothing so full of the spirit of Christmas as making paper chains.

Of course the moment the chains were made they had to be hung up. This I think must have been done by the grown-ups, for I don't remember being allowed up a ladder which was necessary and which I would have enjoyed.

I don't think paper chains went beyond the nursery for down-stairs we trimmed everything that was trimmable with holly. Holly was on everything: lights, pictures, clocks, ornaments—it must have driven those who dusted mad before Christmas was over. In the middle of the hall there was a light to which a big bunch of holly and a few sprigs of mistletoe were attached. The mistletoe was put in the bunch surreptitiously by my mother, who thought it looked pretty. My father did not believe in putting up mistletoe because it might turn minds to kissing. But whose minds? We three little girls were too young to have thought of such a thing and who was there to kiss? Only the curate and who would want to kiss him? Perhaps Father thought of visitors and those who worked for us. I shall never know but I do know that, thanks to Mother, mistletoe always appeared.

Looking back it is strange that that very pretty custom, which comes to us from abroad, of hanging a holly wreath on the front door never existed when I was a child. Certainly we never had one and I do not remember seeing one. Stranger still, we never had a crib in the house. There was one of course in the church, but in those days the charming custom of making a crib for the home never reached us. Today, when so many people give immense imagination and talent to building exquisite cribs which they look at with joy until Twelfth Night, I regret that as a child I never had the chance to build one.

For those of you who want to build a crib but do not know how, here is a description of the way she sets about it by Rumer Godden. Rumer Godden, as I expect you know, is a most beautiful writer. Her books are mostly for grown-ups but some are for children and, as you will discover farther on in this book, she is a poet. But now, thanks to her Great Aunt Emily, she is describing how you make a Christmas crib.

RUMER GODDEN

St Francis, My Great Aunt Emily and You, or How to Make a Christmas Crib

The customs we keep for Christmas have almost all come down to us from long ago but none, I think, is as old as the Christmas Crib; for it is more than seven hundred years since the first was made by St Francis of Assisi. It is just the sort of thing he would think of—he is the saint most marked by joy and simplicity—and he made it, we are told, with intense love, dressing his kings and angels in gay medieval clothes and giving his Holy Family the golden wigs that were used then for haloes.

The first Crib I ever saw was not made by anyone at all saintly but by a severe old lady who was my Great Aunt Emily; she was severe but she gave wonderful children's parties and at one, given for Christmas, there, in her drawing-room, was a Crib. I do not remember how it was made but I know it had a rustic cave, moss, a silver star and that, while we sang carols, the parlourmaid held slides of coloured paper in front of a lamp shining down on it, so that the cave was in moonlight or rosy dawnlight or in the yellow sunshine of midday. I was five years old and thought it the most beautiful and poetical thing I had ever seen.

I still think a Crib a beautiful and poetical idea; it brings the true spirit of Christmas into a home but, up to a year or two ago, very few were seen in private homes like my Great Aunt Emily's: they were in churches, sometimes in schools, but nowadays more and more children seem to be having them in their own homes. Sets of figures are sold now in the shops, sometimes with a cave or a stable for a complete Crib, but most of these are expensive and, beautiful though they are, a Crib you have made yourself always seems most beautiful of all. Perhaps owing to that long ago memory of Great Aunt Emily's, I and my children make one, though very simply every year: I thought you might like to know how we do it.

Just before Christmas Eve, or on Christmas Eve itself, we go out and gather moss, trails of ivy, leaves and berries—even in London there are places where you can find all these. We also choose three or four small logs of more or less even size with, if possible, the bark still on them, and we try to find a little sawdust or bran: this can be bought at any pet shop very cheaply. Then, on a deep windowsill or table, or on a large box covered with paper, we spread several thicknesses of newspaper, thick because moss is always damp and might, for instance, take the polish off a table.

For the cave we use a basket without a handle or a bowl in plain brown or blue china. The bowl gives quite a good effect if a third of it is sunk between the logs and covered with moss: but a basket looks more rustic and cosy and has the advantage that sprays of ivy and sprigs of holly can be fastened into its weave. Of all baskets a bicycle basket is the best for, if laid on its flat side, it is the shape of a cave: it does not need to be sunk into the moss and, of course, it has no handle.

We place it, on the papers, on its flat side and put a log each side to steady it, letting the log project about four inches in front to form a setting. The others we put at the back and then, all round the cave and over the logs, we build a small landscape of moss, stones, chips of bark, holly and ivy. Besides the two side logs, and safely away from the basket, we set two nightlights in small jars or pots and heap them round with moss so that the pots are not seen. Nightlights are safer than candles and, lit on Christmas Eve, will burn all night, giving a soft and lovely light.

When the landscape is finished we fasten sprays of ivy over the top of the basket, with a twig or two of holly berries, and perhaps thatch it with moss. Then the floor of the cave is spread with sawdust or bran and it is now ready for the figures.

You can have all sorts of these, bought ones or modelled by yourself in clay, allowed to dry and then painted: or you can make little figures of pipe-cleaners and dress them, or cut them out in paper, making each a bent paper stand. For years we used figures out of an old Noah's Ark. Mrs Noah was in blue and white and made a perfect Virgin Mary, Noah in pink was St Joseph. We made them haloes, drawn round halfpennies, on stiff gold paper and then cut out and gummed onto the back of their heads.

Shem, Ham and Japhet were the Three Wise Men and of course there was an ox and an ass and two lambs. Sometimes now we use carved wooden ones and we have also collected a small set in plaster. Sometimes the children put in the Shepherds, sometimes an angel but, however we arrange them, it is always a rule that St Joseph and the Virgin Mary should be in the cave itself—as, of course, they were.

I made our first Jesus, a tiny bundle of white wrappings sewn round a painted face and laid Him in a manger made from twigs bound together: it looked extremely real. If you keep the real spirit of Christmas the Holy Child should not, of course, be put into the cave until late on Christmas Eve. It is a good idea to ask your mother to do this for you so that when you go to bed the cave is ready, its lights burning, all the figures waiting, but is empty of Him: when you wake in the morning, He is there.

On Christmas Day, if you liked, you could do what my Great Aunt Emily's parlourmaid did, but with a torch or, rather, two. Arrange them so that they shine into the Crib, darken the room and, with coloured blue, red, yellow talc paper stretched over cut-out cardboard frames, change the time of day: you could have 'Hail! Thou ever blessed morn' with a pink dawn; 'On Christmas Day in the morning' with yellow for sunshine, and blue moonshine for 'Holy night, peaceful night'.

When St Francis made his Crib the legend tells us that he was afraid the Pope would think him irreverent to use wooden dolls for the Holy Family but when St Francis knelt and took up the wooden Bambino, or Child, it came alive in his hands and blessed him, so the Pope dared not be angry. We, of course, are not St Francis but I think a little lit Crib in a home does give a feeling of blessedness.

I don't know about you, but I plan to have a little lit crib in my home next Christmas.

Before Christmas there never seem enough hours in the day to get through all you have to do. First on the list of course is shopping. All my life I have tried to get ahead with my Christmas shopping, but I have never succeeded. I make careful lists months beforehand and by October I have started to shop, but I never catch up with my own tail. You know how it is—something somebody wants which you could have bought anywhere a month or so ago suddenly disappears. In London, where I live, this means travelling miles from one shopping area to another wearing out both the feet and the temper. I suppose if you live in the country it's worse for it means going from one town or village to another. It's worth the effort though if you run what you want to earth. You feel as if you had won an Olympic Gold Medal, and when you see the face of the person you give it to all your labour is worth while. 'Oh, bless you! It's what I most wanted and I was scared stiff nobody would give it to me.'

I got my first watch off the Christmas tree, and you know what a first watch means. I must have been about eleven. You would laugh if you saw it today, it was made of what was called gunmetal fastened onto me by a metal bow attached to a pin. A watch like that was all the rage in those days, just as much in fashion as the latest craze in watches is today. I forget who gave mine to me, but I do know however much of a search the giver had to find it, he or she must have thought every second worth while if they saw my face when I opened the box in which it arrived. In fact even now, all those years later, if I flag in my search for a special present I see again my little gunmetal watch and I plod on.

How easy it was when one was tiny. My brother when he was just four gave everybody who had to have a present a sugar mouse. Sugar mice complete with pink noses and wool tails in those far-off days cost one halfpenny each. The only person who did not get a mouse was me. When I asked my brother why he said: 'I only had four pennies which is eight mice, with you it would have been nine. I like you least so I left you out.' Even at just four I thought that showed a poor Christmas spirit.

Present buying is only half the business of present giving. Thank goodness, when I was a child there was none of the elaborate parcel doing up there is today. It was plain brown paper and string with perhaps a piece of holly stuck in the string. How children manage today with elaborate paper, ribbons, bows and sticky tape I can't imagine. They must be exhausted by Christmas Day.

Whether a parcel is done up in glorious colours or brown paper and string, have you ever thought about the people who have nowhere to go at Christmas? Perhaps no parcels to undo? Here is an Irish story about a boy who had nowhere to go for Christmas. It was written by that gloriously Irish writer Patricia Lynch whose books you must all have read. I know southern Ireland fairly well for I go there every year, and always I am enthralled at the way so many of the Irish do not know where fact ends and fancy begins. Patricia Lynch, thank goodness, was one who had never known and all her books prove it. Here is a lovely story of Miheal who had nowhere to go for Christmas. Just read what can happen in such a circumstance in Ireland.

PATRICIA LYNCH

Last Bus for Christmas

'Hurry up there, Miheal! Will ye bring over two red candles, quick!'

'More strawberry jam, Miheal! Two one-pound jars! And raisins: four one-pound bags!'

'Miheal Daly! I'm wore out wid waitin' for twine. How can I parcel the customers' groceries wid ne'er an inch of string?'

Miheal grabbed a handful of string from the box in the corner behind the biscuit tins and ran with it to Mr Coughlan. He brought the jam and the raisins at the same time to Peter Cadogan, and rolled the candles along the counter to Jim Reardon. Then he went back to his job of filling half-pound bags with sugar.

Miheal was the shop-boy and, one day, if he worked hard and behaved himself, Mr Coughlan had promised to make him an assistant.

'There's grandeur for an orphan!' Mrs Coughlan told him. 'Ye should be grateful.'

Miheal was grateful. But, as he watched the women crowding the other side of the counter, filling market bags and baskets with Christmas shopping, he was discontented. Yet he had whistled and sung as he put up the coloured paper chains and decorated the window with yards of tinsel and artificial holly.

He nibbled a raisin and gazed out at the sleet drifting past the open door.

'Everybody's going home for Christmas but me,' he thought.

The Coughlans always went to their relations for Christmas. Mrs Coughlan left Miheal plenty to eat and Mr Coughlan gave him a shilling to spend. But Miheal never ate his Christmas dinner until they came back. After Mass he spent Christmas Day walking about the streets, listening to the noise and clatter that came from the houses.

'Only two more hours,' whispered Peter Cadogan, as Miheal brought him bags of biscuits and half-pounds of rashers as fast as Mr Coughlan could cut them.

'Two more sugars, Miheal,' said Jim Reardon. 'Where d'you get your bus?'

Jim was new. He didn't know Miheal was an orphan, and Miheal was ashamed to tell him he had no home to go to for Christmas.

'Aston's Quay,' he muttered.

'We'll go together,' said Jim over his shoulder. 'I've me bag under the counter. Get yours!'

The next time Miheal brought Jim candles and raisins the new assistant wanted to know what time Miheal's bus went.

'I'll just make it if I run,' said Miheal.

'Then get yer bag, lad. Get yer bag!'

Miheal slipped through the door leading to the house. He ran to his little dark room under the stairs. He didn't dare switch on the light. Mrs Coughlan would want to know what he was doing. And a nice fool he'd look if she found out he was pretending to go home for Christmas.

'Home!' said Miheal to himself. 'That's where a lad's people come from and mine came from Carrigasheen.'

He wrapped his few belongings in an old waterproof. He grabbed his overcoat from the hook behind the door and was back in the shop before Mr Coughlan could miss him.

'Hi, Miheal! Give me a hand with this side of bacon. I never cut so many rashers in me life!'

Miheal pushed his bundle under the counter and ran to help.

'Isn't it grand to be going home for Christmas!' cried Peter, as they closed the door to prevent any more customers from coming in.

'Isn't it terrible to be turning money away!' groaned Mr Coughlan.

But Mrs Coughlan was waiting for him in her best hat and the coat with the fur collar.

'Can I trust you lads to bolt the shop door an' let yerselves out be the side door?' demanded Mr Coughlan.

'Indeed you can, sir!' replied Peter and Jim.

The last customer was served.

'I'm off!' cried Peter.

'Safe home!' called the others.

Then Jim was running down the quay, Miheal stumbling after him, clasping his bundle, his unbuttoned coat flapping in the wind.

They went along Burgh Quay, pushing by the people waiting for the Bray bus, then across to Aston's Quay.

'There's me bus!' shouted Jim.

''Tis packed full!' murmured Miheal. He was terribly sorry for Jim. But maybe he'd come back with him and they could spend Christmas together.

The bus was moving.

Jim gave a leap, the conductor caught his arm and pulled him to safety. He turned and waved to Miheal, his round red face laughing. He would have to stand all the way, but Jim was used to standing.

Two queues still waited. Miheal joined the longest.

'Where are ye bound for, avic?' asked a stout countrywoman, with a thin little girl and four large bundles, who came up after him.

'Carrigasheen!' replied Miheal proudly.

'Ah, well! I never heard tell of the place. But no doubt ye'll be welcome when ye get there. An' here's the bus.'

'I'll help with the bundles, ma'am,' said Michael politely.

Now every seat was filled. Still more people squeezed into the bus. Miheal reached the step.

'One more, an' one more only!' announced the conductor.

'In ye go, ma'am!' said Miheal, stepping back.

'One only!' repeated the conductor firmly.

The little girl was in. Miheal pushed the bundles after her and everyone cried out when the conductor tried to keep back the stout woman.

'Sure ye can't take the child away from her mammy!' declared a thin man. 'Haven't ye any Christianity in yer bones?'

'Can't she sit on me lap?' demanded the stout woman. 'Give me a h'ist up, lad. And God reward ye!' she added, turning to Miheal.

He seized her under the arms. She caught the shining rail and Miheal gave a great heave.

He stood gazing after the bus.

'Now I'm stranded!' he said, forgetting he had no need to leave Dublin.

A dash of sleet in Miheal's face reminded him. He could go back to the lonely house behind the shop. His supper would be waiting on the table in the kitchen. He could poke up the fire and read his library book.

The quays were deserted. A tall garda strolled along. He stared curiously at Miheal and his bundle.

'Missed the bus, lad?' he asked.

''Twas full up,' explained Miheal.

'Bad luck!' sympathized the garda. 'Can ye go back where ye came from?'

Miheal nodded.

''Tis a bad night to be travelling!' said the garda. 'That's the way to look at it.'

He gave Miheal a friendly nod and passed on.

'I'd as well be getting me supper,' thought Miheal.

But he did not move.

Over the Metal Bridge came a queer old coach drawn by two horses. The driver was wrapped in a huge coat with many capes and a broad-brimmed hat was pulled down over his twinkling eyes.

He flourished a whip and pulled up beside Miheal.

The boy edged away. He didn't like the look of the coach at all.

The driver leaned over and managed to open the door at the back with his whip.

'In ye get! Last bus for Christmas!'

'Whoever saw a bus with horses!' thought Miheal. 'But I suppose they use any old traps at Christmas.'

Still he held back.

'All the way to Carrigasheen widout stoppin'!' said the driver.

Miheal could see the cushioned seats and the floor spread thick with fresh hay. The wind, which was growing fiercer and colder every moment, blew in his face. He gave one look along the desolate quay and, putting his foot on the iron step, scrambled in.

At once the door slammed shut. The driver gave a shout and the horses trotted over the stones.

The coach bumped and swayed. Miheal tried to stretch out on the seat, but he slipped to the floor. The hay was thick and clean. He put his bundle under his head for a pillow and fell asleep.

An extra bump woke him up.

'I never thought to ask the fare,' said Miheal to himself. 'Seems a long way, so it does. Would he want ten shillings? He might—easy! Well, I haven't ten shillings. I've two new half-crowns. He'll get one and not a penny more!'

He tried to stand up, but the coach was swaying from side to side and he had to sit down again.

'Mister! Mister!' he shouted. 'How much is the fare?'

The rattling of the coach and the thunder of the horses' hooves made so much noise he could scarcely hear himself. Yet he would not keep quiet.

'I won't pay a penny more than two and six,' he shouted. 'Mind now! I'm telling you.'

The door of the coach swung open and Miheal was pitched out, his bundle following him. He landed on a bank covered with snow and lay there blinking.

The road wound away through the mountains in the moonlight—an empty desolate road. The wind had dropped but snow was falling.

In the distance he could hear a strange sound. It was coming nearer and nearer, and soon Miheal knew it was someone singing '*Adeste Fideles*' in a queer cracked voice.

The singer approached, tramping slowly along: an old man with a heavy sack on his back.

'What ails ye to be sitting there in the snow, at this late hour of the night, young lad?' he asked, letting his sack slip to the ground.

'I came on the coach from Dublin,' replied Miheal, standing up.

He was ashamed to say he had fallen out.

The old man pushed back his battered caubeen and scratched his head.

'But there hasn't been a coach on this road in mortal memory!' he declared. 'There's the bus road the other side of the mountain and the last bus went by nigh on two hours ago. I suppose ye came by that. Where are ye bound for?'

'Mebbe I did come by the bus and mebbe I didn't!' exclaimed Miheal. 'But I'd be thankful if you'd tell me am I right for Carrigasheen?'

The old man wasn't a bit annoyed by Miheal's crossness.

'D'ye see the clump of trees where the road bends round by the mountain? There's Carrigasheen! I'm on me way there an' I'll be real glad of company. So ye're home for Christmas? I thought I knew everyone for miles around, yet I don't remember yer face. What name is on ye, lad?'

'Miheal Daly.'

The old man stared.

'There are no Dalys in Carrigasheen now. That I do know! But we can talk as we go. Me own name is Paudeen Caffrey.'

Miheal caught up the sack. He was a strong lad but he found it heavy. He wondered how the old man had managed to carry it at all. Paudeen Caffrey took the boy's bundle and they set off. The snow piled on their shoulders, on the loads they carried, on their hair, their eyebrows, but they did not notice, for Miheal was telling the old man all about himself.

'So me poor gossoon, ye're an orphan,' asked the old man.

'I am indeed!' agreed Miheal.

'An' ye haven't a father or mother, or brother or sister to be a friend to ye?'

'Not a soul!'

'An' these people ye work for, what class of people are they?' continued old Paudeen Caffrey.

'Not too bad!' declared Miheal. 'Aren't they going to make me an assistant one of these days?'

'Suppose now,' began the old man. 'Mind, I'm just saying suppose—ye have a chance to be shop-boy to an old man and his wife that needed help bad in their shop and couldn't get it? Mind ye—I'm only supposing. Ye'd have a room wid two windas, one lookin' out on the market square, the other at the mountains. Ye'd have three good meals a day, a snack at supper, ten shillings a week, an' if ye wanted to keep a dog or a cat, or a bicycle, ye'd be welcome. What would ye say to that?'

He looked at Miheal sideways and Miheal looked back.

'It wouldn't be with Paudeen Caffrey, that kept the corner shop next the post office, would it?' asked Miheal.

'It would so,' replied the old man.

'I'm remembering now,' said the boy. 'Me father told me if ever I needed a friend to write to Paudeen Caffrey.'

'Why didn't ye, lad? Why didn't ye?'

'I was ashamed. Me mother told me how they left Carrigasheen after telling everyone they were going to Dublin to make their fortunes an', when they came back, they'd be riding in their carriage. Ye see?'

The old man laughed.

'An' didn't ye come back in a carriage? But there's the lights of Carrigasheen. Do ye come home wid me, Miheal Daly?'

'If you'll have me, Mr Caffrey.'

The old man chuckled.

'An' to think I went out for a sack of praties an' come back wid a shop-boy! Wasn't it well ye caught the last bus for Christmas, Miheal?'

'It was indeed!' declared Miheal Daly.

He could see the corner shop with the door open and an old woman looking out. Beyond her he caught a glimpse of firelight dancing on the walls, of holy pictures framed in holly and a big red Christmas candle on the table waiting for the youngest in the house to light it.

Amongst the Christmas cards there are usually several in fancy envelopes inviting you to parties. Sometimes the parties are not in anyone's home, but you are asked to a play, a film or a pantomime with a meal in a restaurant afterwards. A few years ago you might also have been asked to a circus for huge circuses performed in all the big towns. Nowadays there are almost no big circuses because of that thing grown-up people always talk about called 'the cost of living'. In the case of circuses that is the true reason why they have disappeared. Just think of one elephant. Imagine, with food more expensive every day, what one elephant costs to keep. Then imagine him travelling from town to town. You know that travelling for you costs more, then just guess how much more it costs to travel an elephant. Then of course there are all the other things the elephant has to have: a huge Big Top in which to perform and people to put it up and take it down, and look after the elephants and all the other animals, and wages go up and up.

When there were Christmas circuses I took a little girl called Richenda to a Christmas circus. The performance was to finish up with what is called a 'cat act' which means lions. Richenda, who was only four, asked me: 'Do the lions ever eat the men who look after them?' I said: 'Very seldom,' and then, in case she was frightened, I added: 'and never at matinées.' But I need not have worried for when the lions were performing I looked at Richenda. Her lips were moving so I leant down to hear what she was saying and it was: 'Eat him! Eat him!'

Perhaps the most circusy thing about a circus is the clowns. Here is part of the story of one clown and a very famous one. Coco was a circus artist from the time he was a small boy in Russia. His family was very poor so he started to work early as you will read in this extract from his book.

NICOLAI POLIAKOFF

Coco the Clown

One day, a week after my father had left us to serve in the army, we were all sitting round the table at home. There was very little food in the house, and we were too hungry to play. The room was cold because the fire was nearly out, and there was nothing more to put on it. I wondered how I could find something for us to eat.

I got up and went out into the street. When I had trudged through the snow for several minutes I came to a café. I pressed my face against the window. I could see cakes and bread there, and my mouth watered. I was so hungry I decided to go into the shop and ask for a job. But it took me a long time to pluck up enough courage to go in.

At last I could stand out in the snow no longer, and I went in. The shop was kept by an old Turk, and the sight of him nearly sent me out into the street again. He was a short man with an enormous paunch and tremendously long moustaches. His clothes were greasy, and he looked as if he hadn't washed for a long time. But he spoke to me quite kindly.

'Well, little one, what do you want?'

At first I couldn't answer, there seemed to be a lump in my throat. But I swallowed it, and the smell of the bread gave me courage.

'Please, sir,' I said, 'I want a job. My father has gone to the war, and there is no one to look after us, and we haven't any food.'

He looked at me and laughed. 'How old are you?' he said.

'Please, sir, I was five last October.'

'But you're so small, what can you do?'

'I can sweep the floor,' I said. 'I can open and shut the door for your customers. And I can sing, too.'

'What can you sing?' he asked.

I stood up very straight, stuck out my chest, and started to sing '*Tusa Tusa*'. This is a very old Russian song that my mother had taught me.

I was still singing lustily when the door opened and four officers came in. They looked at me and laughed.

'Ha! What's this—a young nightingale?' said one.

'Let's take him to the club with us, and give our comrades a surprise,' said another.

They asked me if I would go with them, and I said I would.

They made their purchases, and we went outside. There was a sleigh with three horses waiting. One of the officers picked me up and threw me to another in the sleigh. He tucked me up in a big black bearskin, and with a jingle of bells we were off to the club.

When we arrived at the club one of the officers told me that he wanted me to stand in the middle of the floor and sing my '*Tusa Tusa*'. I felt very frightened when we got inside. I was still very hungry, and very dirty, and I wanted to cry. But I remembered that I had a father at the war.

Suddenly one of the officers stepped into the middle of the floor and held up his hand. The orchestra stopped playing, and all the people stopped talking.

'Ladies and gentlemen,' he began, 'I have a great surprise for you. Here is the finest singer in all the Russias.'

He beckoned to me to step forward.

There was an expectant hush, and then what a roar there was when the people saw me. But I can remember vividly to this day how the feeling of fear left me, young child that I was, when I was faced with an audience, and what a feeling of confidence suddenly possessed me. When the laughter died down I started to sing my song.

When I had finished they applauded and shouted for more. I didn't know any more songs, so I started to dance, and to tumble like the clowns I had seen in the theatre. This pleased them more than my singing, and I did some more.

Suddenly I thought of my brothers and sisters, and my mother at home, and it seemed a very long way away. I felt I must go home. I ran to one of the officers who had brought me and asked him if he would take me home.

'Certainly, little one, if you want to go home I will take you.'

'I must go home, sir, my mother will be frightened because I've been away so long.'

The officers made a collection and gave me thirty-two copecks. They told the sleigh driver to take me back to the Turkish café.

When we got there the driver asked me if I was very hungry. I said no, but he bought me a basket of pastries, and told me to take them to my brothers and sisters at home.

Clutching my money in one hand and the basket of cakes in the other, I ran home through the snow and darkness as quickly as I could. How proud I was and how happy.

When I reached the house I kicked on the door and shouted: 'Mother, please let me in. It's Nicolai. Hurry, please!'

Alexander opened the door. My mother said: 'Oh, Nicolai, where have you been? We've looked all over the town for you.'

I was half crying with pride and happiness, and couldn't speak, so I just gave her the cakes and the money instead. I looked up into her face, but there was no look of joy and no embrace for Nicolai. My mother looked frightened, and said: 'Nicolai, where did you get all this from?'

'I earned it,' I said. 'I've been working, and I've got all this for you.'

'Oh, Nicolai, you have stolen. You must take it back.'

I started to cry, and tried to explain.

'Please believe me, mother. I have been working, I've been singing and dancing, and people gave me the money and cakes.'

But my mother wouldn't believe me. She picked up the cakes and money, and took me by the hand.

'Come along and show me where you got this,' she said.

We trudged through the snow back to the café. I was tired and hungry, and as bitterly unhappy as only a misunderstood child can be. I wept all the way.

When we got to the café my mother took me inside, and nervously asked the old Turk if that was where I had got the cakes.

'Yes,' he said, 'and the money was given him by the officers at the club for singing and dancing.'

Then my mother kissed me warmly, and I felt proud and happy again.

'Let us go home,' she said, 'we will have the pastries for supper.'

We hurried home, stopping on the way to spend some of the money on fuel for the stove.

I shall never forget my brothers' and sisters' faces when they saw the food. And I shall never forget the happiness of that evening, sitting round the table, the stove bright and warm, eating those cakes.

About a year later, when I was six and a half, we heard that a travelling theatre was coming to the town. This made everyone very excited, because a travelling theatre was a rare treat. At last the great day arrived, and the whole town turned out to greet the troupe. Needless to say I wormed my small body well to the front. We followed them right to the theatre, where the first performance was to be given on the Saturday.

This event made everything seem like a holiday, the sun shone, and I was so excited I did not know how I should wait until Saturday came.

That night my father who was home from the war came in with his face all smiles.

'I have a job. I am property man at the theatre.'

At this my mother almost wept for joy. Father didn't very often have a job. A job meant food and warmth, and new clothes for the winter, which in Russia always comes too soon.

My father was away at the theatre all next day, preparing the stage and props for the opening performance.

When he came home in the evening he said to my mother: 'I have everything ready, but what am I going to do? They need a little girl for the show.'

For some time they talked and argued about who they could find. And all the time some strange excitement was mounting in me, until I could bear it no longer.

'Father,' I said, my voice trembling, 'wouldn't a little boy do instead?'

My father glanced down at me. 'No, of course not, it must be a girl.'

'But father, I can dress up like a girl, and talk like one too.'

But my father wouldn't hear of it, and I felt the tears stinging my eyes, when my mother said: 'You could take Nicolai to the theatre tomorrow, and see what the manager says.'

'Very well,' said my father, 'I will.'

I hardly slept all that night. I tossed and turned, and never had a night seemed so long. I got up very early and dressed, and was ready a long time before my father was.

At last the time came, and we went off to the theatre. My father explained the situation to M Trafiloff, the manager, who said: 'Well, at any rate we will see what he looks like.'

While he rummaged in a chest which stood in a corner I stood gazing with delight at the dresses and costumes which hung round the walls.

'Come here, little one,' he said, and put a wig on my head. He stood back to look at me.

'It is good,' he said, 'just what I want.'

I felt rather silly in the wig, it wasn't very comfortable and I was afraid it would fall off.

Then they dressed me up in a girl's frock, and told me the few words I had to say. I repeated them until I knew them by heart.

Then my father came to me and told me to go on the stage and say my words as I would in the show.

As I walked out of the wings onto the stage I was so happy I nearly forgot about my few lines. I, Nicolai, was on a stage. I looked out into the empty auditorium and said my lines.

'Good, Nicolai,' said my father. I am sure I felt more pleased than the leading man in the show.

That afternoon, just before the play was due to start, my father took me to the back of the stage and asked the fireman there to look after me until I was wanted.

Here I stood, and gazed open-mouthed at the actors and actresses as they hurried to and fro. Everyone seemed excited, and there was a great deal of noise. There were orders from Trafiloff, shouts from the dressers, and everyone seemed to talk at once, no one seemed to listen.

'Poliakoff, come here at once.'

'Poliakoff, where's the curtain?'

It seemed to me that my father must be everywhere at once.

No one took any notice of me except my fireman, and he didn't speak unless I moved from where he had put me.

In one corner I could see the band tuning its instruments, and when the curtains sometimes blew aside a little, I caught glimpses of the people crowding into their seats. I thought the whole town had come. They moved and scraped their chairs, talking loudly among themselves, adding to the noise and clamour.

At last a bell rang loudly somewhere near me. My fireman told me that it was to warn the players that the play was about to start. The bell rang again, and all the players assembled at the back of the stage, ready to go on in their turn. The bell rang a third time, and the curtain went up almost at the same moment.

I held my breath with excitement. As the curtain went up the audience became very still and quiet. But when Trafiloff appeared in the middle of the stage they all clapped and cheered. He held up his hand.

'Ladies and gentlemen, I have much pleasure in presenting to you "The Bell", a drama in four acts.'

How the audience clapped and cheered! Trafiloff disappeared at the back of the stage, and the curtain was lowered.

The bell rang for the last time. The curtain rose. The play had really started. One could have heard a pin drop.

I stood as close as I dared. I drank in every word, and watched every movement the players made. But all the time I felt I could hardly wait for the third act. Then I began to wonder if my wig would fall off. And did I know my lines? I repeated them feverishly to myself. My legs ached, but I couldn't sit down.

Between the second and third acts my father came and asked me if I felt all right.

'Why, yes, father,' I said.

I could hear the audience applauding the second act. I imagined them applauding me, only even louder.

The curtain went up on the third act. My mouth felt dry. I felt my turn would never come. I pressed closer to the stage. I leant against the curtain and peered through the crack. I pushed nearer and nearer. Suddenly I fell through the curtain and onto the stage.

A large hand grabbed me by the back of my frock. I looked up into the angry face of my fireman. But all the time I could hear roars of laughter from the audience. M Trafiloff, when he came round, was even angrier than the fireman.

'You, what do you think you are doing? You nearly spoilt the whole play. It's a good thing for you that the audience have taken it the right way.'

I felt sad and ashamed. 'I'm very sorry, sir. I was excited. I didn't know what I was doing.'

'Well, don't do it again. Get ready for your turn.'

I felt my wig to see if it was still on my head. I once more repeated my lines to myself. Then as though from a long way off I heard someone say: 'Are you ready, Nicolai? Do your best, little son.'

Then M Trafiloff came to me with the jug that I was to carry onto the stage. He took my hand and led me to the players' entrance. 'On you go,' he said. 'Don't be frightened.'

I walked onto the stage. For a second I lifted my eyes and looked into the crowd of people. Then I said my lines and went off the stage.

It was over. I felt very tired. But I was happy because I had thought I heard people in the audience say: 'That wasn't a girl, that was Nicolai Poliakoff dressed up.' And I was proud that they should know me. But I don't know if they really said that or if I imagined it.

When the play was over the players gave me chocolate and sweets. My father said he was proud of me, M Trafiloff said: 'Well done, little one, you will make a good actor one day.'

After this I played several times with this troupe. Sometimes as a boy and sometimes as a girl. And once—the part I enjoyed more than any of the others—as a dwarf with a long beard.

I felt that life had really started the day I was apprenticed to Truzi's Circus. To be sure, I was the youngest and most insignificant part, but there I was.

We stayed in Riga all the winter, and I used to go and see my parents every day.

There were four other apprentices besides myself. I got on well with all of them except the eldest one. At first he disliked me, and wouldn't speak to me because I was so young. I didn't mind this, though; all I cared about was being in the circus.

We all lived together in lodgings in the town. Every morning we had to get up at six o'clock and be at the circus at seven. I was given all sorts of jobs—helping with the horses, cleaning the ring, mending ropes.

Then one day Truzi told me that I was to start my proper training.

'First of all you must learn to be an acrobat and to work on the trapeze,' he said.

'But I don't want to be an acrobat, I want to be a clown,' I said.

'My boy, if you want to be a successful clown first you must be an acrobat, then a trapeze artiste and a tumbler: in fact you must be able to do everything, and then you can think about being a clown.'

At first I thought that this was rather silly, but when I saw how the other clowns practised, I came to see that Truzi was right.

Every morning we would hurry into our practice clothes, and then we would line up in a row, ready for Rudolph Truzi to inspect us. After this the day's work would begin. We had to learn how to tumble, we had to learn to ride: we had to learn trapeze work, juggling, and, in fact, nearly every one of the arts of the circus. We started work on a miniature trapeze or wire near the ground, and then, as our work improved, the apparatus would be moved higher and higher. The finished apprentices would work high up in the big top. How we smaller ones envied them!

During the summer the circus was divided into two parts. Each part toured a different part of the country. There were two other apprentices besides myself in the circus I went with. We had a very happy time. The hours were long and the work was hard, but we didn't mind that. At each show one of us had to take a small part in the ring. It was really only more training, but we loved this. It gave us a chance of showing what we had learned, and it made us feel like real artistes.

We had a bear act with us—a baby bear and his trainer, a man called Bono. One day at Revel having been sent to the stables

to chop wood, I couldn't see the chopper. Then I saw it just inside the little bear's cage. Quite without thinking I opened the door to get the chopper. And then I saw the little bear running towards the door.

I turned and ran, the bear after me. I was so frightened that I didn't realize he only wanted to play with me, and wasn't nearly big enough to hurt me. In and out of the stalls I went, expecting all the time that I should feel his claws in my back. At last I found myself in the ring. But I went on running. Suddenly just by my ear there was a furious shout.

'Who has let that bear out?' It was Bono himself.

'Please, sir, it was me.'

Without another word Bono seized hold of me and gave me a terrible beating with a stick he always carried.

'That will teach you not to let any more bears out,' he said. And picking up the bear he carried it back to its cage.

I got up cautiously and felt myself all over. Suddenly I heard a shout of laughter. The two apprentices were looking at me and laughing until they cried. For a long time they kept reminding me that I had run away from a baby bear.

At the end of the last performance in Revel, we apprentices were so excited we didn't know what to do with ourselves. The circus was going to Vilno.

The Circus Truzi was the biggest of its kind in Russia in those days. From Revel to Vilno was over four hundred miles, and the whole circus was to be transported by a special train. This meant a great deal of work for everybody. There were one hundred and twenty-five horses, and the five other apprentices and myself had to lead these to the station and hand them over to the grooms, who then got them onto the train.

It seemed as if the whole town had gathered at the station to watch the work. The crowds would roar with laughter at the many little accidents that are bound to happen when a circus entrains. One of the horses took an instant dislike to the train, and it was over two hours before it was coaxed into it. And then one of the bears got loose. He was only caught after he had climbed onto the top of the station and got stuck there.

On the afternoon of the second day we were ready. Soon we were pulling out of the station, the crowd cheering lustily. I loved that journey. I seemed to have passed so many journeys hidden under the carriage seats to save the fare that I never tired of looking out at the countryside. The corn was ripening, and yet on top of the hills the sun shone on snow. And then, as by contrast, we would pass through dark deep forests that I thought would never come to an end.

I had to spend a good deal of time with the horses. They

travelled eight in each truck, and each truck had a groom in charge of it.

We first sighted Vilno during the afternoon of the second day. We could see the town down in a valley about fifteen miles away. Immediately the whole train was in a bustle. We had to have all the animals, and everything else, ready to unload when we stopped so that we could get them to the circus ground before dark.

Again, at this station, were crowds of excited people. And here again I started my job of leading the horses from the train to the fairground. It was three miles from the station to the circus, and we had to make the trip three times. At the end of the last trip my feet were sore, and I was very tired. But there was still work to be done. Bales of luggage, props, and cages had to be sorted and unpacked, and with one thing and another it was in the small hours of next morning when I lay on a heap of hay in an empty stall and fell asleep.

Next morning I had time to look at the circus. You see, in those days nearly every town in Russia had its own circus ground. Markets and fairs were held in them, and the travelling theatres performed there. A big circus like the Circus Truzi was a very important event.

This circus ground was a big place—bigger than any I had yet seen. We had booked it for a month. However, as I will tell you, we were to stay there only a week.

All through the week every performance was packed. During the night of the sixth day there was a big storm. It rained so hard that the ground was turned into a great quagmire of mud.

The force of the wind made the circus building shake and shudder. The building itself was a wooden structure, about thirty feet high. The roof was also of wood, except for a large area of canvas in the centre, which let in the light. From the roof to the ground ran very big ropes, which helped to support the building. The ropes were attached to large stakes, which were driven into the ground. But the wind was so strong that these stakes were continually wrenched out of the ground.

However, the storm did not keep the people away. In the afternoon and again in the evening we had to put the 'house full' boards out. Half way through the evening performance the wind rose even higher. It roared and shrieked around the building until it seemed to me that it must fall any minute. As fast as we replaced the stakes in the ground they were pulled out again.

After inspecting the building, M Truzi decided that every single person who was not actually in the ring must come out and hold on to the ropes. Gingek acted as call-boy. As one artiste would dash in to give his turn, another would take his place on the ropes.

How we hung on those ropes. By now one side of the building was lifted nearly a foot off the ground. We wondered how long we should have the strength to hold it down. We hung on there, slipping and sliding in the mud, wet and cold, deafened by the wind. I was so small that I was often blown right off my feet, and I do not think that my weight could have helped very much. Several times I fell flat on my face in the mud, until I was rolled in mud from head to foot.

At last the show was over, and the audience filed out. To us, nearly at the end of our strength, it seemed as if they came out very slowly. But at last we were told that there was no one else inside. Unable to hold on any longer, one by one we slipped from the ropes, our hands torn and bleeding. The building began to rock and sway. The wood cracked and groaned, and cracks appeared in the walls.

Then there came a terrific blast of wind. It picked me up and dropped me several feet away. I heard a terrifying noise, and, as I picked myself out of the mud, I saw the whole circus falling. It went slowly at first, as if it were loath to give in to the wind, then more quickly. Then there was one more fierce gust of wind and the whole place collapsed like a pack of cards.

It was pitch dark, and we could do no more that night. Almost as though satisfied with what it had done, the wind abated, and the rain stopped. Most of us just found a sheltered place, dropped down, and slept from exhaustion.

The next day Truzi decided that as the summer was coming to an end it was useless to wait in Vilno for the circus to be rebuilt. So it was decided that we should go straight back to Riga, the winter quarters of the circus.

So once again we had to load up our train, but this time the journey only took us just over a day. As the train passed through the town we could see the terrible havoc wrought by the storm. Houses were blown down and wrecked, trees were lying completely uprooted, and we passed raging torrents that had been peaceful streams.

It seemed a long time since I had seen my father and mother, and so I was longing to get to Riga. As we drew near the town I became very excited.

When the train had been unloaded and everything was settled and orderly once again, I went to Rudolpho Truzi and asked him if I might go home for three weeks.

'Yes, Nicolai,' he said, 'but before you go there is something we have got to decide. We have to find a name for you—something short and easy to say.'

I had often noticed that Truzi, being an Italian, had found difficulty in pronouncing my name. He wrote my name on a piece of paper and looked at it. At last he said: 'I know—Coco. It is a bit of both your names. Now, Coco, home you go to your mother, and don't forget to come back.'

From that day onwards my professional name has been Coco, sometimes spelt like that, and sometimes spelt Koko. And very soon I began to forget that I had any other name.

Home I went to my family, and how pleased we were to see each other. My mother embraced me and wept, and could not stop looking at me. My father wanted to hear of my progress and of all I had been doing while with the circus. And I was very happy and proud.

But after a day or two I began to miss the circus sadly. Then I asked my father if he would give me the money to go to Metava.

'Why can't you stay a little with us, your parents?' he asked. 'Why do you wish to go to Metava?'

'Father, I must go, I want to see the Circus Isako.'

He sighed and gave me the money.

When I reached Metava I went straight to the circus and asked for M Isako.

'Well, young man, what do you want?' he said.

'I want a job. I'm a clown now.'

'But you are still very young.'

'I'm nearly thirteen, and I've been with the Circus Truzi,' I said proudly.

'Very well, you can have a job.'

I started to thank him, but he said: 'Don't thank me. If you are no good, why, you will not stay with my show.'

I found some lodgings in the town, and early next morning I was at the circus rehearsing. Isako came out to watch me, and I thought he seemed pleased with me.

I shall never forget that first night, when I did my first turn as an accredited and salaried artiste. I was so happy I wanted to cry all the time, especially when the audience clapped and applauded me. Besides the usual clowning I did some trapeze work.

I spent a happy three weeks with the Circus Isako. I have never forgotten a goat that was there. He was a very vicious goat. The first time I saw him he was looking in a rubbish heap for something to eat. I picked up some cigarette ends and gave them to him. He seemed to enjoy them. I gave him some more. Every day after that he would follow me about until I found him some cigarette ends. After he had eaten a good many he would begin to sneeze, and then the more he ate the more he sneezed. It was so comical to watch him eating and sneezing I would give him all the ends I could find.

One day as I was giving him his usual feed I heard someone laughing behind me. It was Isako. I was frightened. But he said: 'Every morning I watch for you to give him his feed, and I laugh as well as you.'

At the end of the three weeks I told Isako that I must go back to Riga.

'Coco, you will be a very good artiste one of these days. Why don't you stop with me?'

But I told him that I had to go home.

'Very well, but if at any time you want a job, you shall have one here with me.'

Next day I took a train back to Riga.

In London for many years we have been pitiably short of carol singers and bands which play carols. Maybe there are more in other parts of the country. When I was a child there seemed never a minute, in the evenings before Christmas, when some group was not on the doorstep singing 'Away in a manger' or 'Good King Wenceslas'. Near the shops there were bands supposed to have come from Germany who played carol after carol to the great joy of the shoppers. Of course now there are loud-speakers in many shops blaring out carols, but to me loud-speakers have not the charm of live people.

The high spot of our carolling came on Christmas Eve when the hand-bell ringers came to play carols to us. The hand-bell ringers played in the hall and everybody in the household sat on the stairs to listen. When it was over the players were served with mince pies and ginger wine. They left in a gust of 'merry Christmas' and, as the front door closed on the last of them, one could feel the spirit of Christmas creep into the house. It was all done. The decorations were up, the tree was trimmed. Every present lay under it. In the kitchen the turkey was waiting for tomorrow and so was the plum pudding. Upstairs our stockings were ready to be hung up. It was a time to feel and just to soak in what Christmas meant.

In those far-away days, before we went to bed there was reading out loud of some Christmas story. Often Dickens's Christmas Carol. *It is of course a terribly sentimental story, but I would swear there are few who by the end cannot hear the Christmas bells pealing and see the boy running to fetch the biggest turkey in the town.*

Though A Christmas Carol *may not be to everyone's liking it is certain that Christmas Eve is the time to hear a story. So here is a legend for you. A legend, as you know, means a myth, probably from a traditional story. This one is called 'The Legend of the Christmas Rose'. It is told by the famous Swedish writer Selma Lagerlöf. Mind you, though this story is accepted as a legend, I often wonder if it is not true. It is so strange that one quite large beautifully formed flower should bloom at Christmas while almost all other flowers are sleeping.*

SELMA LAGERLÖF

The Legend of the Christmas Rose

The outlaws lived in a cave in Goinge Forest. Mostly they lived on what grew in the forest, but when there was no food about Mother outlaw went down to the village on a begging tour. Father was the one who was outlawed so he did not dare to leave the forest.

One day Mother, with five of her children, went begging, each child bore a sack on his back as long as himself. When the Mother stepped inside the door of a cottage no one dared refuse to give her whatever she demanded: for she was not above coming back the following night and setting fire to a cottage if she had not been well received. The Mother and her brood were worse than a pack of wolves, and many a man felt like running a spear through them: but it was never done, because they all knew that the outlawed man stayed up in the forest, and he would know how to wreak vengeance if anything happened to the children or his woman.

On this day when the Mother went from house to house and begged she came to Ovid. At that time this was a monastery, so she rang the bell of the monastery and asked for food. The watchman let down a small wicket gate and handed her six round bread cakes—one for herself and one for each of the five children.

While the Mother was standing quietly at the gate, her youngsters were running about. Then one of them came and pulled at her skirt, as a signal that he had discovered something which she ought to come and see, so his Mother followed him promptly.

The entire cloister was surrounded by a high and strong wall, but the child had managed to find a little back gate which stood ajar. When his Mother got there, she pushed the gate open and walked inside without asking leave, as it was her custom to do.

Ovid monastery was managed at that time by Abbot Hans, who knew all about herbs. Just within the cloister wall he had planted a little herb garden, and it was into this that the woman had forced her way.

At first glance the Mother was so astonished that she paused at the gate. It was high summer time, and Abbot Hans's garden was so full of flowers that the eyes were fairly dazzled by the blues, reds and yellows, as one looked into it. But presently an indulgent smile spread over the woman's features, and she started to walk up a narrow path that lay between many flower-beds.

In the garden a lay brother walked about, pulling up weeds. It was he who had left the door in the wall open, that he might throw the weeds and tares on the rubbish-heap outside.

When he saw the woman coming towards him with all five children in tow, he ran to her at once and ordered them away. But the woman walked right on as before. The lay brother knew of no other remedy than to go into the monastery to call for help.

He returned with two stalwart monks, and the woman saw that now the lay brother meant business! She let out a perfect volley of shrieks, and, throwing herself upon the monks, clawed and bit at them: so did all five children. The monks soon learned that she could overpower them so all they could do was to go back into the monastery for reinforcements.

As they ran through the passage-way which led to the

cloister, they met Abbot Hans, who had come rushing out to learn what all this noise was about.

He upbraided the monks for using force and forbade their calling for help. He sent them both back to their work, and although he was an old and fragile man, he took with him only the lay brother.

He came up to the woman and asked in a mild tone if the garden pleased her.

The woman had turned defiantly towards Abbot Hans, for she expected only to be trapped and overpowered. But when she noticed his white hair and bent form, she answered peaceably: 'First when I saw this, I thought I had never seen a more beautiful garden: but now I see that it can't be compared with one I know of. If you could see the garden of which I am thinking you would uproot all the flowers planted here and cast them away like weeds.'

The lay brother was hardly less proud of the flowers than the Abbot himself, and after hearing her remarks he laughed derisively.

The woman grew crimson with rage to think that her word was doubted, and she cried out: 'You monks, who are holy men, certainly must know that on every Christmas Eve the great Goinge Forest is transformed into a beautiful garden, to commemorate the hour of our Lord's birth. We who live in the forest have seen this happen every year. And in that garden I have seen flowers so lovely that I dared not lift my hand to pluck them.'

Ever since his childhood, Abbot Hans had heard it said that on every Christmas Eve the forest was dressed in holiday glory. He had often longed to see it, but he had never had the good fortune. Eagerly he begged and implored the woman that he might come up to the outlaws' cave on Christmas Eve. If she would only send one of her children to show him the way, he could ride up there alone, and he would never betray them—on the contrary, he would reward them insofar as it lay in his power.

The woman said no at first, for she was thinking of her

husband and of the peril which might befall him should she permit Abbot Hans to ride up to their cave. At the same time the desire to prove to the monk that the garden which she knew was more beautiful than his got the better of her, and she gave in.

'But more than one follower you cannot take with you,' said she, 'and you are not to waylay us or trap us, as sure as you are a holy man.'

This Abbot Hans promised, and then the woman and her children returned to the forest.

Soon after it happened that Archbishop Absalon from Lund came to Ovid and remained through the night. The lay brother heard Abbot Hans telling the Bishop about the outlaws and asking him for a letter of ransom for the man, that he might lead an honest life among respectable people.

But the Archbishop replied that he did not care to let an outlaw loose among honest folk in the villages. It would be best for all that he remained in the forest.

Then Abbot Hans grew zealous and told the Bishop all about Goinge Forest, which, every year at Yuletide, clothed itself in summer bloom around the outlaws' cave.

'If these bandits are not so bad but that God's glories can be made manifest to them, surely we cannot be too wicked to experience the same blessing.'

The Archbishop knew how to answer Abbot Hans. 'This much I will promise you, Abbot Hans,' he said, smiling, 'that any day you send me a blossom from the garden of Goinge Forest, I will give you letters of ransom for all the outlaws you may choose to plead for.'

The following Christmas Eve Abbot Hans and the lay brother were on their way to the forest. One of the outlaws' wild children ran ahead of them to show them the best route for the horses.

It turned out to be a long and hazardous ride. They climbed steep and slippery side paths, crawled over swamp and marsh, and pushed through windfall and bramble. Just as daylight was waning, the boy guided them across a forest meadow, skirted by tall, naked leaf trees and green fir trees. Behind the meadow loomed a mountain wall, and in this wall they saw a door of thick boards. Now Abbot Hans understood that they had arrived, and dismounted. The child opened the heavy door for him, and the Abbot looked into a desperately poor mountain grotto, with bare stone walls. The Mother was seated before a log fire that burned in the middle of the floor. Alongside the walls were beds of virgin pine and moss, and on one of these beds lay the outlaw asleep.

'Come in, you out there!' shouted the Mother, without rising, 'and fetch the horses in with you, so they won't be destroyed by the night cold.'

Abbot Hans walked boldly into the cave, and the lay brother followed leading the horses. Here were wretchedness and poverty indeed, and nothing done to celebrate Christmas.

The Mother spoke in a tone as haughty and dictatorial as any well-to-do peasant woman. 'Sit down by the fire and warm yourself, Abbot Hans,' said she, 'and if you have food with you, eat, for the food which we in the forest prepare you wouldn't care to taste. And if you are tired after the long journey, you can lie down on one of these beds to sleep. You needn't be afraid of oversleeping, for I'm sitting here by the fire keeping watch. I shall awaken you in time to see that which you have come up here to see.'

Abbot Hans obeyed the Mother and brought forth his food-sack, but he was so fatigued after the journey he was hardly able to eat, and as soon as he could stretched himself on the bed, and fell asleep.

The lay brother was also assigned a bed to rest and he dropped into a doze.

When he woke up, he saw Abbot Hans had left his bed and was sitting by the fire talking with the woman. The outlawed man sat also by the fire. He was a tall, raw-boned type with a dull, sluggish appearance. His back was turned to Abbot Hans, as though he would have it appear that he was not listening to the conversation.

Abbot Hans was telling the woman all about the Christmas preparations he had seen on the journey, reminding her of

Christmas feasts and games which she must have known in her youth, when she lived at peace with mankind.

At first the woman answered in short, gruff sentences, but by degrees she became more subdued and listened more intently. Suddenly the outlaw turned towards Abbot Hans and shook his clenched fist in his face. 'You miserable monk! Did you come here to coax from me my wife and children? Don't you know that I am an outlaw and may not leave the forest?'

Abbot Hans looked him fearlessly in the eyes. 'It is my purpose to get a letter of ransom for you from Archbishop Absalon,' said he. He had hardly finished speaking when the man and his wife burst out laughing. They knew well enough the kind of mercy a forest outlaw could expect from Bishop Absalon!

'Oh, if I get a letter of ransom from Absalon!' said the man, 'then I promise you that never again will I steal so much as a goose.'

Suddenly the woman rose. 'You sit here and talk, Abbot Hans,' she said, 'so that we are forgetting to look at the forest. Now I can hear, even in this cave, how the Christmas bells are ringing.'

The words were barely uttered when they all sprang up and rushed out. But in the forest it was still dark night and bleak winter. When the bells had been ringing a few moments, a sudden illumination penetrated the forest: the next moment it was dark again, and then light came back. It pushed its way forward between the stark trees, like a shimmering mist. The darkness merged into a faint daybreak. Then Abbot Hans saw that the snow had vanished from the ground, as if someone had removed a carpet, and the earth began to take on a green covering. The moss-tufts thickened and raised themselves, and the spring blossoms shot upward, their swelling buds already touched with colour.

Again it grew hazy, but almost immediately there came a new wave of light. Then the leaves of the trees burst into bloom, crossbeaks hopped from branch to branch, and the woodpeckers hammered on the limbs until the splinters fairly flew around them. A flock of starlings from up-country lighted in a fir top to rest.

When the next warm wind came along, the blueberries ripened and the baby squirrels began playing on the branches of the trees.

The next light wave that came rushing in brought with it the scent of newly ploughed acres. Pine and spruce trees were so thickly clothed with red cones that they shone like crimson mantles and forest flowers covered the ground till it was all red, blue and yellow.

Abbot Hans bent down to the earth and broke off a wild strawberry blossom and, as he straightened up, the berry ripened in his hand.

The mother fox came out of her lair with a big litter of black-legged young. She went up to the woman and scratched at her skirt, and she bent down to her and praised her young.

Then the children let out shrieks of delight. They stuffed themselves with wild strawberries that were everywhere. One of them played with a litter of little hares, another ran a race with some young crows, which had hopped from their nest before they were really ready.

The outlaw was standing out on a marsh eating raspberries. When he glanced up, a big black bear stood beside him. The man broke off a twig and struck the bear on the nose. 'Keep to your own ground, you!' he said, 'this is my turf.' The huge bear turned around and lumbered off in another direction.

Then all the flowers whose seeds have been brought from foreign lands began to blossom. The loveliest roses climbed up the mountain wall in a race with the blackberry vines, and from the forest meadow sprang flowers as large as human faces.

Abbot Hans thought of the flower he was to pluck for Bishop Absalon, but each new flower that appeared was more beautiful than the others, and he wanted to choose the most beautiful of all.

Then Abbot Hans marked how all grew still, the birds hushed their songs, the flowers ceased growing, and the young

foxes played no more. From far in the distance faint harp tones were heard, and celestial song, like a soft murmur, reached him.

He clasped his hands and dropped to his knees. His face was radiant with bliss.

But beside Abbot Hans stood the lay brother. In his mind there were dark thoughts. 'This cannot be a true miracle,' he thought, 'since it is revealed to malefactors. This does not come from God, but is sent hither by Satan. It is the Evil One's power that is tempting us and compelling us to see that which has no real existence.'

The angel throng was so near now that Abbot Hans saw their bright forms through the forest branches. The lay brother saw them too, but behind all this wondrous beauty he saw only some dread evil.

All the while the birds had been circling around the head of Abbot Hans, and they let him take them in his hands. But all the animals were afraid of the lay brother, no bird perched on his shoulder, no snake played at his feet. Then there came a little forest dove. When she marked that the angels were nearing, she plucked up courage and flew down on the lay brother's shoulder and laid her head against his cheek.

Then it appeared to him as if sorcery were come right upon him, to tempt and corrupt him. He struck with his hand at the forest dove and cried in such a loud voice that it rang throughout the forest: 'Go thou back to hell, whence thou art come!'

Just then the angels were so near that Abbot Hans felt the feathery touch of their great wings, and he bowed down to earth in reverent greeting.

But when the lay brother's words sounded, their song was hushed and the holy guests turned in flight. At the same time the light and the mild warmth vanished in unspeakable terror of the darkness and cold in a human heart. Darkness sank over the earth, like a coverlet, frost came, all the growths shrivelled up, the animals and birds hastened away, the leaves dropped from the trees, rustling like rain.

Abbot Hans felt how his heart, which had but lately swelled with bliss, was now contracting with insufferable agony. 'I can never outlive this,' thought he, 'that the angels from heaven had been so close to me and were driven away: that they wanted to sing Christmas carols for me and were driven to flight.' Then he remembered the flower he had promised Bishop Absalon, and at the last moment he fumbled among the leaves and moss to try and find a blossom. But he sensed how the ground under his fingers froze and how the white snow came gliding over the ground. Then his heart caused him ever greater anguish. He could not rise, but fell prostrate on the ground and lay there.

When the outlaw and the lay brother had groped their way back to the cave, they missed Abbot Hans. They took brands with them and went out to search for him. They found him dead upon the coverlet of snow.

When Abbot Hans had been carried down to Ovid, those who took charge of the dead saw that he held his right hand locked tight around something which he must have grasped at the moment of death. When they finally got his hand open they found that the thing which he had held in such an iron grip was a pair of white root bulbs, which he had torn from among the moss and leaves.

When the lay brother who had accompanied Abbot Hans saw the bulbs, he took them and planted them in Abbot Hans's herb garden.

He guarded them the whole year to see if any flower would spring from them. But in vain he waited through the spring, the summer, and the autumn. Finally, when winter had set in and all the leaves and the flowers were dead, he ceased caring for them.

But when Christmas Eve came again, he was so strongly reminded of Abbot Hans that he wandered out into the garden to think of him. And look! As he came to the spot where he had planted the bare root bulbs, he saw that from them had sprung flourishing green stalks, which bore beautiful flowers with silver leaves.

He called out all the monks at Ovid, and when they saw that this plant bloomed on Christmas Eve, when all the other growths were as if dead, they understood that this flower had in truth been plucked by Abbot Hans from the Christmas garden in Goinge Forest. Then the lay brother asked the monks if he might take a few blossoms to Bishop Absalon.

When Bishop Absalon beheld the flowers, which had sprung from the earth in darkest winter, he turned as pale as if he had met a ghost. He sat in silence a moment, thereupon he said: 'Abbot Hans has faithfully kept his word and I shall also keep mine.'

He handed the letter of ransom to the lay brother, who departed at once for the outlaws' cave. When he stepped in there on Christmas Day, the outlaw came towards him with an axe uplifted. 'I'd like to hack you monks into bits, as many as you are!' said he. 'It must be your fault that Goinge Forest did not last night dress itself in Christmas bloom.'

'The fault is mine alone,' said the lay brother, 'and I will gladly die for it, but first I must deliver a message from Abbot Hans.' And he drew forth the Bishop's letter and told the man that he was free.

The man stood there pale and speechless, so the woman said in his name: 'Abbot Hans has indeed kept his word and my man will keep his.'

When the outlaw and his family left the cave, the lay brother moved in and lived all alone in the forest, in constant meditation and prayer that his hard-heartedness might be forgiven him.

But Goinge Forest never again celebrated the hour of our Saviour's birth: and of all its glory, there lives today only the plant which Abbot Hans had plucked. It has been named CHRISTMAS ROSE. And each year at Christmastide she sends forth from the earth green stalks and white blossoms, as if she never could forget that she had once grown in the great Christmas garden at Goinge Forest.

Lots of you have more than human beings to remember at Christmas. Presents are of course wanted for pets. I had a black miniature poodle called Pierre, and I cannot tell you what Christmas presents meant to him. His, not so much prettily packed, as made difficult to open, were piled under the tree with everyone else's. In his were simple things like a little squeaky toy, a biscuit or a piece of chocolate : he did not care what, his fun was to open his own parcels. Each time he was handed one he carried it to a corner of the room and only when he and everyone else had received all their presents would he unpack his. Then what an orgy of unpacking went on. Many people said watching Pierre and his parcels was one of the high spots of their Christmas Day.

When I was choosing stories for this book I thought of those of you who take a present to a pony. For all horse lovers here is a very special story by a true horse lover.

JOYCE STRANGER

The Wild White Horses

It was Christmas Eve.

The world was alight with excitement. Children fretted at the slowly passing hours. They made plans and bought presents, and huddled in corners, glowing, as they whispered secrets. Parents glanced at each other with meaning in their eyes. Strange shaped parcels, gaily wrapped, were hidden in odd corners and put on high shelves, and tucked into drawers, insecurely masked by piled shirts or underwear.

The excitement spilled into the seething last-minute streets, where, at night, bright lights glittered. From every lamp post angels danced. Unicorns, splendid in silver and gold, shone above the slowly moving motor cars. Children gazed skywards at giant crowns, jewelled with glory, and Santa Claus sat on his sleigh, his reindeer lifting their antlers high above Market Street.

Shop windows were hung with tinsel, and snow covered the floor inside, while mannequins, in their Christmas splendour, sledged, wrapped in furs, or held pretty baubles towards the idling crowds. Frost flecked the glass. Christmas trees shimmered with shining balls, and small children, faces flushed with cold, pressed their noses against the icy panes and, with eyes brighter than the brilliant balls, lost themselves in a maze of delight.

Market Street was a solid mass of people, homeward bound, hurrying to the bus station and the railway station, anxious to get home, away from the cold, to start preparing for the next day, the greatest day of all, for feast and for fun and for the early present giving. Few of them noticed the three gypsy girls with their long black tangled hair and brown faces and bright patched shawls of orange and green and blue, clutching their baskets.

The girls had saved their money so that they could come to Manchester to shop and to see the big city for the first time, and moreover, see it in all its Christmas splendour. They were in no hurry and going nowhere and had all the time in the world. They looked up at lights that dazzled along the street, and looked down at mock snow and fake frost on shop window floors, and looked in at every scene set to attract and excite them, unaware that this was to lure the people inside and help them spend their money. They had no money left to spend, nor did it occur to them to be envious.

They walked through Piccadilly Gardens, where luminous plaster owls lurked in the trees and goblins peeped from the bushes, enchanting the children, and coloured lights hung, unusual exotic winter fruits, from slender branches. They paused to look at a snow house and a snowman, seeming more real than snow itself. They crossed the road, moving with the throng, unnerved by traffic that snarled and fought its way down the main roads and turned off at every corner, often baulked by the mass of pedestrians attempting to cross from side to side, eyes on the lights above them and not on the streets in front of them. The gypsy girls were thin and ragged and undernourished but laughter was never far from their mouths, and their merry voices and quick movement caught many eyes as they moved through the busy throng. Their world today was an infinite satisfaction, as brave and colourful as any gypsy's wildest dream. The girls asked for nothing and expected nothing. It was enough to look, to caress with every glance, to fold the glory and wonder away in the mind where it could remain. At a later date they would bring it from their treasure house and revel afresh in the colour and excitement and brilliance of a world to which they could never belong and whose splendour they could only admire from outside.

It began to snow. Large flakes drifted slowly through the air, and the city dirt was masked in shining white. Flakes settled on hair and cheek and shoulder, drifted down onto the side street barrows of gold and green fruit, and on those which were massed with yellow and red tawny flowers. The stragglers hurried, anxious for warm fire and tea and television set. Children wailed, hungry and fretful. The girls watched them and smiled. There were small ones at home, inside the brightly painted caravans. They too were preparing for Christmas. They did not want to hasten back. They would wait and see the night-time crowds and sleep, huddled together for warmth, in some arched doorway, or perhaps, if they were lucky, find a deserted hayloft outside the city. They had shopped for Christmas. Romaine had bought her mother a shining brooch, a beautiful thing of glass and beads, the cluster as bright as any real gem in any jeweller's window. She held it in her hand, wrapped in tissue paper, more precious than diamonds. Sarina had found a tinsel scarf that would brighten her married sister's hair. Both her parents were dead, and her sister looked after her. She had also a bag of tiny sweets for her baby niece. Anita had found a fluffy horse, all of four inches high, made of white brushed-up felt, with a curled black wool mane and bright black eyes and nose. A minute scarlet saddle added an air of gaiety. Her little sister would love the toy.

The girls turned into a side street. The high walls closed together and the lights were gone. They had entered a black canyon, lit by the soft glow from one lamp, which illuminated the falling flakes. A black and white timbered building cast its shadow on the cobbles and loured against the dark as it had when Shakespeare was a boy. The windows glowed gold, and voices from the public house spilled into the darkness. The girls moved to catch the warmth from the doorway and savour the smell of frying chips that came from the kitchen.

It was then that they saw the pony, he was tethered to a post. A creamy pony with gold mane and tail, trembling with cold and weariness and hunger. His large wise eyes shone with tears caused by the icy wind that cut into him. The girls stopped.

Anita put her arms about his neck and leaned against him. She was warm and she smelled of comfort and love and his tired tense body relaxed. He was not used to kindness. Her small hand fondled his mane.

'He is just like my pony. See?' she said, and held the toy up to the light. The pony huffed at her.

He was a gentle creature, and life was wearying for him. He found the world a frightening place.

His master drove a cart. Each morning the cream pony was caught, groomed roughly and carelessly, and put between the shafts, where he stood, dejected, until a whip was laid spitefully across his shoulders.

His hooves were painful, needing paring, and he clip-clopped along in shoes lacking a nail, so that often he was lame, but not lame enough for his master to know or care.

Sometimes a bright balloon was tied to his harness, to attract the children who swarmed on his route. He hated it. He hated the flabby feel and the bat, bat, bat against his neck when he trotted, and even worse, the terrifying bang when some boy, grinning with mischief, punctured it with a pin, or a man pushed a glowing cigarette butt against it.

He hated the days spent dragging a cart that became heavier and heavier as the hours went by: and the evenings standing in the rain and mud in the seven-acre field where the grass grew thin and spare and thistly and the food his master gave him was sparse and stale.

He longed for lush green grass, for the feel of summer meadow, rich with buttercups, beneath his tired hooves, and the dip and trickle of running water, remembered dimly from a time long ago when freedom had been his. Freedom to gallop under a summer sun, to roll in long, clean grass, and stand swishing his tail against the flies, fetlock deep in cool clear water where tiny fish arrowed in darting flight brushed against his legs, tickling them.

The pony had often stood with his head over the gate, longing for a human to stop and give him a kind word, or a titbit, and he had grown more and more sorrowful. His head had drooped, his tail had hung behind him, useless for flicking flies as it had been docked by his master who objected to a swishing tail in front of him all day.

Slowly the years had passed. The pony had wilted finding no pleasure in living. How should he? His days were spent trotting on hard roads, the whip ever ready to flick at his shoulders.

At night he had grown too tired to run in the seedy field. Sometimes he had watched the moon slide over the sky, and leaves, moon-flecked, shiver in the wind.

When the wind had blown he had turned his tail to it and stood patient, feeling the strange unseen creature ruffle his hair and tease his mane, tangling it even more. He had longed for someone to brush the grit from his coat and smooth the jagged tangles in mane and tail, and he had sighed more deeply as the years went by.

He had also longed for company. Another pony to lean against, and lick in friendship; to run against, and to call joyously when he had come back from the streets at night.

He had nothing.

Now he looked at the girls, feeling the friendship that radiated from them, warming him. He leaned his head against Romaine, who was standing in front of him, crooning to him as no one had crooned in his life before, and he pushed her gently, wishing he could communicate both his gratitude and his need.

Snow was drifting over them. The pony shook his head, hating it. He yearned for food, for warmth, for love and for kindness, for an owner who would groom him and soothe him and comfort him, for a warm stable and for hay that smelled of summer, and not of damp and mould.

Romaine put both her arms round him and he turned his head and nuzzled her with velvet lips. His brown eyes gazed at her, wishing that he could be hers, that her gentle hands might always stroke his coat and play with his mane, that he might be free for ever of the rumbling jolting cart that dragged behind him uphill and chased after him downhill and always hurt his back. He longed to be free of the confining chafing harness that made him sore, and of the hateful batting balloon.

'We ought to do something about him,' Romaine said.

Sarina and Anita looked at her. The alleyway was dark, light from the street lamp spilling onto the pony's head. The cart, piled high with old clothes, with tyres, with bits and pieces once treasured and now discarded, was in deep shadow. They gave the pony a last kiss each, then one by one they crept under the old clothes, making no sound, showing neither face nor arm nor hand.

The man came out of the public house, stumbling and swearing. He fumbled at the reins and when the pony did not acknowledge him, slapped its neck. The pony breathed sadly and softly and dropped his head lower. He did not want to start again, did not want to pull the heavy cart, did not want to clop over the cobbles, with the wind knifing at him. The snow had turned to rain, which had just begun to fall, wetting him.

The man clambered onto the cart, tugged at the reins, and slashed with his whip. The pony moved, heaving with his shoulders, feeling the weight of the cart. The wheels gripped and began to turn.

They walked out of the alley and into the main traffic. Cars sped past him, and a policeman looked at him sourly. He was holding up all the traffic behind him. Hooters sounded, and men glared at him when they found room to overtake. Children looked back, seeing not an old and shabby pony, but a dream horse, piebald and beautiful, his head looking towards them, mild eyed, the gay balloon a banner at his neck, the man a figure of mystery, as he drove through the night.

The rain, which had succeeded the snow, turned once more to sleet, and finally to snow again. Huge wet flakes drifted down and the trees were masked and shone in the lamplight. The world turned from everyday to fairytale magic and houses lay secret under whitened roofs, and hedges and roads alike were smooth and beautiful. The thud of the dragging hooves was muffled, and the pony slipped, and stopped. The flicking spiteful whip drove him on again.

The girls, warm under the old clothes, but almost stifled by the dust and stuffy smell of them, peeped out through the cracks, and watched the world they knew change. In the fields where the caravans stood, there would be even more beauty for all the daytime mud would be hidden, while the silent snow turned the trees to Christmas glory.

They clopped on. The traffic was less. Most people were

home by now, and the road beyond Fallowfield station stretched broad and quiet. The shops were closed, some of them lit for Christmas, so that trees and tinsel and shining baubles glittered invitingly.

It seemed a long journey to the girls and even longer to the pony. He thought of food, hung in bags for him to tug, of grass, long and green and luscious, of water, and of sunshine and warmth. He shivered. Other creatures would spend the night indoors, but his only shelter was a shed without a door to it and with only half a roof and with the floor sodden. He had little protection from the weather. If he was lucky there might be some mouldy hay bought cheap because it was useless to anyone else. He would have to dig through the snow and nose out the grass that remained in the muddy field. He was cold and he was hungry and he was tired. His hooves dragged but the whip stung his neck again so he speeded his pace. Once he got the man home the cart would be removed and the chafing harness hung on the wall and there would be a little moment of peace before the galls that chafed him began to hurt again, and hunger remind him of his misery.

When they reached Didsbury they turned by the church and came into a tiny lane that the girls had never seen before. It was part of the old village, hidden away between the houses, a memory of long ago when there had been fields and trees, and the mist that still straddled Fog Lane in autumn and winter had come from the low lying fields now succeeded by rows of houses.

Anita caught a glimpse of the lane and the name at the end of it. Paradise Meadow.

The meadow was small, hardly big enough to keep a pony, but here there was a ruined shed and a five-barred gate and beside the meadow was an old house, tumble-down and decrepit, long ago condemned but for some reason forgotten by the authorities.

The man left the horse and cart for a moment and went inside to light his fire so the gypsy girls slipped out of their hiding place and climbed into the field and hid behind the hedge, shivering in the wicked wind that showered the field with snow, hiding its ugliness.

The man came back. His fingers were clumsy with drink and pulled and tugged at the buckles. He was cold, and he kicked the unresisting pony in temper, wanting to be by his fireside and safe with his bottle of beer again. He had neither wife nor child to comfort him.

At last the pony was free and the man pushed him into the shed, and flung hay at his feet. There was not much and it was not good, but the pony had no choice. He began to eat. The man left the cart and went indoors and the girls watched as the light went on in the decrepit house, and his shadow fell across the thin curtain, as he settled himself in his chair and kicked off his boots before the fire that now blazed, logs burning brightly.

The girls went to the shed. The pony saw them come and lifted his head, and made a tiny whinny of welcome.

'Hush,' Sarina said and rubbed his soft muzzle, and put her arms round his neck. She felt the galls on his back.

'He has harness sores,' she said angrily.

Anita, who had learned the art of healing from her grandmother, felt with her soft fingers.

'No one has taken care of him, ever,' she said passionately. 'That man is wicked. We ought to teach him a lesson.'

'How?' Sarina asked, but Anita did not know.

Romaine had vanished, and only her footsteps showed in the snow. Anita and Sarina waited, and Anita picked out the better pieces of hay and gave them to the pony, and he held his head towards her and rubbed against her dress, to show how much he loved her company and appreciated not being alone.

The slender ghost of a moon slipped up the starry sky and magic spilled over the field. The girls looked at the new-made world, revelling in its beauty. They loved beauty. Their eyes shone, and their small bodies, leaning against the pony, one on either side, warmed him and comforted him, and happiness filled him. He sighed deeply, this time with joy.

Anita took her comb and began to tease it through his mane, her fingers gently pulling at the tangles. He bore it patiently and she whispered to him as Sarina fed him.

'I will make you beautiful. You will be the most beautiful pony in Manchester. Your coat will shine and your mane and tail will be silken soft and your hooves will be polished and everyone will turn to look at you.'

The moon was brighter now. The stars hung in the sky, far away, overhead, deep in outer space, and the world whirled on, and Sarina took her sharp knife and began to pare the overgrown hooves, her hands so gentle that he scarcely felt them as she brought him comfort. It was a job that she had often done before for their own ponies.

Anita took a dry wisp of hay and began to rub the dust from the pony's coat. She slapped him gently and the clouds of dust flew around them, and she had to stifle a sneeze. She looked anxiously towards the cottage but all was dark. The man had gone to bed and they were safe for the time being.

'No one has ever groomed him,' she said, and she worked to shift the dust and grime and the mud around his legs. He stood patiently, knowing that he would feel better when she had finished.

Romaine came back, drifting on the wind like a snowflake herself, so silent that she made the other girls jump as she spoke.

'There were some apples on the tree in the old orchard, left from autumn,' she whispered. 'The pony can feed on them. And I found some hay in the corner of the farmyard at the end of the lane. No one will miss it.'

The hay was fresh and the pony ate it greedily. He had never fed so well before, not for long ages, longer ago than he could remember, when he was a colt in a green field and the world was new and young and exciting and he could race on smooth turf and chase with his mother.

It was very long ago. He had raced, he remembered, running against other horses on a wide racecourse, when he was only two years old, but his untried muscles rebelled and his legs were strained and the tendons stretched and he had been sold at an auction to a girl who rode him occasionally and kept him in a big field, and then forgot him.

He had been sold again, this time the man bought him, and ever since he had dragged the cart over the streets and come home at night to the tiny field and waited uncomplaining for day to dawn again.

Sometimes children gave him apples and old ladies gave him carrots: sometimes the sun shone and he savoured the warmth and sometimes there was green grass on the verges and the man let him graze, knowing that it saved money in the end. His thoughts slipped through his mind, pictures without words, memories of people's faces, and of voices that spoke to him, and of weather.

'I have one other apple,' Romaine said. 'The Apple of Peace and Freedom that was given to me by my grandmother's grandmother long ago. It keeps fresh for ever.'

Sarina and Anita looked at her.

'Shall I give it to him?' she asked.

Their eyes were troubled. They looked at the pony, at the coat that would never shine again and the hooves that would never trot fast again. He was old and his wind was broken and his legs were knobbly and worn with age and hard work, and he would never know comfort again. Only the lonely desolate field and the man who drank too much and swore too much and who used the whip too often and did not give him food or water, or comfort, or company.

'Give him the apple,' Sarina said, and her hand stroked the soft neck, and the pony wondered why her eyes suddenly filled with tears.

He took the apple, and ate it. Nothing had ever tasted so wonderful. Nothing had ever brought such a feeling of well being. It was sweet and firm and refreshing and it gave him strange ideas. He lifted his head. Dim memories of far places came to him, of rolling moors where birds called shrill and sweet, and rabbits ran and other ponies cantered, tossing their manes, knowing nothing of roads and carts. The girls, hand in hand, downcast, slipped into the lane, each one kissing the pony as she passed. Silent they turned for home.

The moon was high and the wind was wild, a rushing ecstatic

wind that brought with it the scent of the sea, faint and far away, of driftwood and seawrack and the tossing tumbling waves.

Bewitched by the girl who gave him the apple, the pony nosed open the gate. He stared for a moment into the rustling dark. It was so long since freedom had been his. He was not aware that there had been magic in the apple.

He turned into the lane, pushing through brambles and bracken onto a hill. His familiar world had mysteriously vanished and he was in a land beyond time. Uphill to woodland, where the turf was soft and cool and kind, and where there was grass, grass such as he had never tasted, long and green and clean and cool and sweet smelling. He browsed, shadowy beneath a tree, savouring delight.

The grass gave him new energy. He turned and pricked his ears, wary, listening. A rabbit, bounding under his hooves, startled him, but he knew it did not threaten his safety. He sped over the turf, alone in the windy night, trotting faster than he had ever trotted, racing against the wind.

He began to canter. The night and the wind excited him and the soft ground, kind to his hooves, was tempting, so that he fled through the windy dark leaving the town and the seven-acre field and the world's unkindness far behind him.

Somewhere, he did not know where, he was joined by other ponies, long legged, cream coloured, very like himself, manes and tails silken with loving care, and satin coats shining. Now that the girls had groomed him, he was as beautiful as they.

They called to him, and he answered, lifting his voice in joyous ecstasy, a long neighing call that challenged the moon, and brought answering neighs from the ponies running beside him.

They were almost flying, a frieze of cantering beauties, speeding over the moors. They leaped a running brook where water sparkled, gemlike, under the gleaming light, and sped on, tiny divots of turf flashing up behind the urgent hooves.

The pony raced with them, all tiredness forgotten. Now and again one of his companions brushed against him and it was good to feel the warmth and solidity of a companion of his own kind. He could see the splendid creatures all around him, so that there seemed to be hundreds of cream-coloured ponies on the moors.

Then they were dropping towards the sea and the sea smell was a wild excitement and he could remember, how, he did not know, the sting of salt, the surge and roar and thunder of green waters and the wild exotic fury of the rolling waves.

They plunged through a pinewood, the needles kicked up behind them, the birds just awakening, shouting angry calls as the flying bodies sped amongst the trees.

The cliffs were before them, raking into the sky and, beyond them, the world was amaze with white water as the wind piled the sea to seething fury, and the waves hurled themselves against the rocks and broke high in cascading fountains of white, lacy foam that glittered in the light of the newborn sun.

They were at the edge of the cliffs. They were leaping over, cream ponies dropping from the sky, dropping into the thunder and the foam and fret of the flashing, tumbling sea, bodies arched and beautiful.

The pony did not hesitate. He leaped with his companions, felt the sudden impact of water, the clean coolness, the soothing welcome that told him that, after a lifetime of misery, he had come home.

He was strong, he was powerful, he was gleaming with glory, swimming into the sunrise, calling his kind.

He was power, he was strength, he was beauty, and the years of toil and misery were nothing, and he swam to a life of rousing wonder, of wildness and foam and fret, with his companions, the wild, white horses of the sea.

Far away in a muddy distant field, surrounded by houses that gloomed, and smoke that poured from grimy chimneys, a man whipped his leg and cursed, as he found the body of his dead pony, lying in the mud beside the half-open gate.

Before we leave animals here are two lovely poetry prayers. The first is about a donkey and the second about a camel. Both were originally written in French and both were translated by Rumer Godden. The donkey in this first prayer is of course supposed to be the one who carried Mary into Bethlehem. If you have ever taken donkeys for granted I think you never will again after reading this prayer.

The Prayer of the Donkey

O God, who made me
to trudge along the road
always,
to carry heavy loads
always,
and to be beaten
always!
Give me great courage and gentleness.
One day let somebody understand me—
that I may no longer want to weep
because I can never say what I mean
and they make fun of me.
Let me find a juicy thistle—
and make them give me time to pick it.
And, Lord, one day, let me find again
my little brother of the Christmas crib.

Rumer Godden
(TRANSLATED FROM THE FRENCH)

I always thought camels had very proud faces There was something which lowered my pride in the supercilious curl of their upper lips. Then I read 'The Camel' and I felt quite differently about them. So I pass the poem on to you so that you too can (if you need to) understand them better.

The Camel

Lord,
do not be displeased.
There *is* something to be said for pride
against thirst, mirages
and sandstorms;

and I must say
that, to face and rise above
these arid desert dramas,
two humps
are not too many,
nor an arrogant lip.
Some people criticize
my four flat feet,
the base of my pile of joints,
but what should I do
with high heels
crossing so much country,
such shifting dreams,
while upholding my dignity?
My heart wrung
by the cries of jackals and hyenas,
by the burning silence,
the magnitude of Your cold stars,
I give You thanks, Lord,
for this my realm,
wide as my longings
and the passage of my steps.
Carrying my royalty
in the aristocratic curve of my neck
from oasis to oasis,
One day shall I find again
the caravan of the magi?
And the gates of Your paradise?

Amen

Rumer Godden
(TRANSLATED FROM THE FRENCH)

Although this is a winter holiday book nobody wants ice and snow all the time. So I decided we would visit somewhere really hot. This story comes from a book called My Uncle's Strange Voyages *and, my goodness, they were strange.*

The 'Uncle' of the stories was skipper of a rusty old steamer which was forever heading towards the horizon to pick up, or put down, a cargo. The stories are all (supposedly) told by the Uncle himself.

I do not know where Tahoola is but, if you are like me, it is the kind of place you dream about when the wind comes howling straight from Russia, and the grown-ups say, 'It's too cold for snow.' In weather like that I fix my mind on blue skies and palm trees. There is nothing like a palm tree waving in the sun for warming the blood.

RICHARD G. ROBINSON

The Stowaway

We were loading ship in the port of Tahoola. I was sitting in my cabin, sipping my lime juice and looking out through the porthole at the palm trees wavering in the heat, the thatched store houses, and the procession of native women, with baskets on their heads, passing up and down the rickety gang planks between ship and shore.

They were brown skinned, these women, and they wore dresses of bright reds and blues. Large and strong-armed, they never ceased jabbering the whole time they worked. Some had brought their children with them, and these little imps spent their time running up and down the gang planks and being cuffed and sworn at whenever they were more than usually in the way.

I spotted one young rascal slipping into the galley while the Cook was emptying garbage over the side, and sang out to his mother. She soon had him out and, tucking him under her arm, carried him back to the jetty.

Not two minutes later he was back again. I felt sure it was the same child. I knew him by his fat tummy and his huge eyes which showed the whites as he rolled them about in his brown face. This time I got the Bos'n to see him over the side.

When it happened a third time, I sent for his mother and told her, if she could not look after him better, she would have to stop work. She rolled her eyes—just like her son—threw up her hands as if in despair, and then seized him by the arm and marched him away. The last I saw of him was a small figure amongst the palm trees, turning round to face his mother, who was waving him on towards his home.

Less than an hour later I signed for the cargo and we cast off. The harbour was soon cleared and, making a good ten knots, it was not long before we put the palm trees below the horizon.

A couple of days after this, I happened to be having a word with the Cook.

'The boy's settling down nicely,' I heard him say.

'What boy?' I asked.

'That boy that came aboard at Tahoola. He's doing fine, sir, and the lads have taken quite a fancy to him.'

It was true, I found out. The little rascal had got on board in the end, hidden in a basket, I learned later and, for all anyone knew, may have been carried aboard by his own mum.

What I wanted to know was, why had I not been told of this

before? It was coming on me slowly that there was going to be trouble over this. I could just see it. His large mum, with tears rolling out of those big eyes of hers, rushing to the authorities and the authorities taking a very serious view of the matter. Kidnapping. That's what they would call it. All ports to be notified, and the devil of an inquiry when we put in there again.

'The lads say they want to keep him,' the Cook went on.

'Well, they can't,' I told him. 'They can't do that sort of thing. What about his mum?'

'He says she told him to come. She told him the English sailors would make him a captain if he sailed with them.'

'That's his yarn,' I said. 'I don't suppose she said anything of the sort. There'll be no end of a rumpus and, if we hadn't come so far, I'd turn the ship round this minute.'

After this I thought I had better send the First Mate along to see just how things were.

'It's ridiculous the way they're carrying on,' he told me when he came to report. 'The fuss they're making of the child. He sits at the head of the table, and anything he wants, they give it him. He has a fancy for strawberry jam, and at breakfast, dinner and tea they open a new pot for him. Jam runs down his face, drips from his chin, and spreads round as far as his ears. It's ruinous the way they're digging into the ship's stores.

'I told them it would have to stop,' the First Mate went on. 'They were up in arms at once. It was nothing but cruelty, they said, not to let the boy have his jam. Victimization, they called it. You'd hardly believe it, sir, the way they've gone daft about the boy.'

'Well,' I said, 'seamen always were a sentimental lot, always did have a soft spot for the kiddies. But we'll have to look out they don't make the little fellow ill. Too much jam can't be good for him. A balanced diet is what he needs, with a little cod liver oil every day to make up any deficiencies. If we can send the boy back in good shape, it may go easier with us.'

I decided to ask the Chief, being a family man, to draw up a suitable menu. Then all that was needed was to get the Bos'n to persuade the crew to follow it.

Soon after this I had my first sight of the youngster. He was on the fore deck, stumping about in imitation of the Bos'n. The men were egging him on. He had only to pretend to roll up his sleeves and spit on his hands and there was a roar of laughter. The First Mate was right. The boy could do what he liked with them.

I said nothing then, and we steamed on across the Pacific. But the next evening, at two bells in the first watch, I noticed the man at the wheel had not been relieved.

'Is there a man sick?' I asked.

'No, sir,' was the reply. 'He'll be on directly. He's just reading the nipper his bedtime story.'

'He's what?' I said.

'Well, sir, it's like this,' the man went on. 'The kid won't go to sleep without it. And if he doesn't go to sleep, he won't let anyone else either.'

'I'm not having it,' I said. 'He's upsetting the whole ship,' and I sent for the Chief and asked him if he would have the child in the spare bunk in his cabin. He did not mind, he told me. It was about time, he said, something was done about the boy. He was still having too much jam on his menu.

So the boy fed in the Chief's cabin. And it was not long before I noticed three of the crew hanging about his door. They made some foolish pretence of sweeping the alley way, but I soon discovered they were there to waylay the food on its way from the galley. They were convinced the Chief was trying to poison their pet, and they had drawn up a rota amongst themselves so that two or more should be on duty to inspect every meal.

It was the brown bread and molasses that made them most suspicious, and I must say I could not quite make out what the Chief was at myself, until I remembered seeing him reading a health food magazine.

'He's a lovely boy,' I heard the Chief say, with quite a motherly note in his voice. 'An' you should see the weight he's put on since I've had him.'

When I did see him, my first thought was that the Chief was overdoing it. The child was lolling in a coil of rope, his hands clasped over his tummy, and the satisfied smile on his face of one who had just managed to swallow an elephant. That's not brown bread and molasses, I said to myself. Nor was it, as it turned out.

'The cargo's been broached,' said the First Mate.

'What d'you mean?' I asked.

'You'd better come and have a look, sir,' he said, and I followed him down into the hold. In the light of a torch he showed me where the lid of a packing case had been prised off.

'Damaged in loading,' I told him. 'That's all that is. Nothing wrong with the tins.'

He took one out.

'Look at that, sir,' he said.

In the end of it was a small hole that might have been made by a nail. I took the tin in my hand and shook it. Something soft and heavy thumped from side to side. If it was pineapple, as the label said, then the juice must have been sucked quite dry. Every tin in twenty-four cases was the same.

'It's that boy,' said the First Mate.

'I don't believe it,' I said. 'He couldn't have.'

'Look at this then, sir,' and he took me to another part of the hold and showed me a large hole in a case.

Shreds of paper hung out of it, and a half-eaten bar of chocolate lay on the deck below.

'Rats,' I said.

'I've never heard of rats picking out only the ones with strawberry centres,' he said. 'Not every one out of all six cases. I'm afraid there's no doubt about it, sir, it's the boy.'

'The little devil!' I said.

There was only one thing to do and that was to take over the boy myself. I could not trust anybody. They just let themselves be made fools of. They were soft, the whole lot of them.

It was only when he came to my cabin, I realized I had a way with children. Rough seaman that I am, I had not expected it. The trusting way he waddled up to me, the broad smile that spread right across his face, made me see myself in a new light. Then there was the charming way he brought me a little gift and put it in my hand, and I was so touched by it that it was only afterwards I realized he had pinched it from the Chief.

We had our little troubles to begin with. He managed to break the spring of the ship's chronometer and block up the engine-room speaking tube with breadcrumbs. But we got through the day, and one only had to see him tucked up in his little bunk, his eyes closed and a sweet, innocent smile on his lips, to know that he did not really mean any harm. The mistake the others had made was not to appeal to his better nature. 'You'll do this for me, won't you, sonny?' I would say to him sometimes, and pat him on the head, and if it did not run too contrary to his ideas, he would.

But one thing I could never get him to understand was that it was not a good idea to throw seaboots through the porthole into the sea. We had words about it, and he would stand in my cabin, a seaboot in his hand and a broad grin on his face, defying me.

'No more now, sonny,' I would say. And yet all the time I felt it a pity to stop him. It gave him so much pleasure. It was only when the seaboots were gone and he started on my shirts, braces and ties, I showed him I was angry. I locked them all in a drawer and put the key in my pocket.

But he had not played his last card yet. He gave me a long, calculating stare and then let out a yell. When I did not give in at once, he yelled again. The yells became a howl. I shut the portholes, but not before I had seen the heads of some of my crew, and caught a glimpse of the Bos'n standing outside my door, where he had no doubt been sent to see that their pet was not being ill-treated.

I suppose they thought they could manage him better. That's what it was. I'd like to see them cope with him now.

The little wretch still howled like a foghorn and, in the intervals between each blast, while he was taking in breath, I tried to reason with him. The Bos'n was twisting himself in knots, trying to screw up his courage to knock. Something had to be done quickly. I grabbed a half pound bar of chocolate from the locker above my bunk, stripped off the paper and, waiting until he had his mouth wide open, jammed it in. The noise stopped at once, and I was soon relieved to see the Bos'n on his way back to the crew's quarters.

I was careful after this not to provoke the child too much. I removed out of his way anything that might cause trouble between us, doing my best to hide my charts, which he liked for making paper hats, and my telescope, which he used for jamming he steering gear. I was not always successful.

It was not only the damage he did. It was the embarrassment e caused. There was the time when the First Mate reported a man-of-war about three miles on our starboard quarter, signalling to us.

'I'll be up right away,' I said, wondering what the Navy could want with us.

It was a destroyer, I soon saw. She was overhauling us fast and flashing away at a great speed on her signalling lamp.

'I can't make it out,' said the First Mate.

'I wouldn't try,' I said. 'They only do it on purpose to dazzle us.'

He took another look through his glasses.

'She's got her boats swung out and her crew lined up along the deck,' he said.

'Maybe she's in trouble,' I said hopefully. It would be nice to be one up on the Navy for a change. Perhaps they were lined up ready to abandon ship, I decided, and rang for the engines to stop.

They were alongside us in no time and were blaring across at us on their loud hailer.

'Are you on fire?' they were asking.

I looked aft and saw there was a black plume of smoke curling up from the galley funnel. The Cook was banking up his fires after the midday meal. If that was what they were worrying about, they must be mad. I could see them running out hoses on the deck, and one of their boats was already in the water being rowed across to us. In no time the officer in charge was clambering aboard.

'Where is it?' he shouted.

'You've got us all wrong,' I said. 'We aren't on fire.'

'You're sinking then,' he said. 'Where's the leak?'

I stared at him.

'We came as quickly as we could,' he said. 'As soon as we saw your signal.'

'What signal?' I asked.

'Your S O S. at the masthead,' he said.

I looked up and saw, fluttering in the breeze, the bedspread off my bunk and, above it, a bundle which turned out to be the Chief's trousers.

'That?' I said, and still I could not make sense.

'I suppose you know the International Code?' he said in a haughty voice.

I knew it only too well. A square flag, having either above

it or below it a ball or anything resembling a ball. The signal of distress. What could I say? There are times when a man longs for a thick fog to come down over him.

'Very good, Captain,' the man was saying. 'I'll report the matter to my commanding officer,' and he climbed over the side, while I and my fellow officers hung our heads in shame. We saw him hoisted aboard, heard the telegraph clang, the white foam burst from under the destroyer's stern, watched her swing away and, putting on full speed, tear off towards the empty horizon.

The small boy was at my elbow.

'British Navy very smart,' he said, and I wrenched the engine-room telegraph off its stand rather than wring the little blighter's neck.

The signal halyards was just one more thing to keep out of his reach. I won't go into all the other capers we had: how we found we had been steaming in circles for two days, because our little friend had opened the binnacle, right under the nose of the helmsman, and mucked about with the magnets: how we drifted for six hours with our biggest hawser round the propeller, all because he had been trailing it over the side. 'Me catch big fish,' he had said. In the end I had to confide in the Chief that I could not manage him at all.

'I expect he's missing his mum,' he said. 'That's why he's so troublesome.'

'You may be right, Chief,' I said. 'There's nothing like a mother's love. Let's face it, Chief. We haven't got the touch. We're too rough and ready. It's the tenderness that women have, their gentle ways.'

It had been a worrying voyage, but we were getting near the end of it. Tahoola in twenty-four hours. If nothing dreadful happened, I would get him safely back. What did it matter if the authorities did make a stink? I would have done my best and returned him to his mother's arms.

The harbour was in sight. I spruced him up, smarmed down his hair and parted it in the middle. His mum should see him at his best. There were only three people on the jetty. Two were the men waiting to take our ropes. The other was a woman, a large woman, his mother I felt sure. I was surprised not to see the police and some brass hats as well.

'Are you sure you're feeling all right, sonny?' I said, looking anxiously at him. I had a sudden panic he might be sickening for something. His eyes had not got their usual twinkle. His smile had gone. 'Never mind,' I said, 'you'll soon have your mum.'

The heaving lines flew through the air. The ropes were hauled to the bollards. I stood with my hand on the boy's shoulder while the gangway was being lowered. It was a touching moment and I saw several rough seamen wipe a tear from the corner of their eyes. The gangway settled on the jetty. Mother stood at the bottom and boy at the top. I gave him a gentle push. At the same moment his mother rushed up to meet him.

All eyes were on the pair, all thoughts on their happy reunion. They met, and the mother flung a large brown arm round her boy. But what was this? In a moment she had turned him upside-down and was walloping his bottom for all she was worth. His little legs kicked frantically in the air, and he howled at the top of his voice. I saw the Bos'n start forward, and then stop. It was not for any of us to interfere between mother and child. She gave him one hell of a hiding, and as she laid it on, I was surprised at a curious feeling creeping over me that I can only describe as satisfaction.

The next story sounds from its title like a pretty legend but, as you will see, Sir Cleges was not made of the stuff around which pretty legends grow.

CHRÉTIEN DE TROYES

The Christmas Cherries

In the days of King Uther Pendragon, who was King Arthur's father, there lived near Cardiff a noble knight named Sir Cleges. He was tall, good-looking and powerfully built, and he was wealthy too, for he owned many manors and farms. He spent all his money in helping others and there were many people who needed help, because the whole country was plagued by war. Many of the knights and barons fought among themselves, so that no one was safe and there was much suffering. Sir Cleges kept open house for anyone in distress, for he was the kindest, most hospitable of men, and every Christmas he gave a great feast to which he invited everyone, rich and poor, for miles around his castle. You may be quite sure that after the feast Sir Cleges gave rich gifts, gold and silver, horses and clothing, to the minstrels who had entertained his guests by telling tales, such as this which I am telling you now.

For years the good knight lived happily in this way, with his gentle wife, Dame Clarice, and his two sons, but he grew steadily poorer. Yet he was too proud to change his way of life. He sold one manor after another to pay for all this hospitality, until he had only one manor left, and this was almost too small to keep him and his family. All their followers and servants deserted them one by one and they were left alone in miserable poverty.

When Christmas came round again Sir Cleges grew very sad, thinking of the feasts he had given, and his pride was humbled at last. He wept and wrung his hands and prayed aloud to God to have pity on him.

Dame Clarice heard that cry. She came and took him in her arms and said:

'My lord, my dear love, it will not help us to mourn for the past. Let us thank God for all his gifts to us, for he has given us a great many. This is Christmas Eve, when everyone should rejoice. Come in to dinner, and let us all do our best to be happy together.'

What could Sir Cleges do but smile at her? They went in to their humble meal of bread and herbs, and made merry for their sons' sake all that day.

On Christmas morning they all went to church, and Sir Cleges felt much happier. Afterwards he went alone into his little garden, where he knelt on the grass under a cherry tree, thanking God with all his heart for God's gift of poverty. As he rose to his feet he put his hand on a low bough—and stood staring in amazement. The bough, the whole tree, which had been completely bare before, was now covered with green leaves and fine ripe cherries.

'Dear God,' he cried, 'what miracle is this?'

Plucking a large red cherry, he put it into his mouth. It was delicious. It was the best cherry he had ever tasted. He broke off a little bough laden with fruit and hurried into the house, calling to his wife:

'My dear, my dear, look at this! Our cherry tree is covered with fruit. I am afraid it's a bad omen, it means more trouble coming to us.'

His wife took the bough and marvelled at it, but her heart rose.

'This is a good sign,' she said. 'This means better fortune for us. But whatever happens we will thank God for it.' She thought for a moment. 'Now, let us fill a large basket with these wonderful cherries, so that tomorrow morning early you can set out for Cardiff with it, to give it to the King. He will be so astonished and pleased that he will give you a rich gift in return.'

Sir Cleges kissed her and said: 'I will do just as you wish.'

At daybreak next morning he set out. He had not one horse left of the many which had once stood so proudly in his stables, so he had to use the poor man's pony, a strong staff, but his elder son went with him to carry the heavy basket of fruit.

When the two reached Cardiff Castle it was nearly dinner time. Sir Cleges had been away from the court for so long that no one recognized him as he was now, old and worn and wearing shabby clothes. When he and his son went in boldly at the main gate the porter stopped them at once.

'Churls,' he said, 'how dare you come in here! Get out, both of you, before I break your heads with my staff. Go and wait with the beggars outside.'

'Good sir,' replied Sir Cleges humbly, 'I beg you to let me come in. I have brought a wonderful present for King Uther from the King of Heaven.'

The porter lifted the lid of the basket, and as soon as he saw the cherries he had wit enough to realize that the King was likely to give a rich reward to the bringer of such a wonderful gift.

'By heaven,' he said, 'you shall not come into the castle unless you promise to give me a third of anything the King gives you, whether it be gold or silver.'

Sir Cleges could see no hope of avoiding this, so he said reluctantly, 'I promise,' whereupon the porter let him and his son pass.

At the door of the great hall the usher stopped them, swinging his staff of office menacingly.

'You churls,' he said, 'what are you doing here? Begone at once, or I will have you beaten from head to foot.'

'Good sir,' answered Sir Cleges meekly, 'for the love of God, do not be angry with me. I have brought the King a present from Him who created all things. See for yourself.'

The boy brought the basket forward, and when the usher saw the cherries he could hardly believe his eyes.

'By St Mary,' he said, 'you shall not go into the hall unless you promise to give me on your way out a third of anything which you may get.'

Very sadly Sir Cleges gave his word, and he and his son made their way into the hall. It was full of lords and ladies, whose fine clothes made the poor knight look shabbier than ever. The King's steward came striding up to him angrily.

'How dare you enter the King's hall in those rags! Get out!'

But Sir Cleges stood his ground. 'I have brought the King a wonderful present,' he said, 'from Him who died for our salvation.' He lifted the lid of the basket, and the steward stared and stared.

'By St Mary,' he cried, 'never in my life have I seen such a thing at Christmas. This is a marvel indeed. I will not allow you to take it to the King unless you promise to give me a third of everything that the King gives you.'

Sir Cleges was so cast down that he could not answer. He told himself sadly that all his trouble would go for nothing, for those three men would take everything.

'You rascal,' growled the steward, 'have you lost your tongue? Give me your promise at once or I'll have you beaten and flung out of the hall.'

Sighing heavily, the poor knight replied: 'You shall have a third of anything which the King may give me, I promise you.'

Without another word the steward led him and his son to the dais at the top of the hall, where King Uther sat in state, under a wide canopy of cloth of gold.

Sir Cleges knelt before the King and opened his basket

wide, so that everyone could see the cherries, red and ripe and glistening among their fresh green leaves. A silence fell. The fine lords and ladies looked at each other and looked again at the wonderful fruit. The King leaned forward to see the better.

'Sire,' said Sir Cleges, 'our Saviour, Lord Jesus, has sent you these cherries by me.'

'I give thanks to Him with all my heart,' replied the King, 'for this is a great marvel. Bring the basket here.'

Sir Cleges put the basket in front of the King, who looked wonderingly at the cherries and ate two of them. 'They are as delicious as they are marvellous,' he said. 'They shall be passed round so that everyone in this company can taste one of them, and you who brought them shall join our feast—and your son.'

Sir Cleges and his son bowed low, and thanked the King, and then found humble places for themselves at one of the long trestle-tables which ran the whole length of that great hall. The King and the noblest of the court took their seats at the high table on the dais. The trumpets sounded, and the feast began. There was rich food in plenty: all kinds of meat, fish and fowl, good wine and good ale, elaborate cakes and pastries, but for everyone present the crowning wonder was a fresh, ripe red fruit. For the rest of their lives they told the story of the Christmas cherries.

When the feast was over the King said to a squire: 'Ask the poor man who brought the cherries to come to me.'

Sir Cleges came at once and knelt on one knee before the King.

'You have done great honour to our feast and to me,' the King said, 'and I will reward you gladly. I will give you anything you ask, in gold or silver, goods or lands or anything else.'

'Thank you, my liege,' replied Sir Cleges, 'but there is only one reward I wish: your gracious permission to give twelve blows with my staff to three men in this hall.'

The King looked at him in astonishment. 'You make me regret that I gave you that promise,' he said. 'Will you not change your mind, and let me give you gold or precious stones from my treasury? Do you not need money?'

'Alas,' said the knight sadly, 'it would be of no use to me. All I ask is twelve blows.'

'Then you must have my permission to give them, because I gave you my word.'

Sir Cleges and his son bowed low once again. The King rose from the table, and as soon as he had left the hall the knight looked round for the steward.

There he was, at the far end of the hall, keeping watch at the great door. Grasping his heavy staff more tightly, Sir Cleges strode towards the door, and the steward turned to meet him.

'You are to give me one-third of everything which the King gave you,' he said harshly, 'or I will have you whipped and take it all.'

'The King gave me twelve blows,' replied Sir Cleges, 'and I will gladly give you your share.' He swung his staff above his head. 'One, two, three, four.'

The steward howled with pain, the bystanders laughed, for no one liked him, and Sir Cleges went on into the antechamber. The usher came scurrying after him at once, calling out: 'Churl, churl, curses on you, give me my reward.'

'Gladly,' replied the knight. 'Here you are. Five, six, seven, eight.'

He went into the courtyard, towards the main gate, and at once the porter barred his way.

'What did the King give you, churl?' asked the porter, glowering.

'Twelve strokes,' the knight answered, 'and you shall have your fair share. Nine, ten, eleven, twelve.'

The last blow beat the porter to his knees. Leaving him to the crowd, Sir Cleges went back to the great hall, with his son still close behind him. The tables had all been cleared. A score of serving men were busy lifting them from their trestles, to be carried away, while others strewed fresh rushes on the floor.

The King was in his parlour, with a few of his lords and ladies, drinking spiced wine beside a blazing log fire, while one of his court minstrels sang a lay of knightly deeds.

Sir Cleges stopped at the door and listened in amazement for the minstrel was singing of him.

When the song was finished the King gave a gold coin to the minstrel. 'Sir Cleges was a brave and worthy knight,' said the King. 'It is years since he came to court, and I miss him sadly. Where is he now?'

'I do not know,' answered the minstrel. 'He has gone away from this country.'

Sir Cleges came forward, bowing before the King.

'Ah,' said the King, 'now tell me, why did you ask only for twelve strokes?'

The knight told him the whole story, and the King and all his courtiers laughed and laughed.

'This is a noble jest!' he said at last. 'Bring the steward to me.' And when the steward came, still rubbing his back, the King cried, 'Well, Sir Steward, you got your deserts from this poor man. What have you to say for yourself?'

'May the devil fly away with him!' roared the steward. 'I'll never speak to him again!'

The King laughed again, and said to the poor knight, 'What is your name?'

'Sir Cleges, sir. As I hope for salvation, I am he.'

'What!' cried the King. 'Are you indeed that noble knight whom I have missed for so long?'

'Indeed, sire, I am. God has brought me low, as you see, but I am Sir Cleges.'

'I see now that you are,' said the King, 'and I welcome you with all my heart. You shall not remain in poverty. I will make you governor of this Castle of Cardiff and lord of all its lands. I will give you from my own treasury all the gold and silver that you may need, and you shall not leave me again.'

'I thank you, sire,' answered Sir Cleges, 'and I thank God for the Christmas cherries.'

I love this next story because Bridget is in many ways like I was at her age. I remember as clearly as if it happened yesterday my sisters and I being asked to a party. The card said '7–11 dancing'.

In those days many people gave dances, for all that was needed was to roll up a carpet and provide someone to play the piano. Very like today in fact except that you use a tape recorder. What was different was clothes. Today you go as you are, but in my childhood you wore a party dress. We were the daughters of a poor parson so we only had two party dresses each. Our best were white, so very much kept for best to keep them clean. Our second best were pink, of cheap material, and we hated them.

I cannot remember now why but my mother had decided that party would be a second-best so we were sent wearing our pinks. Unknown to us the party givers were being visited by their only rich relations. Because of their arrival they had laid on the grandest party they ever gave. The carpets were not just rolled back, workmen had carted them away and polished the floors so they shone like a skating rink. The children of the house all had new frocks and so did those of their friends who were in the know. There was a buffet served by proper waiters. Every light in the house was turned on. But the final touch was a band. Truly only three-piece but renowned throughout the whole county and very expensive. Imagine the glory that we three saw and the shame of our second-best pinks.

I was never given to humility but I was near to feeling it that night and at last I could bear it no longer. Dragging my unwilling sisters with me I settled us down on the stairs where many of the rich relations of our host had parked themselves to eat some supper. I then began a loud cross-talk with my sisters (much to their embarrassment).

'If,' I said, 'we'd known it was going to be this sort of party we would have worn our blue silks trimmed with sequins or our scarlet taffetas.'

'Or our whites,' my eldest sister put in, struggling to get me back on to the path of truth.

By then I knew even our whites were unworthy of this party. My imagination ran riot.

'I'd rather have worn our gold. Everybody says how lovely we look in them.'

On I went, imagining a wardrobe fit for a princess. I did not stop until the rich relations had moved away back to the dance floor. Of course they hadn't believed us, why should they care what three shabby little girls in pink might have worn? But the fairy tale I had made up had done me good. I danced with my head high for the rest of the evening.

In this story Bridget's troubles are different from mine. She too was a snob but of another kind, but my goodness I understood how she felt.

The story is by Helen Cresswell, a writer for whom I have the greatest admiration for she not only writes perfect English but she understands people. You read this wintry story and see how well she understands not only Bridget but everybody else.

HELEN CRESSWELL

A Shower of Snow

'But I wanted to go skating! What if it thaws? I wanted to go down to the lake.'

'Thaw? You heard what the forecast said. Hard frost with occasional snow showers.'

‘Oh, that!’ Bridget clattered the saucers she was drying. ‘You don’t believe that, do you? I’d as soon believe in witch doctors. Sooner.’

‘They’re usually about right,’ said her mother stolidly. She turned, wiping her thick red hands on her apron—the hands that always made Bridget feel obscurely sad, and even more obscurely guilty. It was seeing them that made her give in now.

‘All right, Mum. I’ll come.’

‘Only for an hour or two,’ her mother said. She was apologetic now that she had gained her point. ‘Just to give a hand with the silver, that’s all. I’ve my hands that full, and you’ve no idea how particular Mrs Penfold is about things.’

‘She’s lucky to get you, then,’ Bridget said. ‘There’s no one else in this village’d slave for her the way you do.’

‘And she’s got people coming over Christmas,’ her mother went on. ‘Two dinner parties, she’s got, and her children coming back from school.’

‘You don’t think *they*’ll care if the silver’s cleaned or not, do you?’ Bridget said.

‘It’s just one of those things. People *clean* silver at Christmas. Traditional, like. *We* always did—what bit we had.’

‘Bit is right,’ said Bridget. She immediately regretted saying it so she rushed on to cover up. ‘Don’t *worry*, Mum. I’ve said I’ll do it. I’ll go with you in the morning and stay till I’ve done it.’

‘You can sit down to it, in the kitchen.’ Her mother, who always carried on with her own line of thought, held a kind of one-sided conversation with herself. ‘I’ll put you out plenty of clean rags, then fetch the things to you. Cutlery first, I think. Yes. Then the things off the sideboard—you’ll be interested in them, Bridget, trophies and all sorts. Then the things . . .’

‘Look, Mum. You’re not planning a campaign. I’ve said I’ll come up and clean the silver, and that’s all there is to it.’ A thought struck her. ‘Shall I be paid?’

‘We—ell.’ Her mother paused, leaning on her hands in the soapy water. ‘Nobody *said* anything. All I says to Mrs Penfold is that I’m a bit behindhand, and p’raps you’d come up and give me a hand with the silver. In a way, see, it's *my* job you'll be doing.'

'You mean she's too mean to have you in five days a week,' Bridget said. 'Expecting you to keep that barn of a place clean in three mornings—it's daft.'

'I can always give you a bit myself . . .'

'Oh Mum!' she cried in exasperation. Her mother was too humble, thought too little of herself. It maddened Bridget, who wanted her mother to *be* somebody.

'But I daresay, with it being Christmas . . . I've told Mrs Penfold ever so much about you. *Her* girl's clever as well, you know, taking . . .'

'Yes. I know. You told me. And playing Hamlet in the school play. Have we finished? I want to go to the Bring and Buy. Thousands of second-hand clothes, Jenny says. She's running the stall.'

'There's no need at all for you to go buying things second-hand. Poor we may be, but we can afford clothes.'

'Oh *Mum*!' But it was useless to explain. To come up against her mother's ideas about respectability was to meet a brick wall, head on.

She fetched her coat and purse and a minute later was out of the light and warmth, the soapy, linoleum smell of the kitchen and into the cold night. Her eyes adjusted (she often tried to *feel* the slow dilation of her pupils) and the cold became visible, a gleam of white. Her nostrils, too, were aware that the frost had a subtle and mysterious scent of its own—'I'd know it was frosty, even with my eyes shut!' she thought. Then, with sudden excitement, 'The forecast was right! No thaw!'

She broke into a run, a special kind of flat-footed run, because of the slipperiness—then took the short cut over the green to the Village Hall.

'Get there before it starts,' Jenny had told her. 'Then I'll let you have first pick.'

Inside the hall her eyes were dazzled and she stood half blinded in the suddenly thicker and warmed air.

'Yoo-ee! Bridget!'

And then she was with Jenny, picking through the piles of cast-off clothing, holding things against herself, exclaiming.

'What about this? No—nothing to go with it. See me in this? Oh, this—yes, I'll have this. Twenty pence? Put it on the chair, Jenny. I'll pay later when I've finished. Oh! This! Look!'

It was a mini skirt—suède! Five pounds it would cost new —which was why she had never had one.

'Twenty-four waist—perfect! How much, Jen?'

'Fifty pence. That's what it says. On the bottom, look. I'd have it myself, if I could afford it.'

'A gift!' sang Bridget. 'I'll have it. And what's this—look, perfect! Could've been made to go with it!'

'Came in the same bundle,' Jenny told her. 'Twenty pence.'

'Both, I'll have,' said Bridget. 'Rags to riches. And that's that. I've only got a pound—and that earned by the sweat of me own brow, running newspapers.'

'You've done all right for ninety pence,' Jenny said. 'Whose stuff, I wonder? Wish *I* could afford to throw out stuff like that. Hush now, will you, for the vicar.'

The sale was opened, Bridget handed over the ninety pence, and for her the sale was over. Back at home she tried them on in her room, the pinkish suède skirt and skinny jumper to match.

'Swish, I am,' she thought, and nodded to her blotched reflection in the half-silvered glass. 'Posh!' she told herself, and went down to show her mother.

'Oh, I know they're the *thing*,' she said. 'But I can't bring myself to like them. I don't see the beauty at all, Bridget.'

And next day, when Bridget came down wearing the outfit, the pair came very close to a quarrel.

'It's not what *I* think,' her mother said. 'I know *that's* not important. It's what Mrs Penfold will think.'

'What does her kid wear, then?' Bridget demanded. 'Twin sets and pearls, does she?'

'I've not set my eyes on her yet, Bridget, as you very well know. But something ladylike, I'll be bound.'

'Oh *cor*! Ladylike!'

Her mother pursed up her lips and assumed an expression

Bridget knew only too well—and detested. It was an air of being totally and beyond question in the right, but too saintly to say so.

'Anyway I shall go skating, after,' Bridget said. 'You need a short skirt for skating. And I daresay it won't affect the shine on the silver.'

She was being sarcastic again, and was aware that she disliked the tone of her own voice as she spoke, but equally aware that she had a right to choose her own clothes, and would fight for it, if need be.

The two of them walked in silence through the village. There was rarely any conversation between them unless Bridget herself started it, and this morning she did not feel like talking. The frost had deepened in the night, it was as if the world were held tight in a mailed fist. The road rang, the air rang, and they each walked in a private halo of smoke from their own breath. Everyone they met wore the cloudy halo, and were oddly changed and made mysterious because of it, just as the very houses in the street were changed, all white-roofed and standing in stiff white plots. Above the wood beyond the lake a round red sun was showing in a perfectly blank and pearly sky.

'Here we are, then.' Her mother's voice broke into her thoughts. 'First time you've been up here, isn't it, Bridget?'

She nodded. Gravel and frost crunched underfoot.

'Long drive, isn't it?'

Bridget nodded again. She was torn between the desire to seem unimpressed and shame at disappointing her mother.

'Not up there, Bridget. Round the side.'

'Tradesman's entrance,' Bridget thought. 'No hawkers or circulars,' and followed. Her mother gave a little knock at the back door and let herself in.

'Here we are then. This is the kitchen.'

She took off her things and hung them on a hook behind the door. She was already wearing her overall underneath. Despite herself, Bridget was impressed. She had never seen a kitchen like this before—or only in advertisements.

'Finish stacking the washer, that's the first job,' her mother was saying.

'What's that, then?' She went and looked over her mother's shoulder. 'A dishwasher?'

Bridget saw her mother in an entirely new light.

'You never told me it was like this, Mum.'

'You never asked. Take your coat off, Bridget, and hang it next to mine. Mrs Penfold'll be here in a minute.'

'Ah, Freda. And this is your daughter, is it?'

Mrs Penfold, wearing a blue silk housecoat and looking as if she were just off to a dance, stood in the doorway. Bridget smiled politely, and stared too. Her mother began the explanations.

'It's like I said, Mrs Penfold. With me being so behindhand, Bridget can give me a hand with the silver. This is Mrs Penfold, Bridget.'

'Pleased to meet you,' Bridget said.

'And I thought I'd bring the silver in here and Bridget can do it while I'm——'

'That will be perfect, Freda. And it's kind of Bridget to come. And now—I wonder if you'd get some breakfast for Anna? Nothing much—grapefruit and some toast. She only came home last night, and I like to spoil her on her first day—give her breakfast in bed.'

'I'll see to it right away, Mrs Penfold.'

'And perhaps Bridget would like to take it up to her? She and Anna are more or less the same age, aren't they? Though Anna's a tall girl—she's often taken for seventeen or eighteen.'

'Yes, Mrs Penfold. Bridget'll take it when I've got it ready, won't you?'

'I'll leave it to you, then, Freda. Thank you.'

She was gone.

'There you are,' said Bridget's mother. 'Nice, isn't she?'

'What did you want to go and say I'd take that tray for? *I* don't want to take any tray. Why doesn't she get up? And why should you run round after her? You're not a——'

She had been going to say 'a servant'.

She did take the tray too. She had known that she would, in the end. Swiftly she mounted the deep carpeted stairs, holding the tray at arms' length, disowning it. She paused outside the second door along the landing.

'Enter chambermaid,' she thought, and knocked.

'Come in!'

Anna Penfold was sitting up in bed reading a magazine by the light of a bedside lamp. She had long dark hair, properly out, and it swung enviably when she lifted her head.

'Hullo! Who are you?'

'Bridget Carter. I've come to give a hand with the silver—but my mother thought I'd p'raps just bring this up to you.'

'Honestly, I feel ridiculous, sitting here like this being waited on. It's not like this at school, *I* can tell you.'

'Here you are then.' Bridget approached the bed, still holding the tray at arms' length.

'Pretty, she is,' she thought. 'Nice—could be.'

'I say—Bridget—could you just pull the curtains back? Is it still freezing?'

'Hard.' Bridget pulled back the heavy curtains and the room filled with the queer, cold, upward-slanting light that always comes with frost and snow.

'Are they skating? The minute I knew we were coming to live here, I prayed for the lake to freeze.'

'Be all right for skating, I reckon. Going down there myself later.'

'Well, if you're——' Anna broke off. 'Here, that's——' She started to giggle. Bridget, already at the door, turned back.

'If that isn't the—where did you get that outfit?'

'This?' Bridget was half nonplussed, half pleased. 'This skirt and things? Second-hand actually. Got them down at the Bring and Buy last night.'

'I knew it!' Anna flung up both hands and the tray tilted dangerously. 'They're mine! Of all the coincidences! Fancy your walking in here wearing my skirt and my sweater!'

She began laughing again. Bridget shut the door behind her and heard Anna's voice.

'Hey! What's wrong? Hey—Bridget!'

She ran down the stairs two at a time. If her mother had

not been in the kitchen, she would have grabbed her coat and gone.

'There you are, Bridget! Found the room all right, did you? Nice, is she?'

'Oh, very,' Bridget said. 'Proper little lady, just like you said. And this is *her* outfit I'm wearing, you'll be pleased to hear. Got something better, I suppose, and flung this out.'

'Well, fancy! Hers, is it?'

'*Was.*'

'Well, if it was *hers* . . . Your taste's better than I thought it was, Bridget, I'll admit that.'

'I doubt,' said Bridget, 'if I'll ever want to wear it again. Come on, where's the things?'

She cleaned the Penfolds' silver with furious speed and thoroughness. She rubbed at dishes, goblets, plates, till they gave her back her own image.

'I'm stamped in silver,' she thought. '*Their* silver.' And the thought pleased her.

By eleven o'clock she had finished, and escaped into the frost.

She ran with careful loping strides towards the lake. And the cold and the impact of all that whiteness were so great that soon she no longer felt anything—not anger, nor shame, nor anything else. She was reduced to a marvellous innocence, like that of an animal, knowing only the overpowering witness of her own senses, and was happy again. It was as if the world had been wiped like a slate and made new, with the possibility of new beginnings.

Several figures were already wheeling on the frozen distances. Sitting on the bank she put on her skates, feeling her fingers go thick and clumsy with cold. For a moment the sun gleamed and lit the golden winter sticks of the willows. Just as suddenly it went in again, and there followed a little moaning gust of wind, fresh and smelling of snow.

Then she was away, running with knees bent, exploring the barely scarred acres of ice. And all the time she was filled with a curious sense of exultation, that was partly to do with her own flying speed and partly because the very act of cutting the printless ice, making her mark with the steel of her blades, seemed to make the lake belong to her, and her alone. Deliberately she kept away from the other skaters, fostering the illusion.

'Bridget! Bridget!'

It was a voice she did not know. Half turning her head she had a glimpse of a girl in red, a girl with flying dark hair. Anna Penfold. Bridget looked away, pretended not to have heard, and began to drive for the far end of the lake. When she reached the farthermost bank she looked back, and there was no one within a mile of her. She saw tiny anonymous figures in the far distance and could only guess that one of them was Anna Penfold.

After that, she skated leisurely. Thrust and glide, thrust and glide—she wove wide patterns and her eyes were bent down, watching the curls and spirals she was making. And after a time she was calm again, hypnotized almost, swung in space and time, perfectly alone.

Then the snow began to fall. It fell in great tissue-like flakes, and she looked up to find that everything had disappeared. The sky, the woods, the banks, the skating figures, all were gone. She strained into the dizzying swirl. The loneliness she had courted and won was all at once a threat. She was as if walled in by the snow, imprisoned by it.

The very quality of the silence changed. Even the hiss of her own blades was muffled. She stopped and listened. She heard only the soft pattering of snow on ice.

'Keep your head, girl,' she said out loud.

She skated on, but slowly now, as if she were half blind. She knew there was nothing she could run into, and yet some deeper instinct was afraid. She even groped ahead with her hands as if she were playing Blind Man's Buff. And within minutes, she might as well have been blindfold, always ringed round by the same snow, as if she were not travelling at all, merely marking time.

She talked to herself inside her head.

'Steady does it, Bridget girl. Keep on and on, and I'm bound to get to the shore in the end. The lake's only a mile long, remember, and half that wide.'

But she was on the edge of panic and knew it.

'Thinking of those tales you've heard, are you? People going round and round in circles, then collapsing and dying, and safety not ten yards away. But that's not for you, Bridget Carter. Not a chance. You just keep your eyes ahead, and you'll get there.'

But there *was* no way ahead.

'North south east west north south east west . . .' she muttered the words under her breath, comforted by them because they reminded her that there *were* directions, perspectives, paths to follow.

Another thing she was rapidly losing track of, was time.

'Light-hearted, you're getting, Bridget Carter,' she told herself. Yet she could not rid herself of the sense that she was moving forward neither in space nor time.

'If this is eternity,' she thought, 'you can keep it.'

Then:

'Surely, if you've been skating in a straight line you'll be at the edge by now.'

Then she could not be skating in a straight line. She was going in circles. Like those other travellers.

'Another minute, you'll be praying,' she told herself.

Her hands encountered something wet and woollen! She let out a little breathless scream, there was a jarring thud, and she was down on the ice.

'Oh!' she gasped. 'Oh!' She was aware of painful knees and elbows, of cold and wet stinging her skin, of muffled sobs—surely not her own! Above all, she was aware of enormous relief, of being anchored again in space and time—someone else was there, near by! She heaved herself to her knees and looked wildly about her.

'Don't go! Where are you?' she cried.

Then there was an answering cry and she saw a blur of red, then a face appearing through the snow on a level with her own. They crawled towards one another and stared into each other's eyes.

'Oh, thank heaven!' sobbed Anna Penfold. 'Thank heaven!'

And they helped one another to their feet, and stood for a moment leaning against the blizzard. Then Bridget held out a hand, and wordlessly they began to skate on together, through what was, after all, only a heavy snow shower, and towards what must, eventually, be a safe shore.

This is not a Christmas story but it is a very wintry one. When I was a child a story like this was read out loud to us on a winter's evening. An icy wind would howl round the house and we children would roast chestnuts on the fire feeling glad we were safe and warm.

This next is not exactly a fairy story—more perhaps a magic story. I know when I read it first I got the same shiver down the spine that I got when as a child I first read Keats's 'La Belle Dame sans Merci'. It was the last verse that made me shiver.

'And this is why I sojourn here
Alone and palely loitering,
Though the sedge is wither'd from the lake
And no birds sing.'

You try saying that out loud and you will see what I mean. Now here is the story.

GODFRIED BOMANS

The Lady of the Lake

On a Friday night, when the moon is full, take care, for the world is bewitched. If on such a night you come to a lake, you will see the Lady of the Lake. She rises silently to the surface;

not a ripple disturbs the water. She says nothing, but looks at you with her ice-cold eyes. Then with her white hand she beckons and into the water you go, whether you want to or not. No one can help you. The water closes over your head and no mortal man knows what happens after that.

Now, once upon a time there lived a king and a queen who had only one child. He was the prince, and the prince was very spoiled. When he was still in his cradle he was given a golden rattle. He ate from a golden plate and he drank from a golden mug. All his toys were of gold and as he grew older it became more and more difficult to give him anything that he did not already possess.

By the time he was to be eighteen he had everything he could wish for, and all in pure gold. But he must be given something for his birthday. The prince stood by the window as his uncles and aunts filed in. Each one had brought him a present, but they felt very awkward, for they knew that he would have it already. The prince unwrapped the paper and took one look. 'I have one of those,' he said each time and flung the present out of the window. Down in the snowy street stood the poor children of that country. They gathered up the presents and hurried home with them, where they could be put to good use.

A young girl was standing there too. She loved the prince dearly. She did not dare to say so, for she was very poor, but she was very fond of him all the same. She picked up a golden fiddle the prince had tossed away, and slipped it into her apron. But she did not go home. She waited and watched in the falling snow. All the children had gone, because they thought that there was nothing more to come, but the girl stayed on. It was already twilight when she caught a gold mug. She tucked it into her apron, but still she did not go home. She waited there in the darkness, gazing silently upwards. It was bitterly cold and she could see the prince standing by the window, while a bright fire flickered behind him. There! He had been given yet another present. He unwrapped the paper, yawning and a moment later a golden dagger flew out of the window. The girl picked it up and tucked it silently into her apron. Only then did she turn and go slowly home.

At that very moment the prince looked out of the window and saw the girl walking away. A trail of red drops of blood lay behind her in the white snow, for she had cut herself on the sharp blade, although she did not know it. The prince leaned out of the window and called:

'Ho, maiden, bid you stay!
Did I harm you in some way?'

The girl turned swiftly and replied:

'More than you know
You cause me woe.'

The prince quickly forgot her, for other visitors arrived and he hoped that at last he would receive something that he did not already possess. But he had everything already and he yawned so hugely that the tears sprang into his eyes.

'How boring it is when you already have everything,' he said irritably. 'I really think I will go to bed now.'

And he would have done so, too, had not an old woman arrived just before midnight. The old woman was called the Princess Bobbelink. Princess Bobbelink had a strange, deep voice and a long, pointed nose, which always had a drip hanging on the end of it. She lived in a distant palace, where she opened the door to no one, for no one ever came to see her.

'So, dear boy,' she rumbled, 'have you had many presents?'

'Yes,' said the prince, 'but I have thrown them all out of the window. Have you brought something that I do not possess already?'

'I believe I have,' answered the old woman. 'Here it is.'

And she gave him a big black book, wrapped in cobwebs.

'Bah!' said the prince. 'Is that all?' He had already started towards the window, to fling the book out with the rest.

'Not so fast!' warned the old woman. 'This is a book of spells. Think of the oddest things you like, and you will find them there.'

This promise aroused the prince's curiosity. Without even a

word of thanks, he hurried off to his bedroom and began to read. The old witch was right. The oddest things you could think of were to be found there. First there were spells to turn the whole dinner service into silver. The prince passed over them, for he had already seen this done years ago. Then there were five pages about turning all the cups and saucers into gold. The prince flipped over these pages too, for he had been given golden cups and saucers on his last birthday. Then came the spells for conjuring roast venison out of nothing, and producing from two half-burned matches a stuffed hare which would melt on your tongue. The prince passed over these too because he had often eaten such things before. Then he read that diamonds could be found under toadstools when there was a rainbow in the sky, and how to change hailstones into pearls just by standing quite still and thinking of nothing else.

The prince read on and on, but no matter how many pages he turned he could find nothing that he did not already know about or possess. And he was just about to pitch the book out of the window when he came to a page which was stuck down by its two outer corners. The old woman had written on it in large letters: 'DANGER! DO NOT OPEN!' for well she knew that was just what the prince would do.

And so he did. The prince tore open the page and read the story of the Lady of the Lake. 'Friday and full moon,' said he. 'I would dearly love to see that Lady, because seeing her is the only thing I have not already done.'

He looked out and saw that the moon was full in the sky. Then he called his chamberlain and asked what day it was.

'Friday, your Highness,' answered the man, 'and tomorrow it will be Saturday.'

The prince gave him a florin because he knew more than he had been asked. Then the prince put on his ermine cloak and went out. The snow had stopped, it was a cold, bright night and the stars stood still in the sky. The prince looked curiously about him. The whole world was white and all the paths were covered with snow. And because he did not know which way to go, he followed the trail of the crimson drops of blood leading to the house of the young girl who had been cut by the gold dagger. She was standing by the window of her room, with a lighted candle in her hand.

'Can I come and sleep in your warm bed?' asked the prince.

'I shall have to ask my father,' answered the maiden, 'and I dare not wake him.'

'But I am so cold,' said the prince.

'That is not reason enough,' said the maiden. 'You must also love me truly.'

'All right,' said the prince, 'I love you.'

The girl shook her head. 'Saying so is not enough,' she said again. 'You will have to prove it too.'

'How can I do that?' asked the prince.

'You must give up your plan to go to the Lady of the Lake,' said the girl. 'And if you promise that, then I will open the door to you in one hour.'

'All right,' said the prince. 'I promise.' For he really did find the girl very charming. But he did not love her truly, for he had never been taught to love anyone.

'An hour is a long time,' warned the girl. 'Will your love be equal to it?'

'Oh, yes, indeed,' answered the prince. 'I will prove it to you.'

'We shall see,' said the girl, 'but I do not believe it.'

And she was right, for after a quarter of an hour the prince felt so cold, standing in the snow, that he could not bear it any longer.

'I am going home,' he said to himself. 'I cannot bear it any longer, and we will see what happens tomorrow.'

He had thought he would find the way home quite easily, but he was wrong. More snow had fallen meanwhile, covering the crimson spots of blood, and there was no sign of them. Hour after hour the prince wandered through the white snow and he was truly sorry that he had not waited, but now it was too late. He shouted for his valet and his coachman and all his servants, but they were all safe in bed and deaf to everything. He even shouted the names of his father and mother and all the aunts and uncles he could think of, but they did not hear him either.

At last the prince grew so cold that he could scarcely walk. His hands were frozen and he felt sleep slowly overwhelming him. The prince knew that if he slept in the snow he would never wake again, and he forced his eyes wide open. Suddenly he saw a wide, glassy lake. The moon was reflected in the still water and in the very middle of the lake the head of a woman rose slowly to the surface. She looked at him with her cold eyes and stretched out her arms to him. The prince felt an irresistible power drawing him as he stepped into the ice-cold water. It almost stopped his breath, but he walked on, for he could not do anything else. The water was up to his hips. It rose to his chest and reached his lips. Then the woman threw her arms about him, and swift as an arrow she plunged with him into the depths.

In the morning the palace was in an uproar. The servant who always carried the prince's breakfast up on a golden tray had found the bed empty. He immediately rang the silver bell which hung above the bed and when the king heard it he sounded the great golden bell which hung in the tower and soon all the bells in the land began to ring, because the prince was missing.

The young girl heard them, but she said nothing. She tucked the golden fiddle, the mug and the dagger in her apron, said goodbye to her father and mother and went straight to the palace.

All the wisest men in the land were gathered there. They stood before the king's throne, taking turns in guessing where the prince might be. One thought he had been swallowed by a whale, another was sure that he was flying through the air on the back of a black swan, a third said that a magician had changed him into a willow tree. The king listened attentively, for he was anxious to know the answer. At last he saw the young girl standing there and asked her what she thought.

'The prince is with the Lady of the Lake,' she said. The wise men laughed, for they did not believe in the Lady of the Lake.

'Sire,' said one of them, 'that is nonsense. The Lady of the Lake does not exist. The prince has been changed into a bluetit and is sitting on a roof somewhere.' That was his own idea.

'Right,' said the king, 'you can all go home. The maiden will stay here.'

When he was alone with the girl he said: 'Let go of your apron.'

The maiden let go of her apron, and the golden fiddle, the mug and the dagger clattered to the floor.

'Strange,' said the king, 'how did you come by those?'

'The prince threw them all out of the window,' answered the girl. 'And what is thrown out of the window belongs to everyone.'

'That is true,' said the king. 'And what are you going to do now?'

'I am going to look for him,' answered the girl, 'and when I have found him I will bring him here.'

'Do that,' said the king, 'and go with God.'

The girl gathered up the fiddle, the mug and the dagger and went out. When it was evening she reached a wide, frozen lake. She took her fiddle and began to play. A little crack appeared in the ice, but the girl played on. The crack grew wider and at last she could see the water. It was quite black and ran in a narrow channel to the middle of the lake. Then she took her golden mug and began to scoop up the water. It was icy cold, but the maiden went on scooping bravely, until she saw a long passage sloping downwards into the lake. The cold there was so terrible that it pierced through bone and marrow, but she walked down all the same, until she came to a door made of a single block of ice, as smooth as glass. The girl hesitated. There was no bell, no knob and no lock, and she realized that she herself must find a way to open the door. She took the dagger from her apron and blew on it with her warm breath. Then she traced an arch in the ice until she made a whole doorway. She placed her bare hands against the ice and pushed. The archway she had cut fell in and the girl stepped through. There sat the Lady of the Lake, her arms about the prince, staring fixedly at the maiden.

'What have you come for?' she asked.

The maiden shivered, for even the lady's voice was cold.

'I have come to fetch the prince.'

The Lady of the Lake smiled.

'If you can unloose my arm,' she answered, 'then you may take him with you.' Within the circle of her embrace, the prince seemed lifeless.

The girl laid her hand on the lady's arm, and the arm was colder than the coldest ice. Though her fingers froze at once on the marble skin, she did not let go, but grasped the arm firmly.

'I love him,' she said.

'That is not enough,' answered the Lady of the Lake. 'You must prove it.'

'How shall I do that?' asked the maiden.

'My arm is frozen,' answered the Lady of the Lake, 'and no power on earth can release the prince from its clasp. But if you can hold on for one hour my arm will thaw and I will lose my power. Poor child, that you surely cannot do.'

'That I can,' said the maiden, 'for I love him.'

The Lady of the Lake smiled again. 'We shall see,' she said, 'but I do not believe it. An hour is a long time. No love is strong enough for that.'

As the girl held her icy arm, the Lady of the Lake looked into her eyes, until the maiden felt that she could no longer endure the icy gaze. She turned her head away to look at the prince. He was deathly pale and his eyes were closed.

'Look at me,' said the lady.

'No,' answered the maiden, 'I will look at him.' And she did. As she looked, his eyelashes quivered and a little flush came into his marble cheeks.

'Look at me!' commanded the lady.

'No,' said the girl again. 'I shall look only at him, for only then can I bear the pain I feel.'

She ached as the blood froze in her body, but she held on, for she could also see that the prince was slowly coming to life. He opened his eyes and looked round him in amazement. Then he saw the maiden. He could not speak, but he looked earnestly at her, as if to say: 'Keep it up a little longer. I shall be free soon and we will go away together.' The maiden wanted to answer but she could not, for her lips were frozen and not a sound came from her mouth.

At last the prince stood up and took the girl in his arms. He carried her back into the icy passage and walked through the snow and wind, straight to the palace. There he held the frozen maiden fast against his breast until the warmth of his heart restored her and she looked about.

'Where am I?' she asked in astonishment.

'You are in the king's palace,' answered the king, 'and here you will stay.'

And it was as the king had said.

Now the prince put on his best clothes and knelt at the maiden's bedside.

'Will you marry me?' he asked.

She only nodded, for talking was not easy yet, but that was enough. And they were married and were very happy. The fiddle, the dagger and the golden mug were placed on a velvet cushion and whenever the prince and princess had visitors they told their story. And if people found it hard to believe, after all, they could prove it.

This story has nothing to do with the winter, for it comes from a country who do not know winter as we know it. Tayeb Salih is a Sudanese. This is a story which needs reading very carefully for Tayeb Salih has a great deal to say which you might miss. The author is a Mohammedan and you need to remember this because it will help you to understand how his mind works.

TAYEB SALIH

A Handful of Dates

I must have been very young at the time. While I don't remember exactly how old I was, I do remember that when people saw me with my grandfather they would pat me on the head and give my cheek a pinch—things they didn't do to my grandfather. The strange thing was that I never used to go out with my father, rather it was my grandfather who would take me with him wherever he went, except for the mornings when I would go to the mosque to learn the Koran. The mosque, the river and the fields—these were the landmarks in our life. While most of the children of my age grumbled at having to go to the mosque to learn the Koran, I used to love it. The reason was, no doubt, that

I was quick at learning by heart and the Sheikh always asked me to stand up and recite the Chapter of the Merciful whenever we had visitors, who would pat me on the head and cheek just as people did when they saw me with my grandfather.

Yes, I used to love the mosque, and I loved the river too. Directly we finished our Koran reading in the morning I would throw down my wooden slate and dart off, quick as a genie, to my mother, hurriedly swallow down my breakfast, and run off for a plunge in the river. When tired of swimming about I would sit on the bank and gaze at the strip of water that wound away eastwards and hid behind a thick wood of acacia trees. I loved to give rein to my imagination and picture to myself a tribe of giants living behind that wood, a people tall and thin with white beards and sharp noses, like my grandfather. Before my grandfather ever replied to my many questions he would rub the tip of his nose with his forefinger: as for his beard, it was soft and luxuriant and as white as cotton wool—never in my life have I seen anything of a purer whiteness or greater beauty. My grandfather must also have been extremely tall, for I never saw anyone in the whole area address him without having to look up at him, nor did I see him enter a house without having to bend so low that I was put in the mind of the way the river wound round behind the wood of acacia trees. I loved him and would imagine myself, when I grew to be a man, tall and slender like him, walking along with great strides.

I believe I was his favourite grandchild: no wonder, for my cousins were a stupid bunch and I—so they say—was an intelligent child. I used to know when my grandfather wanted me to laugh, when to be silent; also I would remember the times for his prayers and would bring him his prayer rug and fill the ewer for ablutions without his having to ask me. When he had nothing else to do he enjoyed listening to me reciting to him from the Koran in a lilting voice, and I could tell from his face that he was moved.

One day I asked him about our neighbour Masood. I said to my grandfather: 'I fancy you don't like our neighbour Masood?'

To which he answered, having rubbed the tip of his nose: 'He's an indolent man and I don't like such people.'

I said to him: 'What's an indolent man?'

My grandfather lowered his head for a moment, then looking across at the wide expanse of field, he said: 'Do you see it stretching out from the edge of the desert up to the Nile Bank? A hundred feddans. Do you see all those date palms? And those trees—sant, acacia, and sayal? All this fell into Masood's lap, was inherited by him from his father.'

Taking advantage of the silence that had descended upon my grandfather, I turned my gaze from him to the vast area defined by his words. 'I don't care,' I told myself, 'who owns those date palms, those trees or this black, cracked earth—all I know is that it's the arena for my dreams and my playground.'

My grandfather then continued: 'Yes, my boy, forty years ago all this belonged to Masood—two-thirds of it is now mine.'

This was news to me for I had imagined that the land had belonged to my grandfather ever since God's creation.

'I didn't own a single feddan when I first set foot in this village. Masood was then the owner of all these riches. The position has changed now, though, and I think that before Allah calls me to Him I shall have bought the remaining third as well.'

I do not know why it was I felt fear at my grandfather's words—and pity for our neighbour Masood. How I wished my grandfather wouldn't do what he said! I remembered Masood's singing, his beautiful voice and powerful laugh that resembled the gurgling of water. My grandfather never used to laugh.

I asked my grandfather why Masood had sold his land.

'Women,' and from the way my grandfather pronounced the word I felt that 'women' was something terrible. 'Masood, my boy, was a much-married man. Each time he married he sold me a feddan or two.' I made the quick calculation that Masood must have married some ninety women. Then I remembered his three wives, his shabby appearance, his lame donkey and its dilapidated saddle, his galabia with the torn sleeves. I had all but rid my mind of the thoughts that jostled in it when I

saw the man approaching us, and my grandfather and I exchanged glances.

'We'll be harvesting the dates today,' said Masood. 'Don't you want to be there?'

I felt, though, that he did not really want my grandfather to attend. My grandfather, however, jumped to his feet and I saw that his eyes sparkled momentarily with an intense brightness. He pulled me by the hand and we went off to the harvesting of Masood's dates.

Someone brought my grandfather a stool covered with an oxhide, while I remained standing. There was a vast number of people there, but though I knew them all I found myself for some reason watching Masood: aloof from that great gathering of people he stood as though it were no concern of his, despite the fact that the date palms to be harvested were his own. Sometimes his attention would be caught by the sound of a huge clump of dates crashing down from on high. Once he shouted up at the boy perched on the very summit of the date palm who had begun hacking at a clump with his long, sharp sickle: 'Be careful you don't cut the heart of the palm.'

No one paid any attention to what he said and the boy seated at the very summit of the date palm continued, quickly and energetically, to work away at the branch with his sickle till the clump of dates began to drop like something descending from the heavens.

I, however, had begun to think about Masood's phrase 'the heart of the palm'. I pictured the palm tree as something with feeling, something possessed of a heart that throbbed. I remembered Masood's remark to me when he had once seen me playing about with the branch of a young palm tree: 'Palm trees, my boy, like humans, experience joy and suffering.' And I had felt an inward and unreasoned embarrassment.

When I again looked at the expanse of ground stretching before me I saw my young companions swarming like ants around the trunks of the palm trees, gathering up dates and eating most of them. The dates were collected into high mounds. I saw people coming along and weighing them into measuring bins and pouring them into sacks, of which I counted thirty. The crowd of people broke up, except for Hussein the merchant, Mousa the owner of the field next to ours on the east, and two men I'd never seen before.

I heard a low whistling sound and saw that my grandfather had fallen asleep. Then I noticed that Masood had not changed his stance, except that he had placed a stalk in his mouth and was munching at it like someone surfeited with food who doesn't know what to do with the mouthful he still has.

Suddenly my grandfather woke up, jumped to his feet and walked towards the sacks of dates. He was followed by Hussein the merchant, Mousa the owner of the field next to ours, and the two strangers. I glanced at Masood and saw that he was making his way towards us with extreme slowness, like a man who wants to retreat but whose feet insist on going forward. They formed a circle round the sacks of dates and began examining them, some taking a date or two to eat. My grandfather gave me a fistful, which I began munching. I saw Masood filling the palms of both hands with dates and bringing them up close to his nose, then returning them.

Then I saw them dividing up the sacks between them. Hussein the merchant took ten, each of the strangers took five. Mousa the owner of the field next to ours on the eastern side took five, and my grandfather took five. Understanding nothing, I looked at Masood and saw that his eyes were darting about to left and right like two mice that have lost their way home.

'You're still fifty pounds in debt to me,' said my grandfather to Masood. 'We'll talk about it later.'

Hussein called his assistants and they brought along donkeys, the two strangers produced camels, and the sacks of dates were loaded onto them. One of the donkeys let out a braying which set the camels frothing at the mouth and complaining noisily. I felt myself drawing close to Masood, felt my hand stretch out toward him as though I wanted to touch the hem of his garment. I heard him make a noise in his throat like the rasping of a lamb being slaughtered. For some unknown reason, I experienced a sharp sensation of pain in my chest.

I ran off into the distance. Hearing my grandfather call after me, I hesitated a little, then continued on my way. I felt at that moment that I hated him. Quickening my pace, it was as though I carried within me a secret I wanted to rid myself of. I reached the river bank near the bend it made behind the wood of acacia trees. Then, without knowing why, I put my finger into my throat and spewed up the dates I'd eaten.

I am sure you have read many of Sir Arthur Conan Doyle's mystery stories. Here is a Sherlock Holmes story which you may have missed. It is a terrible story, but thrilling because it keeps you guessing.

SIR ARTHUR CONAN DOYLE

The Veiled Lodger

When one considers that Mr Sherlock Holmes was in active practice for twenty-three years, and that during seventeen of these I was allowed to co-operate with him and to keep notes of his doings, it will be clear that I have a mass of material at my command. The problem has always been, not to find, but to choose. There is the long row of year-books which fill a shelf, and there are the dispatch-cases filled with documents, a perfect quarry for the student, not only of crime, but of the social and official scandals of the late Victorian era. Concerning these latter, I may say that the writers of agonized letters, who beg that the honour of their families or the reputation of famous forbears may not be touched, have nothing to fear. The discretion and high sense of professional honour which have always distinguished my friend are still at work in the choice of these memoirs, and no confidence will be abused. I deprecate, however, in the strongest way the attempts which have been made lately to get at and to destroy these papers. The source of these outrages is known, and if they are repeated I have Mr Holmes's authority for saying that the whole story concerning the politician, the lighthouse and the trained cormorant will be given to the public. There is at least one reader who will understand.

It is not reasonable to suppose that every one of these cases gave Holmes the opportunity of showing those curious gifts of instinct and observation which I have endeavoured to set forth in these memoirs. Sometimes he had with much effort to pick the fruit, sometimes it fell easily into his lap. But the most terrible human tragedies were often involved in these cases which brought him the fewest personal opportunities, and it is one of these which I now desire to record. In telling it, I have made a slight change of name and place, but otherwise the facts are as stated.

One forenoon—it was late in 1896—I received a hurried note from Holmes asking for my attendance. When I arrived, I found him seated in a smoke-laden atmosphere, with an elderly, motherly woman of the buxom landlady type in the corresponding chair in front of him.

'This is Mrs Merrilow, of South Brixton,' said my friend, with a wave of the hand. 'Mrs Merrilow does not object to tobacco, Watson, if you wish to indulge your filthy habits. Mrs Merrilow has an interesting story to tell which may well lead to further developments in which your presence may be useful.'

'Anything I can do——'

'You will understand, Mrs Merrilow, that if I come to Mrs Ronder I should prefer to have a witness. You will make her understand that before we arrive.'

'Lord bless you, Mr Holmes,' said our visitor; 'she is that anxious to see you that you might bring the whole parish at your heels!'

'Then we shall come early in the afternoon. Let us see that we have our facts correct before we start. If we go over them it will help Dr Watson to understand the situation. You say that

Mrs Ronder has been your lodger for seven years and that you have only once seen her face.'

'And I wish to God I had not!' said Mrs Merrilow.

'It was, I understand, terribly mutilated.'

'Well, Mr Holmes, you would hardly say it was a face at all. That's how it looked. Our milkman got a glimpse at her once peeping out of the upper window, and he dropped his tin and the milk all over the front garden. That is the kind of face it is. When I saw her—I happened on her unawares—she covered up quick, and then she said, "Now, Mrs Merrilow, you know at last why it is that I never raise my veil."'

'Do you know anything about her history?'

'Nothing at all.'

'Did she give references when she came?'

'No, sir, but she gave hard cash, and plenty of it. A quarter's rent right down on the table in advance and no arguing about terms. In these times a poor woman like me can't afford to turn down a chance like that.'

'Did she give any reason for choosing your house?'

'Mine stands well back from the road and is more private than most. Then, again, I only take the one, and I have no family of my own. I reckon she had tried others and found that mine suited her best. It's privacy she is after, and she is ready to pay for it.'

'You say that she never showed her face from first to last save on the one accidental occasion. Well, it is a very remarkable story, most remarkable, and I don't wonder that you want it examined.'

'I don't, Mr Holmes. I am quite satisfied so long as I get my rent. You could not have a quieter lodger or one who gives less trouble.'

'Then what has brought matters to a head?'

'Her health, Mr Holmes. She seems to be wasting away. And there's something terrible on her mind. "Murder!" she cries. "Murder!" And once I heard her, "You cruel beast! You monster!" she cried. It was in the night, and it fair rang through the house and sent the shivers through me. So I went to her in the morning. "Mrs Ronder," I says, "if you have anything that is troubling your soul, there's the clergy," I says, "and there's the police. Between them you should get some help." "For God's sake, not the police!" says she, "and the clergy can't change what is past. And yet," she says, "it would ease my mind if someone knew the truth before I died." "Well," says I, "if you won't have the regulars, there is this detective man what we read about" —beggin' your pardon, Mr Holmes. And she, she fair jumped at it. "That's the man," says she. "I wonder I never thought of it before. Bring him here, Mrs Merrilow, and if he won't come, tell him I am the wife of Ronder's wild beast show. Say that, and give him the name Abbas Parva." Here it is as she wrote it, Abbas Parva. "That will bring him, if he's the man I think he is."'

'And it will, too,' remarked Holmes. 'Very good, Mrs Merrilow. I should like to have a little chat with Dr Watson. That will carry us till lunch-time. About three o'clock you may expect to see us at your house in Brixton.'

Our visitor had no sooner waddled out of the room—no other verb can describe Mrs Merrilow's method of progression —than Sherlock Holmes threw himself with fierce energy upon the pile of commonplace books in the corner. For a few minutes there was a constant swish of the leaves, and then with a grunt of satisfaction he came upon what he sought. So excited was he that he did not rise, but sat upon the floor like some strange Buddha, with crossed legs, the huge books all round him, and one open upon his knees.

'The case worried me at the time, Watson. Here are my marginal notes to prove it. I confess that I could make nothing of it. And yet I was convinced that the coroner was wrong. Have you no recollection of the Abbas Parva tragedy?'

'None, Holmes.'

'And yet you were with me then. But certainly my own impression was very superficial, for there was nothing to go by, and none of the parties had engaged my services. Perhaps you would care to read the papers?'

'Could you not give me the points?'

'That is very easily done. It will probably come back to

your memory as I talk. Ronder, of course, was a household word. He was the rival of Wombwell, and of Sanger, one of the greatest showmen of his day. There is evidence, however, that he took to drink, and that both he and his show were on the down grade at the time of the great tragedy. The caravan had halted for the night at Abbas Parva, which is a small village in Berkshire, when this horror occurred. They were on their way to Wimbledon, travelling by road, and they were simply camping, and not exhibiting, as the place is so small a one that it would not have paid them to open.

'They had among their exhibits a very fine North African lion. Sahara King was its name, and it was the habit, both of Ronder and his wife, to give exhibitions inside its cage. Here, you see, is a photograph of the performance, by which you will perceive that Ronder was a huge porcine person and that his wife was a very magnificent woman. It was deposed at the inquest that there had been some signs that the lion was dangerous, but, as usual, familiarity begat contempt, and no notice was taken of the fact.

'It was usual for either Ronder or his wife to feed the lion at night. Sometimes one went, sometimes both, but they never allowed anyone else to do it, for they believed that so long as they were the food-carriers he would regard them as benefactors, and would never molest them. On this particular night, seven years ago, they both went, and a very terrible happening followed, the details of which have never been made clear.

'It seems that the whole camp was roused near midnight by the roars of the animal and the screams of the woman. The different grooms and *employés* rushed from their tents, carrying lanterns, and by their light an awful sight was revealed. Ronder lay, with the back of his head crushed in and deep claw-marks across his scalp, some ten yards from the cage, which was open. Close to the door of the cage lay Mrs Ronder, upon her back, with the creature squatting and snarling above her. It had torn her face in such a fashion that it was never thought that she could live. Several of the circus men, headed by Leonardo, the strong man, and Griggs, the clown, drove the creature off with poles, upon which it sprang back into the cage, and was at once locked in. How it had got loose was a mystery. It was conjectured that the pair intended to enter the cage, but that when the door was loosed the creature bounded out upon them. There was no other point of interest in the evidence, save that the woman in a delirium of agony kept screaming, "Coward! Coward!" as she was carried back to the van in which they lived. It was six months before she was fit to give evidence, but the inquest was duly held, with the obvious verdict of death from misadventure.'

'What alternative could be conceived?' said I.

'You may well say so. And yet there were one or two points which worried young Edmunds, of the Berkshire Constabulary. A smart lad that! He was sent later to Allahabad. That was how I came into the matter, for he dropped in and smoked a pipe or two over it.'

'A thin, yellow-haired man?'

'Exactly. I was sure you would pick up the trail presently.'

'But what worried him?'

'Well, we were both worried. It was so deucedly difficult to reconstruct the affair. Look at it from the lion's point of view. He is liberated. What does he do? He takes half a dozen bounds forward, which brings him to Ronder. Ronder turns to fly—the claw-marks were on the back of his head—but the lion strikes him down. Then, instead of bounding on and escaping, he returns to the woman, who was close to the cage, and he knocks her over and chews her face up. Then, again, those cries of hers would seem to imply that her husband had in some way failed her. What could the poor devil have done to help her? You see the difficulty?'

'Quite.'

'And then there was another thing. It comes back to me now as I think it over. There was some evidence that, just at the time the lion roared and the woman screamed, a man began shouting in terror.'

'This man Ronder, no doubt.'

'Well, if his skull was smashed in you would hardly expect to hear from him again. There were at least two witnesses who spoke of the cries of a man being mingled with those of a woman.'

'I should think the whole camp was crying out by then. As to the other points, I think I could suggest a solution.'

'I should be glad to consider it.'

'The two were together, ten yards from the cage, when the lion got loose. The man turned and was struck down. The woman conceived the idea of getting into the cage and shutting the door. It was her only refuge. She made for it, and just as she reached it the beast bounded after her and knocked her over. She was angry with her husband for having encouraged the beast's rage by turning. If they had faced it, they might have cowed it. Hence her cries of "Coward!"'

'Brilliant, Watson! Only one flaw in your diamond.'

'What is the flaw, Holmes?'

'If they were both ten paces from the cage, how came the beast to get loose?'

'Is it possible that they had some enemy who loosed it?'

'And why should it attack them savagely when it was in the habit of playing with them, and doing tricks with them inside the cage?'

'Possibly the same enemy had done something to enrage it.'

Holmes looked thoughtful and remained in silence for some moments.

'Well, Watson, there is this to be said for your theory. Ronder was a man of many enemies. Edmunds told me that in his cups he was horrible. A huge bully of a man, he cursed and slashed at everyone who came in his way. I expect those cries about a monster, of which our visitor has spoken, were nocturnal reminiscences of the dear departed. However, our speculations are futile until we have all the facts. There is a cold partridge on the sideboard, Watson, and a bottle of Montrachet. Let us renew our energies before we make a fresh call upon them.'

When our hansom deposited us at the house of Mrs Merrilow, we found that plump lady blocking up the open door of her humble but retired abode. It was very clear that her chief preoccupation was lest she should lose a valuable lodger, and she implored us, before showing us up, to say and do nothing which could lead to so undesirable an end. Then, having reassured her, we followed her up the straight, badly-carpeted staircase and were shown into the room of the mysterious lodger.

It was a close, musty, ill-ventilated place, as might be expected, since its inmate seldom left it. From keeping beasts in a cage, the woman seemed, by some retribution of Fate, to have become herself a beast in a cage. She sat now in a broken armchair in the shadowy corner of the room. Long years of inaction had coarsened the lines of her figure, but at some period it must have been beautiful, and was still full and voluptuous. A thick dark veil covered her face, but it was cut off close at her upper lip, and disclosed a perfectly-shaped mouth and a delicately-rounded chin. I could well conceive that she had indeed been a very remarkable woman. Her voice, too, was well-modulated and pleasing.

'My name is not unfamiliar to you, Mr Holmes,' said she. 'I thought that it would bring you.'

'That is so, madam, though I do not know how you are aware that I was interested in your case.'

'I learned it when I had recovered my health and was examined by Mr Edmunds, the County detective. I fear I lied to him. Perhaps it would have been wiser had I told the truth.'

'It is usually wiser to tell the truth. But why did you lie to him?'

'Because the fate of someone else depended upon it. I know that he was a very worthless being, and yet I would not have his destruction upon my conscience. We had been so close—so close!'

'But has this impediment been removed?'

'Yes, sir. The person that I allude to is dead.'

'Then why should you not now tell the police anything you know?'

'Because there is another person to be considered. That other person is myself. I could not stand the scandal and publicity which would come from a police examination. I have not long to live, but I wish to die undisturbed. And yet I wanted to find one man of judgment to whom I could tell my terrible story, so that when I am gone all might be understood.'

'You compliment me, madam. At the same time, I am a responsible person. I do not promise you that when you have spoken I may not myself think it my duty to refer the case to the police.'

'I think not, Mr Holmes. I know your character and methods too well, for I have followed your work for some years. Reading is the only pleasure which Fate has left me, and I miss little which passes in the world. But in any case, I will take my chance of the use which you may make of my tragedy. It will ease my mind to tell it.'

'My friend and I would be glad to hear it.'

The woman rose and took from a drawer the photograph of a man. He was clearly a professional acrobat, a man of magnificent physique, taken with his huge arms folded across his swollen chest and a smile breaking from under his heavy moustache—the self-satisfied smile of the man of many conquests.

'That is Leonardo,' she said.

'Leonardo, the strong man, who gave evidence?'

'The same. And this—this is my husband.'

It was a dreadful face—a human pig, or rather a human wild boar, for it was formidable in its bestiality. One could imagine that vile mouth champing and foaming in its rage, and one could conceive those small, vicious eyes darting pure malignancy as they looked forth upon the world. Ruffian, bully, beast—it was all written on that heavy-jowled face.

'Those two pictures will help you, gentlemen, to understand the story. I was a poor circus girl brought up on the sawdust, and doing springs through the hoop before I was ten. When I became a woman this man loved me, if such lust as his can be called love, and in an evil moment I became his wife. From that day I was in hell, and he the devil who tormented me. There was no one in the show who did not know of his treatment. He deserted me for others. He tied me down and lashed me with his riding-whip when I complained. They all pitied me and they all

loathed him, but what could they do? They feared him, one and all. For he was terrible at all times, and murderous when he was drunk. Again and again he was had for assault, and for cruelty to the beasts, but he had plenty of money and the fines were nothing to him. The best men all left us and the show began to go downhill. It was only Leonardo and I who kept it up—with little Jimmy Griggs, the clown. Poor devil, he had not much to be funny about, but he did what he could to hold things together.

'Then Leonardo came more and more into my life. You see what he was like. I know now the poor spirit that was hidden in that splendid body, but compared to my husband he seemed like the Angel Gabriel. He pitied me and helped me, till at last our intimacy turned to love—deep, deep, passionate love, such love as I had dreamed of but never hoped to feel. My husband suspected it, but I think that he was a coward as well as a bully, and that Leonardo was the one man that he was afraid of. He took revenge in his own way by torturing me more than ever.

One night my cries brought Leonardo to the door of our van. We were near tragedy that night, and soon my lover and I understood that it could not be avoided. My husband was not fit to live. We planned that he should die.

'Leonardo had a clever, scheming brain. It was he who planned it. I do not say that to blame him, for I was ready to go with him every inch of the way. But I should never have had the wit of such a plan. We made a club—Leonardo made it—and in the leaden head he fastened five long steel nails, the points outwards, with just such a spread as the lion's paw. This was to give my husband his death-blow, and yet to leave the evidence that it was the lion which we would loose who had done the deed.

'It was a pitch-dark night when my husband and I went down, as was our custom, to feed the beast. We carried with us the raw meat in a zinc pail. Leonardo was waiting at the corner of the big van which we should have to pass before we reached the cage. He was too slow, and we walked past him before he could strike, but he followed us on tiptoe and I heard the crash as the club smashed my husband's skull. My heart leaped with joy at the sound. I sprang forward, and I undid the catch which held the door of the great lion's cage.

'And then the terrible thing happened. You may have heard how quick these creatures are to scent human blood, and how it excites them. Some strange instinct had told the creature in one instant that a human being had been slain. As I slipped the bars it bounded out, and was on me in an instant. Leonardo could have saved me. If he had rushed forward and struck the beast with his club he might have cowed it. But the man lost his nerve. I heard him shout in his terror, and then I saw him turn and fly. At the same instant the teeth of the lion met in my face. Its hot, filthy breath had already poisoned me and I was hardly conscious of pain. With the palms of my hands I tried to push the great steaming, blood-stained jaws away from me, and I screamed for help. I was conscious that the camp was stirring, and then dimly I remember a group of men, Leonardo, Griggs and others, dragging me from under the creature's paws. That was my last memory, Mr Holmes, for many a weary month. When I came to myself, and saw myself in the mirror, I cursed that lion—oh, how I cursed him—not because he had torn away my beauty, but because he had not torn away my life. I had but one desire, Mr Holmes, and I had enough money to gratify it. It was that I should cover myself so that my poor face should be seen by none, and that I should dwell where none whom I had ever known should find me. That was all that was left to me to do— d that is what I have done. A poor wounded beast that has wled into its hole to die—that is the end of Eugenia Ronder.'

We sat in silence for some time after the unhappy woman had told her story. Then Holmes stretched out his long arm and patted her hand with such a show of sympathy as I had seldom known him to exhibit.

'Poor girl!' he said. 'Poor girl! The ways of Fate are indeed hard to understand. If there is not some compensation hereafter, then the world is a cruel jest. But what of this man Leonardo?'

'I never saw him or heard from him again. Perhaps I have been wrong to feel so bitterly against him. He might as soon have loved one of the freaks whom we carried round the country as the thing which the lion had left. But a woman's love is not so easily set aside. He had left me under the beast's claws, he had deserted me in my need, and yet I could not bring myself to give him to the gallows. For myself, I cared nothing what became of me. What could be more dreadful than my actual life? But I stood between Leonardo and his fate.'

'And he is dead?'

'He was drowned last month when bathing near Margate. I saw his death in the paper.'

'And what did he do with this five-clawed club, which is the most singular and ingenious part of all your story?'

'I cannot tell, Mr Holmes. There is a chalk-pit by the camp, with a deep green pool at the base of it. Perhaps in the depths of that pool——'

'Well, well, it is of little consequence now. The case is closed.'

'Yes,' said the woman, 'the case is closed.'

We had risen to go, but there was something in the woman's

voice which arrested Holmes's attention. He turned swiftly upon her.

'Your life is not your own,' he said. 'Keep your hands off it.'

'What use is it to anyone?'

'How can you tell? The example of patient suffering is in itself the most precious of all lessons to an impatient world.'

The woman's answer was a terrible one. She raised her veil and stepped forward into the light.

'I wonder if you would bear it,' she said.

It was horrible. No words can describe the framework of a face when the face itself is gone. Two living and beautiful brown eyes looking out from that grisly ruin did but make the view more awful. Holmes held up his hand in a gesture of pity and protest, and together we left the room.

Two days later, when I called upon my friend, he pointed with some pride to a small blue bottle upon his mantelpiece. I picked it up. There was on it a red poison label. A pleasant almondy odour rose when I opened it.

'Prussic acid?' said I.

'Exactly. It came by post. "I send you my temptation. I will follow your advice." That was the message. I think, Watson, we can guess the name of the brave woman who sent it.'

People like me who write books often get letters from strangers. The letters are of all types, but by far the largest are written by people who want to know what happens next to some characters in a book in whom they have become interested. The real answer is nothing happens next. An author has planned what his or her book is about and when they reach the end that, as far as they are concerned, is the finish. Of course this does not apply to authors who write serials: they can write perhaps as many as six books about the same characters.

Of all the books I have written none has brought in as many requests for a sequel as a book I wrote called Ballet Shoes. *For those of you who have not read it, the story is about three babies who were adopted by an old man who collected fossils. His name was Great Uncle Matthew or G.U.M. for short.*

Great Uncle Matthew had a great-niece who lived with him in a house in the Cromwell Road, London. She was called Sylvia, and she and her old nurse, called Nana, together with a cook and a housemaid called Clara, ran the house for Gum. This, in his fossil-collecting days, was quite a job, for he travelled a lot and brought back hundreds of fossils, some very large which he parked all over the house. In fact the house would have been full of fossils and nothing else if it had not been for Nana, who now and then would make Sylvia tell her uncle that not another fossil came into the house until a large number had gone out. Gum hated parting with a fossil, but when Nana got firm he had to. Then workmen would arrive with crates and in time there would be a notice in The Times *saying that Professor Matthew Brown had given another generous gift of fossils to a museum.*

One year poor Gum, when fossil hunting on a mountain, had a terrible fall, as a result of which he lost a leg. That put an end to his fossil hunting for good but not to his travels, for he decided to see the world by sea. That is how the first baby came to the house. Gum's ship struck an iceberg and all the passengers had to take to the boats. One of the boats overturned and everybody was drowned except a baby found coo-ing in a life belt. Gum, used to collectiug things, picked up the baby, wrapped her in his coat and, when they were rescued, took her to the Cromwell Road.

The baby was christened Pauline after St Paul who, you remember, had also been rescued from the sea. Gum argued a bit because he wanted her called after a famous fossil, but Nana said:

'Babies in my nurseries, sir, never have had outlandish names, and they're not starting now. Miss Sylvia has chosen a nice sensible name, and called after a blessed saint, and no other name is going to be used, if you'll forgive me speaking plain, sir.'

A year later Gum turned up with a second baby. He had found this one in a hospital where he had gone to have urgent treatment for his leg. There he made friends with a poor young Russian whose wife had died giving birth when her baby was born. To Gum it was a matter of course, when the young Russian also died, that he should adopt the baby.

'We have a baby at home that I have adopted,' he said. 'We shall have another.'

The new baby was called Petrova. Nana accepted her quite calmly.

'Very nice for Pauline to have a companion,' then she added: 'Let's hope this one has brains, for it's easy to see who's going to be Miss Plain in my nursery.'

But to Gum she spoke very firmly.

'Now, sir—two babies in the nursery is right and proper, and such as the best homes have a right to expect, but two is enough. Bring one more and I give notice.'

Probably it was fear of what Nana would say that made Gum send the third and last baby by district messenger. She arrived in a basket and with her came a note and a little pair of ballet shoes. Gum said in the note that he was sorry not to bring the baby himself, but he was off on a friend's yacht to visit some strange island. He was expecting to be away for some years. He had arranged for the bank to see Sylvia had all the money she needed for five years. About the baby he said that her mother was a dancer and her name was Posy, to which he added: 'Unfortunate but true.'

About four months later a parcel arrived addressed to 'The Little Fossils'. In it were three necklaces—a turquoise one for Pauline, a string of tiny seed pearls for Petrova and a string of coral for Posy.

'Well,' said Nana, 'I expect that's the last of him we shall hear for some time.'

She was quite right.

Gum did not come back in five years, so the bank stopped paying Sylvia money. To help out she took in boarders: two Doctors of

Literature, a Mr and Mrs Simpson from Malaya and a Miss Theo Dane who taught dancing at The Children's Academy of Dancing and Stage Training.

It was these boarders who changed the children's lives. Theo Dane got them into the theatrical school where she taught. Mr Simpson encouraged Petrova in her love of engines and the Doctors of Literature gave the children lessons. Still Gum didn't come home and often money was very tight, so as soon as Pauline and Petrova were old enough they became professional child actors. Posy, who was the dancer of the family, did not appear professionally, for she was not old enough when the book finished.

Now we come to the end of the book about which children write and ask 'What happened?'

First I must explain what had happened. Pauline had acted in a film and had been an instant success. Posy, who showed signs that she might be a great dancer, had sneaked off alone to persuade a Monsieur Manoff, whose Czechoslovakian ballet was visiting London, to see her dance. Petrova, whose eyes were always on the stars, knew there was only one career for her and that was to be a flier.

In the last scene in the book a film agent is with Sylvia trying to persuade her to bring Pauline to California. Pauline can't make up her mind, even for a lot of money, to break up the family. Posy is still out and no one knows where. Pauline and Petrova are discussing Pauline's film offer when Posy, hysterical with happiness, rushes in to say Manoff will take her as a pupil in his dancing school in Czechoslovakia.

Petrova gasped:

'But, Posy, how do you think Garnie'—which is what the children called Sylvia—'is going to afford to send you there?'

Posy was past reason.

'She'll have to get the money. I must go. I must.'

That was when Pauline knew the answer.

'You shall go, Posy,' she said, and went back into the other room and told Garnie to sign her contract.

'That's settled,' she said to Posy when she came out. 'I'm going to make an awful lot of money, enough to keep you and

Nana in Czechoslovakia as well as Garnie and me in Hollywood.'

Petrova managed not to cry, but she did wonder what was to become of her.

It was then Gum came back. He stamped in expecting to find everything just as he had left it, including three babies in the nursery. Of course the girls soon put him wise.

'I'm going to Hollywood with Garnie to be a film star,' Pauline told him.

'And I'm going to Czechoslovia with Nana to train for ballet under Manoff,' Posy said, thumping his good knee.

Gum looked at Petrova.

'That seems to leave you and me. What do you want to do?'

Posy answered for her.

'Flying and motor cars.'

'That suits me,' said Gum. 'Cook and Clara still here?' They told him they were. 'Good,' he said. 'Then they shall look after us. Might hire a car tomorrow, Petrova, and find a house near an aerodrome where you could study.'

I know that all these plans happened, but of course the children who read Ballet Shoes *do not. Now I am going to tell a little about the way things turned out for the three girls, and I hope in such a way that those of you who have not read the book are interested.*

NOEL STREATFEILD

What Happened to Pauline, Petrova and Posy

The first to leave were Sylvia and Pauline. In a way, although they all hated to say 'goodbye', it was a relief when Pauline was really off.

'There wouldn't be as much fuss if it was royalty moving,' Posy whispered to Petrova.

The film company was determined that as they intended to make a star of Pauline she should travel like one. A lady from the company arrived and for three days took Pauline shopping. Pauline had never worn outgrown clothes as Petrova and Posy had to do because she was the eldest. But during the years when they were poor while Gum was away she had cheap clothes, even for the first night of her film her frock was made at home by Nana. Pauline was now fifteen and the lady from the company made sure she was dressed as the most up-to-date teenager to be found anywhere.

Then there were interviews and photographs.

'They wear me out,' said Posy. 'Here's me chosen to join Manoff's ballet company but nobody cares, but because Pauline is going to Hollywood to make a film people from papers come all day long.'

However, at last the day of departure came. It was in May, so Pauline, looking lovely in a tweed travelling coat over a light-weight frock, stepped into a huge hire car. Her wonderful matching luggage all marked 'Pauline Fossil' was packed in by the chauffeur and she and Sylvia rolled away.

Nana had the last word:

'Don't forget. Wool next the skin, dear. Warm climates can be treacherous.'

Posy left next. She and Nana in a taxi with their rather shabby suitcases piled beside the driver. Nobody could cry when Posy left, for she was radiant. They had not far to go,only to Victoria Station to join Monsieur Manoff and his ballet.

The final move was when pantechnicons came to fetch all the contents of the house in the Cromwell Road. When everything was gone Gum, Petrova, cook and Clara got into a car and drove to the midlands. There, until the house Gum had bought was ready for them, they stayed in an hotel. Petrova was in a daze of excitement, for near the new house was an aerodrome, and at the aerodrome a man called Nobby Clark who had undertaken to train her to be a mechanic. Already a governess called Miss Potter came daily to give her lessons.

'Can't have you going to a school,' Gum explained. 'You see, I'm used to travelling. Now if you want to you can come too and we'll take the Potter with us.'

Petrova, crooning over the overalls she was to wear when training at the aerodrome, could not imagine ever wanting to go away, but she could understand that Gum might.

'But if he does,' she told cook and Clara, 'we'll see we know where he is. We don't want him going away for years and leaving us with no money.'

The part for which Pauline had been given her Hollywood contract was the girl in an English book. The girl, who was called Sara, had run away from home when she found out that her father and mother no longer loved each other, so were not going to share a home any more. Sara adored both parents and the thought of living first with one and then with the other was more than she could bear. So she ran away to Europe where she got mixed up with extraordinary events. Of course in the end her father and mother, having found Sara, were so happy that they joined together again.

It is not easy to act in a film, as Pauline had found when she made her first. Then she had only played a small part, now she had the leading part. She was, of course, rehearsed by a coach, but that too was difficult. When Pauline understood why she was to say something in a certain way she could do it, but if she did not understand she would go on asking 'Why?' until she did understand. At first the coach thought Pauline a horrible girl, but later she came to see how her mind worked and then she and Pauline became friends. It was in fact largely due to her coach that Pauline made the enormous success in that first film that she did.

Her film being such a success Sylvia signed, on Pauline's behalf, a long contract. They rented a very nice house with a swimming pool on the lawn and bought a car and hired a chauffeur. 'It all sounds very grand,' Sylvia wrote to Petrova, 'but for Hollywood we live very simply.'

Two things Pauline insisted on. She must have a private governess. She would not go to the studio school and every eighteen months she must have time off to visit England and Czechoslovakia.

'After all,' she told Mr Silas B. Shoppenhanger, who owned the film company. 'I have two sisters and I must see them. We're family.'

Meanwhile in the midlands Petrova too was a success. She had taken examinations in mechanics and passed them with ease, and now she was promoted to studying aeroplane engines.

'You see,' she explained to Nobby on her fourteenth birthday, 'I want, as soon as I can, to get my pilot's licence. Then, the moment I am eighteen, I can fly alone.'

To Gum she said:

'You wait until I'm grown up—then, if you can buy a little aeroplane, I can fly you anywhere in the world you want to go. And we can visit Czechoslovakia and Hollywood on the way.'

Posy was superbly happy training under Manoff, which well she might be, for Manoff thought her a genius and did not hide how he felt.

'Posy,' he would say, 'soon I am taking this company to America. Before that happens you will be dancing for me. I plan two new ballets written specially for you.'

One plan came true. Pauline took a three months' break and did visit both Petrova and Gum and Nana and Posy. This was a great success. Pauline seemed unchanged. She always had been the star performer in the family and of course the eldest, and she still was. Cook and Clara were a bit in awe of her to start with, but they soon got over it when they found she still liked to come into the kitchen and sit on the table and talk to them.

Posy was charmed to see both Sylvia and Pauline again, but with her dancing was all her life. But Nana was thrilled to see them.

'Oh dear, Miss Sylvia, you wouldn't believe how I've counted the days until you came. Of course I'm glad Posy is doing so nicely at the dancing, but such a language they talk here. And the food! You wouldn't believe the trouble I have to get the simplest things, like oatmeal for porridge and treacle for puddings.'

Sylvia, listening, could see life was hard on Nana. She knew not a word of the language and made no effort to learn. What with school and dancing classes Posy was out all day. It must be a lonely life.

She thought things over and made a suggestion.

'I tell you what we'll do, Nana. We'll change places. You go back to Hollywood with Pauline and I'll stay here and look after Posy. We might at least try it out.'

That was what happened and it was a great success. It was also very fortunate, for the next year the war started which began in 1939.

To take a huge ballet company plus stage staff, wardrobe and scenery across the world takes immense organization at any time, but during a war it is a nightmare. Transport was hard to arrange and the company moved in isolated groups. Nana, without a word of the language, would have found things terribly difficult, but Sylvia took it in her stride and somehow arrived safely in New York with a wildly excited Posy.

For many of the ballet company life was to be very hard, for the war lasted five years and of course no theatre wanted to engage the company for that long. But Posy never suffered: when, having made a huge success in the new ballets, the company divided into small groups and went on tour, she and Sylvia went to stay with Pauline until the next ballet season started in New York.

As soon as she was old enough Petrova joined a flying service which transported new aeroplanes from the factory where they had been built to the air base which was waiting for them.

'I am so lucky,' she would say to Gum. 'I could so easily have been born at a time when girls didn't fly.'

When they were children living in the Cromwell Road the girls had made a vow on their birthdays. It was: 'We three Fossils vow to try and put our name in history books because it's our own and nobody can say it's because of our grandfather's.'

I don't know if the Fossils ever got their name in history books. Pauline certainly didn't—film stars don't. Posy would for ever be part of ballet history, but not I think ordinary history. Petrova? I don't know, but I sometimes wonder.

Jumble sales happen all the year round. They are enormously popular, people travel quite long distances to visit them. I have never known why because the ones I have attended never have objects of vast value going for 5p. But to many a jumble sale is a grand treasure hunt holding out splendid opportunities for making a fortune.

Miss Teazle in this next story was not selling jumble, but she had a white elephant stall, which can be the next best thing.

I have heard startling stories of the bargains people have found on white elephant stalls, but what I find is exactly the sort of things Miss Teazle was offered for her stall: two Cornish pottery jugs that leaked, a battered set of saucepans, a poached egg boiler, an old mincing machine, a fly swatter, a bunch of plastic daffodils, two jig-saw puzzles with several pieces missing, an egg timer attached to a fret-saw model of a crinolined lady and other equally useless rubbish. But Miss Teazle had advertised for white elephants for her stall. Now read Margaret J. Baker's story and see what turned up.

MARGARET J. BAKER

Miss Teazle and the White Elephants

'As white elephants it is best for us neither to be seen nor heard,' Trumpeter always told his youngest son, Little Hooter, and the other small elephants. 'That is how things have always been arranged.'

'From time immemorial,' added his mother, Blancmange, who was fat and comfortable, and wobbled when she walked just like a blancmange, especially from the back.

'We must keep ourselves to ourselves,' went on Trumpeter. 'It's best to stay in the very middle of this state forest where even the most lively parties from the picnic areas will never penetrate.'

The state forest where the white elephants lived was planted with conifer trees to be used one day as telephone poles, newspaper pulp and pit props in coal mines. Every December some of the smaller trees were thinned out and sold as Christmas trees. In the centre of the forest the fir trees made it almost dark and the troop of white elephants was private. Only at dawn or late at night the elephants took their exercise, marching up and down the long rides which separated one plantation of trees from the next. Sometimes the younger elephants broke into a canter or filled their trunks from the water tanks which were placed here and there in the forest ready to put out a forest fire. Little Hooter and the other young elephants squirted the water at each other while Blancmange, who had done the same thing herself in her younger days, pretended not to see, and Trumpeter strode forward breathing deeply and thinking of other things.

'But why do we have to keep ourselves to ourselves?' asked Little Hooter. 'Why can't we go out into the world to work like other elephants pushing and pulling heavy objects or giving rides in zoos and standing about for buns?'

'We have to keep ourselves to ourselves and remain unseen because we are white and different from all other elephants,' Trumpeter told him patiently. 'Only grey elephants are meant to work. It's not expected of us.'

'It happens that way,' said Blancmange before Little Hooter could question his father further, 'and I am sure we are all very contended and happy as we are.' She brushed some pine needles from Little Hooter's back as she spoke and straightened one of his ears which had flapped inside out.

The only time all the white elephants left the state forest was after a snowstorm when none of them would show—though people often puzzled over the sight of their round footprints in the crisp snow. Trumpeter's footprints were as big as a potato saucepan lid and Little Hooter's as large as a milk saucepan lid. The elephants were white all over from the tips of their trunks to the end of their tails. Only their eyes were bright blue like cornflowers.

Besides snowstorms, which he loved best of all, Little Hooter liked anything white. From the heart of the forest he sat watching the white clouds sail by high above the fir trees. He admired the white sheets and handkerchiefs, and Sunday shirts blowing on the washing lines of the cottages on the outskirts of the forest where the men who looked after the trees lived, and he was never tired of staring at the daisies, and tiger lilies and cabbage roses which they grew in their gardens.

Little Hooter was strong and determined. He could toss several pit props up into the air from the piles left beside the forest tracks for the lorries to collect. Trumpeter and Blancmange had to tidy the piles up later before the lorries arrived, but they did not grumble because playing with the logs was good exercise and it helped to keep Little Hooter amused. Even as it was, Little Hooter argued a lot and caused Trumpeter and Blancmange to swish their tails and flap their ears and breathe hard down their trunks, and to be as annoyed as a white elephant could be, which wasn't very much for they were kind and patient creatures. Little Hooter twirled small logs round and round in his trunk and caught the fir cones as they fell from the trees—

just for practice in case, one day, he might have the chance to do it in a real zoo for buns. Often he stared at himself in the water tanks and however long he looked he could never see anything wrong with being white.

On snowy mornings, long before anyone else was about, Little Hooter would leave the forest and walk down the village street looking in the shop windows and blowing on the glass. That was how he saw Miss Teazle's advertisement written on a postcard in her best italic writing, and fastened in the post office window with a piece of Sellotape.

White Elephants Urgently Wanted by Miss Teazle for her stall at the Christmas Bazaar in Aid of the Church Restoration Fund to be held in the Village Hall on December 20th at 2.30 p.m. Any gifts will be gratefully received—nothing will be too small or too large! Please send to Miss Teazle at the Nook or deliver to the Village Hall on the day of the Sale.

'And that's today,' Little Hooter told Blancmange and Trumpeter and all the other elephants with his blue eyes flashing. 'All we need to do is to report to the Hall. There are double doors so even the widest of us will be able to squeeze in.'

Miss Teazle was tall and thin with straight grey hair, a long kind face, a tweed trouser suit and flat-heeled brogue shoes. She was shy and didn't like bothering people for goods for her stall. That was why she had put up the card in the shop window so that her neighbours in the village could give her what they chose. So far, on the morning of the sale, they had only chosen to bring her two Cornish pottery jugs that leaked, a battered set of saucepans, a poached egg boiler, an old mincing machine, a fly swatter, a bunch of plastic daffodils, two jig-saw puzzles with several pieces missing, an egg timer attached to a fret-saw model of a crinolined lady, a toy panda with one loose ear, three tins marked SUGAR, FLOUR and SAGO, a cake plate engraved with a picture of a pop group, two lace mats from a dressing-table Duchess set, a white shoulder handbag with a broken zip and a press for men's neckties. The dictionary said white elephants were objects for which their owners had no further use, and looking at the contents of her stall Miss Teazle could well believe this to be true.

'Dear me, Miss Teazle, you don't seem to have been very fortunate,' Mrs Chumleigh from the Cake and Sweet Stall said, as she looked up from her own stall that was crowded with chocolate-layer cakes, meringues, fruit cakes, Victoria sponges, three varieties of fudge, coconut-ice and bright green peppermint creams. She strolled over and picked up the panda by his good ear, then put it hurriedly down again. 'However, no doubt one of the things will sell. It's amazing for what some folk will find houseroom.'

'And I must bring you along some padded coat-hangers and lavender-bags which are only a little the worse for wear,' said young Miss Spencer, who was in charge of the Fancy Goods stall next door. 'I really am a little pushed for space and they will brighten up your stall.'

'Wait till this afternoon, Miss Teazle, and some more white elephants are sure to come along,' said the Vicar cheerfully. 'On these occasions it's remarkable what sometimes turns up, especially at the last minute. I shouldn't be a bit surprised if you didn't do amazingly well.'

But that afternoon, even with the extra coat-hangers and lavender-bags, Miss Teazle didn't feel at all hopeful. No more had arrived for her stall but a fur tippet smelling of moth balls and a bundle of old magazines. For the sake of the Restoration Fund she wished that she had been bolder and had bothered more people to turn out their cupboards, and to give her more interesting merchandise for her stall. It was as she stared down at the egg timer and the tie press that the swing doors of the hall were pushed open. In the doorway, holding their breath to take up less room, stood Trumpeter with Blancmange beside him, while Little Hooter hung onto her tail, and all the other elephants stretched in a procession down the snowy village street.

The elephants were like great white clouds. They stood with their ears flapping gently and their blue eyes bright. Miss

Teazle blinked and blinked again. On the Cake and Sweet Stall Mrs Chumleigh paused with a packet of Turkish Delight pressed to her best Crimplene dress. At the Fancy Goods Miss Spencer upset a jar of bath-salts over a crocheted woollen tea cosy. The Scouts and Guides helping at the Bottle Stall and with the Raffles giggled and clapped, and the Vicar stood stock still, like a figure in an advertisement for a bedtime beverage.

When Trumpeter spoke the sound echoed all round the hall. Even the balloons and paper chains fastened to the rafters wobbled and rustled.

'Would you be so kind as to direct us to Miss Teazle's stall?' he asked the man taking the entrance money at the doors seated at a baize-topped bridge table. 'We do not pay to come in. My youngest son, Little Hooter here, saw a notice that Miss Teazle was in need of white elephants in the shop this morning and naturally we have all come along.'

'It distinctly said size was no objection,' added Blancmange, 'though if you are pushed for space I dare say one or two of the younger ones could wait outside.'

'But we should much rather come in,' said Little Hooter hurriedly. 'It's beginning to snow really hard now, and the flakes do melt when they lodge behind our ears.'

The man at the bridge table overturned a pile of two-pence pieces, and the table rocked as Little Hooter and the other young elephants pushed their way forward to stare longingly into the hall. At the Cake Stall Mrs Chumleigh gathered her cash box and the most expensive Walnut-Cream Layer cake in her arms, and Miss Spender at the Fancy Goods gave a stifled scream. Only Miss Teazle stepped forward. She loved all animals however large.

'What these elephants say is quite correct, Mr Parkinson,' she told the man at the door. 'My appeal in the post office was worded just as they have said, though I never dreamt it would produce such a generous response. Now if everyone will kindly make way I shall be most happy to escort these good animals to my stall. Please be so good as to step this way as carefully as you can,' she added to the elephants. 'It's most good of you to come and naturally there must be no question of even the smaller ones waiting outside, especially in this weather.'

'No doubt we shall be a little pressed for space,' said the Vicar coming suddenly to life and striding forward, 'but I'm sure if the other stall holders will all move their stalls up just a trifle we shall manage admirably and everyone can be fitted in. For the sake of St Martin's Restoration Fund I'm certain any little inconvenience will be well worth while.'

Led by Trumpeter and Blancmange the elephants moved in like white-topped breakers rolling up a sandy beach. Everyone shifted and pushed and pulled at the heavily laden trestle tables. On the tea tables cups and saucers were rearranged and plates stacked. Urns of tea and dishes of bread and butter, potted meat sandwiches and jammed cut-rounds were pushed hither and thither. Parents lifted their young children aloft, and latecomers peered through the windows as the elephants ranged themselves round Miss Teazle's stall. At either end Trumpeter and Blancmange stood with their forelegs on the table, and the rest of them bulging over the fruit and Chicken Dinner on the raffle stall, and the pot holders and poodle-shaped bottle covers on the Fancy Goods. Little Hooter stood with his brothers and sisters behind the stall or lay on the floor in front.

'Now I must write all your price tickets,' Miss Teazle told the elephants. 'There's no time to waste. The Bishop's wife will be arriving at any moment to declare the bazaar open, and then people will be able to choose what they want to buy.'

With a purple felt-tipped pen and a steady hand Miss Teazle wrote large labels to hang round the elephants' necks. She used the lids of the cardboard boxes in which she had packed her rummage, and a whole washing line and two skipping ropes in place of string.

'Would five pounds for the very largest of the elephants be fair?' she asked the Vicar. 'And I thought four for the medium size and three pounds for the smallest or five pounds for a pair.'

'That sounds very fair,' said the Vicar, 'and you can always reduce them later if they don't sell. We don't want too many things left on our hands.'

'Indeed not,' said Miss Teazle, as Little Hooter sat on the upright piano at the back of the stall and made a noise like thunder, but the Vicar's eyes were on the doors of the hall where the car belonging to the Bishop's wife had just drawn up, and he didn't even notice.

The Bishop's wife was tall and beautiful. Nothing would ever surprise her, or if it did she would be too well mannered ever to let it show. As the Vicar led her to the platform at the end of the hall the elephants stared in admiration and waved their trunks to sniff the scent that she wore. Afterwards Little Hooter always said that it was like all the most sweet scented white roses and tiger lilies and lilac blossom that he had ever smelt in one of the cottage gardens.

'Ladies and Gentlemen, Children and Other Helpers,' began the Bishop's wife after the Vicar had introduced her, 'this is the third bazaar I have opened today and quite the most splendid. Your hall is really a most astonishing and inspiring sight. I always tell the Bishop that when the parishioners of St Martin's really put their shoulders to the wheel and all push together anything can be accomplished. I can see that your hall is almost bursting with good things to buy. I hope you will all fling caution to the winds and open wide your hearts and your purses, and I have much pleasure in declaring this bazaar open.'

The people all clapped and the elephants led by Trumpeter flapped their ears and trumpeted. In the excitement Little Hooter swept up three bunches of bronze chrysanthemums from the Flower Stall in his trunk and, pushing his way through the crowd, he laid them at her feet.

'How very kind,' said the Bishop's wife. She smiled straight at Little Hooter and patted his trunk. Little Hooter bent his head and then hurried back to the stall, holding his breath so that he could still smell her scent for as long as possible.

'There was no cause to push yourself forward,' whispered Trumpeter.

£2

'I didn't push, at least not much,' retorted Hooter. 'Most people got out of the way—even that little girl who was meant to give her the bunch of violets and anenomes.'

At the White Elephant stall the reporter from the local newspaper, Mr Dash, in a red spotted tie and a corduroy jacket, interviewed Miss Teazle and took a flashlight photograph. To oblige, Little Hooter stood on his head, Trumpeter waggled his ears and Blancmange swung a green plastic salad shaker from side to side. The younger elephants all held balloons with PLEASE BUY OUR BETTER THAN BUTTER MARGARINE printed on them.

'Yes, real white elephants are a novelty,' Miss Teazle told the reporter, forgetting all about feeling shy. 'I have been very fortunate. They came as it were out of the blue. No, I had no idea there was a troop of them in the locality. It was a complete surprise when they all turned up in answer to my appeal for gifts for my stall. Such a result was beyond my wildest dreams.'

After the reporter had hurried away, and the Bishop's wife had made her last purchase before speeding on to her next bazaar, the hall was suddenly less crowded. The Cake and Sweet Stall was bare except for two rock cakes, the Fancy Goods Stall was also half empty but no one had bought a single elephant.

'You would have thought those priced at two pounds would have gone at least,' Trumpeter remarked quietly to his wife. 'Whichever way you look at it they're a real bargain and, though so small, they're bound to grow in time.'

'It's probably that people haven't had time to get used to the idea of buying one of us yet,' said Blancmange. 'When you've come to a bazaar with a kettle holder in mind, or a jar of pickled onions and a pot of strawberry jam, making the change to an elephant must be rather a wrench.'

Time and time again patrons of the bazaar lingered in front of the stall, but always the expectant elephants and Miss Teazle were disappointed.

'Do let us have one Mummy,' begged a little girl with freckles and a brace to straighten her front teeth.

'No, Peggy, we just haven't the space. With my Mini in the garage as well as Daddy's Jaguar, and your pony in the stables, there just wouldn't be the space,' said her mother.

'And think of the food great creatures like that would get through,' added a farmer's wife. 'It would be buns and bread and cabbages all day long and hay as well most likely, not to speak of the damage they'd do to the hedges.'

A bearded young man in sandals and his wife, in what seemed to be a long dressing-gown, stared at the elephants the longest, but even they turned away at last.

'Of course, Cleo, they're unusual,' said the young man, 'but I really think if we're to have an elephant in the studio grey would be a far more serviceable colour, and with a nicely jewelled howdah it would be every bit as decorative.'

Even Miss Teazle looked a little depressed, especially when Mrs Chumleigh strolled over from the empty cake stall rattling her cash box full of money.

'Dear me, none of your elephants sold yet,' she said. 'I did wonder if they'd really go. I'd take a couple off your hands myself if it wasn't for the Boxer and my two cats.'

'You'd be wise to halve the price,' advised Miss Spencer from the Fancy Goods. 'With everyone having tea and the raffles drawn not many people will come round the stalls now, and those that do always expect reductions.'

But Miss Teazle stood firm.

'Whoever heard of an elephant going for less than an excursion to the Zoo,' she said. 'Rather than reduce the price I'll take the lot of them home myself.'

And that is what she did. Aloft on Trumpeter, with all the remainder of the rummage packed into boxes, Miss Teazle led the procession of white elephants back to the Nook. Plodding through the darkness down the lane with snowflakes swirling round them all the elephants felt disappointed. Even with their margarine balloons still held in their trunks the younger elephants were tired and tearful.

'Now you can see why I've always insisted that we should keep ourselves to ourselves,' said Trumpeter. 'People may stare at us from curiosity but when it comes to the point no one really wants us.'

'Except Miss Teazle,' pointed out Little Hooter. 'She wouldn't reduce the price of one of us even by a halfpenny.'

Back at the Nook Miss Teazle did her best to cheer them up and to make them all comfortable. Far into the night she baked batches of buns in the oven of her small electric cooker. Fortunately she always baked her own bread and she had plenty of dried yeast and flour. Housing them all in the cottage was quite a problem. Trumpeter and Blancmange were bedded down in the garage and in a revolving summer-house in the garden, while Little Hooter and the smaller elephants crowded into the spare room, the living-room, the kitchen, the bathroom, and Miss Teazle's own bedroom. When they were all inside the cottage there was hardly room to turn round. The bath and the kitchen sink were filled with drinking water for the thirsty animals, and newspapers were spread on the floors to protect them from the elephants' muddy footprints. After one or two accidents the best ornaments and the television set were packed away, and most of the furniture was pushed back against the walls.

Soon, with a fire blazing in the sitting-room, the elephants were comfortable enough, yet they knew that Miss Teazle was worried because she had taken so little money on her stall.

'Two pounds and fifty pence won't do much to cure the damage those beetles and the woodworm have done to the timbers of the church,' she confided to Trumpeter when she took him out a further supply of buns to the garage. 'It's hardly enough to repair one choir stall.'

After Miss Teazle had baked her last batch of buns and had finally gone to bed, Blancmange left the revolving summer house to have a brief chat with Trumpeter. Then she came across the garden to the sitting-room window to say 'good night' to Little Hooter and the other young elephants.

'Miss Teazle has made us all very comfortable,' she told them, 'but Trumpeter and I both feel that tomorrow we ought to go back to the forest. There's not an ounce of flour left in her store cupboard or a banana on the sideboard. We've eaten her out of house and home and Trumpeter thinks we should start before dawn.'

But somehow the next morning they all overslept. Only the doorbell woke them, ringing in the hall.

When Miss Teazle hurried to answer it still clad in her sheepskin bedroom slippers and dressing-gown, outside the door stood an old lady with five pound notes clutched in her gloved hand. She was wrapped in shawls and scarves, and the taxicab in which she had travelled still stood at the gate.

'I've come to buy one of your elephants,' she told Miss Teazle. 'Yesterday I couldn't get as far as the bazaar but I read Mr Dash's account of the white elephants in my newspaper this morning, and I thought one of them would be just the thing to take me to the shops and to church and the village hall.'

'Of course,' said Miss Teazle. 'You shall have the very largest and most dependable elephant we have. He will take you anywhere, even in the roughest weather, and carry all your shopping as well.'

The old lady dismissed the taxi and rode away on Trumpeter five minutes later while all the other elephants looked on and cheered.

Even before the smallest of the elephants had stopped trumpeting and jumping up and down the telephone rang. This time it was a farmer who wanted the strongest elephant Miss Teazle could provide to replace his tractor which had broken down. Blancmange stepped forward this time, determined to be of use and Miss Teazle, who had worked on the land during the last war, gave her an old Land Army hat to wear, and an extra rug.

'You'll manage perfectly,' she told Blancmange, as she accompanied her down the garden path. 'Take things steadily at first, be civil to the cows, and every night go early to bed after a mug of cocoa and a good warm bath.'

Afterwards, Colonel Brown from the next village hurried over with his wife in a Land Rover to buy an elephant to draw his garden roller and the lawn mower on his back lawn.

Soon only Little Hooter and two other elephants were left.

Miss Teazle had ordered fresh currants and flour from the grocer to make another batch of buns for them to eat for lunch but, just as they were sitting down to the table, a whole procession of people trudged up the garden path. There were three mothers pushing prams and nine little girls.

'I hope we're not too late,' said the first mother in tartan slacks and a red anorak, 'but it's for the play centre. We would like to buy three of your smallest elephants for the children, and we've the seven pounds handy that we were saving to pay for a climbing frame and a slide.'

Little Hooter and the others finished their lunch, and then Miss Teazle escorted them herself to the home of the mother in the tartan trousers, where they were to live when they weren't on duty at the play centre. Installed in a barn they were very comfortable and soon quite at home. Little Hooter gave all the children rides and sometimes they went as far as his old home in the centre of the forest.

All over the village the white elephants were hard at work. When, in the course of their duties, they caught sight of one another they trumpeted proudly and waved their trunks. They had never been so happy. All through the spring and summer, long after the snow had melted, they were still free to roam about and enjoy the outside world. By the time Christmas came round again all the repairs to the church were finished.

'It's thanks to the elephants we had just enough money,' the Vicar told Miss Teazle. 'When the Bishop and his wife come for the thanksgiving service I hope every one of your white elephants will be there.'

And the elephants were. They crowded into the back of the church in an orderly line ranged beside Trumpeter and Blancmange. After the service they paraded round outside the church head to tail waving holly in their trunks. Miss Teazle was there with Mrs Chumleigh and Miss Spencer. The old lady who had purchased Trumpeter looked on. Colonel Brown and his wife sat in their Land Rover. The farmer who had bought Blancmange was there with his family, and all the children from the play centre came to cheer.

Afterwards, they all gathered round a giant Christmas tree which Blancmange and Trumpeter had helped drag down from the forest, and they sang songs and carols far into the night, with the stars shining and the snow glistening as white as the elephants themselves.

I am ending this book with a poem. For this who better than John Betjeman? His poetic eye sees everything: notice the bunting on the Town Hall saying 'Merry Christmas to you all', and the oafish louts remembering Mum. Then how exquisitely he turns our eyes to the real meaning of Christmas. No 'steeple shaking bells' for the baby born in the utmost simplicity in a stable stall in Bethlehem.

Christmas

The bells of waiting Advent ring,
    The Tortoise stove is lit again
And lamp-oil light across the night
    Has caught the streaks of winter rain
In many a stained-glass window sheen
From Crimson Lake to Hooker's Green.

The holly in the windy hedge
    And round the Manor House the yew
Will soon be stripped to deck the ledge,
    The altar, font and arch and pew,
So that the villagers can say
'The church looks nice' on Christmas Day.

Provincial public houses blaze
    And Corporation tramcars clang,
On lighted tenements I gaze
    Where paper decorations hang,
And bunting in the red Town Hall
Says 'Merry Christmas to you all'.

And London shops on Christmas Eve
    Are strung with silver bells and flowers
As hurrying clerks the City leave
    To pigeon-hunting classic towers,
And marbled clouds go scudding by
The many-steepled London sky.

And girls in slacks remember Dad,
    And oafish louts remember Mum,
And sleepless children's hearts are glad,
    And Christmas-morning bells say 'Come!'
Even to shining ones who dwell
Safe in the Dorchester Hotel.

And is it true? And is it true,
    This most tremendous tale of all,
Seen in a stained-glass window's hue,
    A Baby in an ox's stall?
The Maker of the stars and sea
Become a Child on earth for me?

And is it true? For if it is,
    No loving fingers tying strings

Around those tissued fripperies,
    The sweet and silly Christmas things,
Bath salts and inexpensive scent
And hideous tie so kindly meant,

No love that in a family dwells,
    No carolling in frosty air,
Nor all the steeple-shaking bells
    Can with this single Truth compare—
That God was Man in Palestine
And lives to-day in Bread and Wine.

John Betjeman

Acknowledgments

The compiler and publishers are grateful to the following for permission to include copyright material:

Helen Hoke Associates Ltd for 'Christmas Day in New Zealand' from *The First Margaret Mahy Story Book* by Margaret Mahy.

Curtis Brown Ltd for 'St Francis, My Great-Aunt Emily and You, or How To Make a Christmas Crib' by Rumer Godden from *Time and Tide*, Christmas 1957.

Patricia Lynch for 'The Last Bus for Christmas' from *Strangers at the Fair* by Patricia Lynch.

J. M. Dent & Sons Ltd for the extract from *Coco the Clown* by Nicolai Poliakoff.

'The Legend of the Christmas Rose' from *The Girl from the Marsh Croft* by Selma Lagerlöf, copyright 1910 by Doubleday & Co. Inc. is printed by permission of the publisher and C. E. Fritze Hovbokhandel A. G. Sweden.

Hughes Massie Ltd for 'The Wild White Horses' by Joyce Stranger, copyright © Joyce Stranger Limited, 1973.

Andre Deutsch for 'The Stowaway' from *My Uncle's Strange Voyages* by Richard G. Robinson.

Macmillan, London & Basingstoke for 'The Prayer of the Donkey' from *Prayers from the Ark* by Carmen Bernos de Gasztold, translated by Rumer Godden. Translation copyright © 1962 by Rumer Godden: and for 'The Camel' from *The Creatures' Choir* by Carmen Bernos de Gasztold, translated by Rumer Godden. Translation copyright © 1965 by Rumer Godden.

J. M. Dent & Sons Ltd for 'The Christmas Cherries' from *Sir William and the Wolf* by Chrétien de Troyes, translated by John Hampden.

A. M. Heath & Co. Ltd for 'A Shower of Snow' by Helen Cresswell. © Helen Cresswell 1973.

J. M. Dent & Sons Ltd for 'The Lady of the Lake' from *The Wily Wizard and the Wicked Witch* by Godfried Bomans. © English translation J. M. Dent & Sons Ltd 1969.

Heinemann Educational Books Ltd for 'A Handful of Dates' from *The Wedding of Zein* by Tayeb Salih.

John Murray (Publishers) Ltd and A. P. Watt & Son Ltd for 'The Veiled Lodger' from *The Casebook of Sherlock Holmes* by Sir Arthur Conan Doyle.

Curtis Brown Ltd for 'Miss Teazle and the White Elephants' by Margaret J. Baker. © Margaret J. Baker 1973.

John Murray (Publishers) Ltd for 'Christmas' from *Collected Poems* by John Betjeman.